D1131575

INTELLIGENCE AND AFFECTIVITY
IN EARLY CHILDHOOD

INTELLIGENCE AND AFFECTIVITY IN EARLY CHILDHOOD

An Experimental Study of Jean Piaget's Object Concept and Object Relations

THÉRÈSE GOUIN DÉCARIE

Foreword by
JEAN PIAGET

Translated by
ELISABETH PASZTOR BRANDT
and
LEWIS WOLFGANG BRANDT

INTERNATIONAL UNIVERSITIES PRESS, INC.
New York

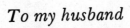

To my husband

CONTENTS

TRANSLATORS' PREFACE

In this experimental study with young children, the author made a first attempt to derive testable hypotheses from a combination of concepts from the theories of Jean Piaget and of the Freudian ego psychologists. We were, therefore, faced with the following difficulties:

1. Piaget's works have been translated by various translators who used different English terms for the same French term used by Piaget.

2. Most of the works by the ego psychologists were written in English but did not have a unified terminology.

3. One work by René Spitz to which the author frequently refers was written in French and has only recently been translated into English.

Under these circumstances we had to decide whether to introduce some new English terms into this translation or to use those existing terms which we considered clearest for the English reader. As one of us (L.W.B.) had pointed out in a critical discussion of the translations of Freud's concepts, further confusion might be created by the introduction of even more fortunate but new terms for concepts for which less appropriate terms have become part of the psychological terminology. We decided, therefore, to use those English terms from Piaget's English translators and from the ego psychologists which seemed best to convey the thoughts expressed by the author. In the few instances where further clarification seemed necessary we added a translators' footnote.

For the translation of the statistical analysis of the data, and particularly of the headings of the tables, we followed the indications of the author whom we wish to thank for her prompt answers to any questions we had concerning her work.

LEWIS WOLFGANG BRANDT, Ph.D.
ELISABETH PASZTOR BRANDT, Ph.D.

FOREWORD

I feel greatly honored and pleased to have the opportunity of congratulating the author of this beautiful and rich study. At the same time, I wish to thank Mme. Gouin Décarie in my own name and in the name of experimental psychology for the service she is rendering to all those who are beguiled by controls and verifications.

The purpose of this investigation is to determine the connection between what psychoanalysis calls "object relations" in the area of the emotional development of the infant, and the developmental stages of the schema of permanent objects which I attempted to analyze in 1937 in the area of the development of intelligence.

It is well known that, although Freud and his followers may have brought to light the existence of an impressive array of new facts, they have hardly insisted on experimental verifications. There are several reasons for this omission: (1) physicians and researchers in clinical psychology work mainly with individual cases and this method hardly allows controls; (2) as soon as a theory becomes the truth of a school of thought, the group opinions delay rather than favor critique and verification. Hence one must welcome with great enthusiasm the present-day attempts, particularly those inspired by the late David Rapaport, of introducing experimental controls in psychoanalysis. The work of T. Gouin Décarie thus appears at the right moment and will certainly evoke a lively interest.

As far as my own research is concerned, if one acknowledges that it is experimentally oriented, it has too often waited for critical and follow-up studies in order to attain a sufficient degree of verification.[1] In an amusing essay on the evaluation of the works of some contemporary psychologists, A. Naess made an estimate in terms of grades of the various requirements which must be fulfilled when one addresses some American researchers. Thus, although I am ranked rather highly for my imagination concerning hypotheses, I received in general a rather low grade for their verifications! Hence, it is very satisfying for me to find in this work the same stages without any change in meaning for the 90 subjects studied by T. Gouin Décarie which I had observed on only 3 subjects. This shows moreover (since the criticism must not be carried too far) that by means of a longitudinal study in which 3 subjects are observed daily over a period of several months, sometimes as many facts can be noticed as in a transversal comparative study of a larger number of subjects. The essentially qualitative study with which, in our opinion, any investigation of previously unknown facts must begin, has, however, to be acknowledged as leading essentially to the determination of levels.[2] On the other hand, in order to get at causal interactions between the factors concerned, one has to make a more quantitative and statistical analysis.

This kind of analysis is inaugurated by Mme. Gouin Décarie in the area of the first 24 months. She presents a series of new and very interesting data which concern not only the verification of

[1] Cf. the many works by M. Laurendeau and A. Pinard, by E. Lunzer, K. Lovell, E. R. Gardner, J. Smeldslund, J. Wohlwill, etc.

[2] I wish to emphasize in this connection, despite Mme. Gouin Décarie's remark (cf. her introduction), that it was not so inappropriate to state a correspondence between the achievement of object relations and that of the schema of permanent objects in terms of "levels."

the order in which the levels follow each other, but also a whole set of instructive correlations: between the stages of the schema of permanent objects and mental age (Griffiths tests), and especially between the development of the object and that of "object relations" in the affective sense of the term. The latter constitutes the central goal of her study.

Two important problems still remain unsolved and it is to the author's credit that she delimits their boundaries while keeping a reserved attitude toward the relationship between intelligence and affectivity and the beginnings of mental representation.

The first problem boils down to the question as to whether the object relations *qua* affective manifestations entail the cognitive progress which consists of the stages of the formation of the schema of the object as Charles Odier among others maintained or whether, as we believe, the affective dynamics and cognitive structuring represent two inseparable aspects of all behavior regardless of whether relationships to people or to things are involved. Mme. Gouin Décarie hardly expresses herself on this central issue, since, although (or because?) she is an excellent experimenter, she distrusts any answer which "remains a theoretical one." Yet, a well-constructed theory does not only guide experimentation, but also offers the great advantage of clarifying the concepts and underlining the connections which are implicit and whose victim one may otherwise be rather than their master. Thus, when the author shows how the advances in psychoanalysis lead to a consideration of the beginnings of emotional development as tied to an entire structural system (Hartmann's ego autonomy, etc.) so that this development can no longer be interpreted as due to mere "displacements" of cathexis, the line of reasoning actually leads to an integration of cognitive (structural system) and affective factors (dynamics). Thus the second solution is clearly pointed to as the better one.

In this connection, we wish to point out that the analysis of the concept "schema" which is interrelated with that of assimilation, seems somewhat brief. Mme. Gouin Décarie retains only the analogy with a Gestalt, but a schema is much more than that: it is a tool for intelligent generalization and even for the satisfaction of needs and the organization of interests. As a result, the inseparability of the affective and cognitive aspects of behavior becomes clear as soon as one discusses the concept of the assimilatory schema.

On the other hand, the author constantly comes back to the problem of the beginnings of mental representation which the Freudians place earlier than we do. We are here confronted with a delicate problem which has not yet been solved in detail and concerning which the greatest caution is indicated. We congratulate Mme. Gouin Décarie for exercising such caution. However, it may be useful to remember that such a problem is not only a question of levels, because it depends above all upon a much more serious and deeper question, namely the mode of formation. When, like the Freudians, one refers to a "hallucinatory mental representation" of the desired object (Freud, 1911, etc.) or to a "hallucinated image," the constitution or origin of such mental representations becomes the central question. Within the context of associationism in which Freud had been brought up and from which he had freed himself only partially, the image is only an extension of the perception, and the problem is therefore not disturbing. But all works on recall as distinguished from recognition (cf. particularly the role of the schemata in F. Bartlett) and also both the psycho-physiological and the genetic analyses of mental images (we have been working on this latter subject with B. Inhelder for years) show that the matter is not that simple. In particular, a close connection seems to exist between the formation of the image and imitation. Thus the image contains an element of active reproduction which makes it into an internalized imitation. Since 1936 we have insisted on this aspect of the problem. We find repeated confirmation for it in our studies with children between the ages of 5 and 10 years of the belated character of the simplest images of kinetic reproduction. As for Wallon, he has insisted on this point by tying imitation and imagery to the manifestations of the postural system (Mme. Gouin Décarie expresses astonishment regarding the role of attitudes which actually does not concern the operative aspect of intelligence, but which is important with respect to the figurative aspect, including precisely imitation and images). Now, imitation develops in successive stages over entire months and is hardly capable of lasting in deferred and internalized forms before the middle of the second year. Thus there is actually good reason for caution with respect to the beginnings of mental representation!

Furthermore, it may be mentioned that one might foresee the existence of different levels of imitative images in accordance with the functional role it may play in specific situations. Eye movement recordings during sleep (Dement, Kleitman, Assermensky, and others) seem to indicate the intervention of imitative eye movements in the arousal of dream images. In some elementary-level dreams an action seems to continue in sleep (e.g., a dog may bark in his sleep). If by means of electroretinograms the existence of eye movements during sleep could be demonstrated in higher animals or in infants of a few months of age, the existence of early perceptomotor imitations might thereby be indicated. In that case, the hypothesis concerning a link between hallucinations and wishes could be confirmed, at least in terms of activities[3] without, however, implying the use of images in the area of sensorimotor intelligence or in the formation of the permanent object schema before stage VI.

But all this constitutes only the hypothetical frame of the research to be undertaken or continued. Meanwhile, we can only congratulate Mme. Gouin Décarie for her clear description of the points of agreement and disagreement between the Freudian school of thought and our own point of view, a work destined to promote further studies and to be useful to everybody.

Geneva, April 1962   JEAN PIAGET

---

[3] I.e., without knowledge of which behavioral perceptomotor imitations correspond to which states of dream consciousness.

ACKNOWLEDGMENTS

I wish to thank all those who, in one way or another, have shown their interest in this work.

I am especially grateful to the Reverend Father Noël Mailloux, o.p., founder of the Institute of Psychology of the University of Montreal who made me love Freud; the Reverend Father Adrien Pinard, Director of the Institute; M. Jacques Saint-Pierre, Director of the Statistics Center, who, through his collaboration, made the quantitative analysis of the data possible. I should also like to thank Mrs. Elisabeth Hone-Bellemare, L.Ph. (Ps.) and Pauline Gratton-Lemyze, L.Ph. (Ps.) who collaborated directly in this research.

To Dr. Ruth Griffiths and Dr. René Spitz, I am very grateful for their comments and judicious advice.

And finally I wish to express my deep gratitude to M. Jean Piaget for the warm welcome he gave to the results of this investigation.

To my husband, I want to give the last words of appreciation; without his infinite understanding this work would never have been finished.

This work has been undertaken and published with the help of a grant from the Social Science Research Council, using funds provided by the Canada Council.

THE PROBLEM

"What we need is an observational check on our hypotheses concerning object formation" (Hartmann, Kris, Loewenstein, 1946, p. 36).

This investigation has, as its point of departure, a paper by Dr. René Spitz and a book by Jean Piaget.

In his paper "Autoerotism. Some Empirical Findings and Hypotheses on Three of Its Manifestations in the First Year of Life" (1949) written in collaboration with Katherine M. Wolf, Spitz considers rocking or "rocking-hypermotility" (1954, p. 553) and fecal and genital play of infants as clues to the quality of their object relations. He suggests the following hypotheses. Rocking indicates the absence of a satisfactory object relationship: the libidinal cathexis remains entirely centered on the body of the infant. Fecal play appears in infants who have reached some level of object relations but who, due to the loss of the love object, use their feces as substitutes. Genital play evidences the existence of adequate object relations and a healthy availability of libidinal cathexis.

On first reading, it seemed to us that these suggestions might contain some operational criteria which would allow for an experimental evaluation of the stages of object relations in the young child. At the time we were especially interested in the seeming parallelism during the first year of life between the emotional and the intellectual developments. In this regard a statement by Jean Piaget had interested us for a long time.

1

In 1945 Piaget stated in *Play, Dreams and Imitation in Child-hood*, "Corresponding to the affective level of 'object choice' there is construction of substantial objects and organisation of external space . . ." (p. 185). This statement appeared to be somewhat categorical since there was very little experimental support for it. But in the light of Spitz's suggestions, it seemed to us that the above statement might become a most precise starting point for the empirical study of the relationship between intelligence and affectivity.[1] This, after all, is the fundamental problem, and in the area of genetic psychology it presents, at this time, a point of special sensitivity. Only a few indications of this situation will be discussed here.

Psychoanalysis, though at first little concerned with the cognitive aspects of human development, for the last thirty years has become increasingly preoccupied with the ego, and today is more and more concerned with epistemological questions (cf. especially Hartmann, Kris, Loewenstein, Rapaport, Anthony, Bowlby, Schachtel, Wolff). Courses by Piaget at the Sorbonne during the academic year 1953-1954 dealt precisely with the relationship between affectivity and intelligence (1954); a more recent paper by Bärbel Inhelder (1956a) discusses the same subject, and one is astonished to find the names of authors such as Bowlby, Anna Freud, Hartmann, Spitz, Deutsch, and Erikson in her list of references.

Even though other schools of psychology are interested today in the dualism intelligence-affectivity,[2] we are taking into consideration here only these two great streams of thought, because the data from the Geneva school, on the one hand, and the psy-

---

[1] *Translators' note.* "Affectivity" is used in this book as a translation of the French term *affectivité*. It denotes the emotional aspects in contradistinction to the cognitive-intellectual aspects of personality. See also Chapter III, footnote 5.

[2] This problem, which at the time of the first meetings of experts arranged by the World Health Organization was more or less restricted (Tanner and Inhelder, 1956), has since become the center of the latest discussions (Tanner and Inhelder, 1960).

choanalytic concepts, on the other, served as framework for our research. We are ready to admit that we find it hardly necessary to justify this choice.

Indeed it seems to be more and more generally admitted that in the area of the development of intelligence, Piaget's theory remains the one which is most coherent and has the best empirical basis (see Laurendeau and Pinard, 1962). Even some psychoanalysts are of this opinion:

"To date, the most fruitful studies on the nature and development of thinking in children have been those of Jean Piaget [Rapaport, Reichard et al., 1944, p. 156]."

" ... outside of psychoanalytic theory I consider this theory [i.e., the one of Piaget] to be the only one worth any serious consideration [Anthony, 1956a, p. 270]."

However, as far as the child's emotivity is concerned, psychoanalysis remains indisputably the most fruitful and penetrating of the contemporary genetic theories. Even Piaget, who has been highly critical of this theory, wrote:

"Freud's work contains a number of other valuable discoveries, and on the level which we are discussing now,[3] I even think that we shall have to retain the main points of the Freudian descriptions [Piaget, 1954, p. 56]."

And yet, even with these two solid points of departure, the problem intelligence-affectivity remained so immense that we could not hope to approach it experimentally. The paper by Spitz and Wolf (1949) and Piaget's statement (1945), mentioned before, made it possible for us to crystallize our working hypotheses by limiting the research to the notion of the cognitive object and to that of the libidinal object.[4] This limitation is easily

---

[3] That is, at the level of narcissism and object choice.

[4] This is exactly what has been suggested by Anthony (1956a) as first application of Piaget's theory to what he calls the psychodynamic theory. Anthony (1958) has undertaken some work in this direction, in a clinical setting. It should also be added that this suggestion by Anthony is of a much later date than the initial steps of our research.

justified, not only for practical reasons, but also in the theoretical outline.

One need be only somewhat familiar with Freudian concepts in order to realize that, for psychoanalysts, object relations constitute both the point of departure and the barometer of emotional life:

"These [i.e., certain well-known psychoanalytic hypotheses regarding personality development] state in effect that the core of healthy adult personality is the ability to make conscious stable and co-operative relationships with other persons, especially love objects, and that the satisfactory development of this ability in the adult is dependent on its healthy development in childhood, especially during the first three or five years of life, when the child is making his first social relationships—those with his parents. These psychoanalytic hypotheses state further that the majority of personality disturbances, and of neurotic and even psychotic symptoms, are the end results of a dysfunctioning of the personality in the field of object relations [Bowlby et al., 1956, p. 211]."

On the other hand, in the context of Piaget's theory, it seems just as valid to study the first steps of mental development starting from the very concept of object as in terms of the six stages of sensorimotor intelligence.

"What, in fact, is the schema of the object? In one essential respect it is a schema belonging to intelligence. To have the concept of an object is to attribute the perceived figure to a substantial basis, so that the figure and the substance that it thus indicates continue to exist outside the perceptual field. The permanence of the object seen from this viewpoint is not only a product of intelligence, but constitutes the very first of those fundamental ideas of conservation which we shall see developing within the thought process [Piaget, 1947, pp. 107-108]."

Our subjects ranged in age from three to twenty months; consequently the age range is very limited and our conclusions are valid only for certain infants. We shall, however, speak loosely of the infant, the baby, or the young child and mean in each case "the infant" as that term is used by Anglo-Saxon psychologists.

Indeed, Zazzo used this English form in his French translation of Carmichael's (1954) text. Etymologically, "infant" (*in*, not +
fari, speak) designates the subject who does not yet speak; technically, it includes the first postnatal period during which the individual depends completely upon the care of his parents, i.e.,
the first two years of life.

More specifically, it is the aim of this work to correlate the development of the concept of object and the development of object relations during the first two years of life, and to do so within
an experimental setting.

Finally, without this experimental setting, our work would have been meaningless in view of Piaget's courses. In these courses, Piaget doubtlessly states the question of intelligence and affectivity with a precision which one finds only rarely in modern research; he states the question and he answers it, but his reply remains a theoretical one, for when he writes:

"Our study aims at examining the relationship between affectivity and intelligence from a genetic viewpoint. If our previous hypotheses are correct, we shall be able to parallel, stage by stage, the intellectual structures and the levels of emotional development. Since no structure exists without dynamic and since, respectively, a new form of energizing regulation must correspond to any new structure, a certain type of cognitive structure must correspond to each new level of emotional behavior [Piaget, 1954, p. 10]."

he proposes an objective which goes further than ours and includes it, but remains outside of a rigorous experimental context. Actually, the correlation which follows is made between two sets of data which rest upon a fragile empirical basis.

The series of intellectual structures used by Piaget for the first two years of life rests upon his systematic observations of his own three children. The sampling is therefore most limited and, even though we bow before the admirable scientific rigor of these observations, it did not seem superfluous to us (in order to assure the accuracy of the parallelism) to verify this seriation with a larger number of subjects.

Similarly, some of the stages of emotional development used by Piaget were borrowed from psychoanalytic theory. The majority of these stages are both the result of interesting but not experimentally verified hypotheses and of more or less systematic observations. Here, again, some rigorous experimentation would seem to be useful.[5]

Let us add that the correlation itself of the two series of phenomena frequently remains an imperfect one. Indeed, Piaget uses chronological age, besides internal coherence of genetic processes, to compare a given intellectual stage with a level of emotional development. However, the chronological age of the intellectual stage has no statistical basis: not only is it the function of only three subjects, but even these three show tremendous individual differences. As for the levels of emotional development, we shall see repeatedly that psychoanalysts are reluctant to specify the chronological age at which these levels are to be located.

This by no means indicates that our research, which was limited to ninety subjects from widely varying environments, closes the question; or that we have succeeded once and for all in relating a given Piagetian stage with a given phase of emotional development. It simply means that we have tried to answer the question, which Piaget recently addressed to Bowlby, concerning precisely this point (Piaget, 1960, p. 25), and that we have arrived, in the end, at asking new questions rather than at answering them. In the realm of intelligence and affectivity, we are still in an exploratory stage; it is our only merit to have undertaken to clear a bit of land. Nevertheless, we hope that this investigation may constitute the first step of a work of much larger dimensions which would compare not only the formation of the concept of object with the stages of object relations, but also the other dimensions of reality:

[5] "The psychoanalyst should apply certain methodological norms and techniques of research when they are compatible with the nature of the facts upon which his work depends. He should not conform to certain procedures simply because they are characteristic of a highly regarded physics or are in some questionable way associated with a vague and arbitrary abstraction like the general notion of 'science'" (Ritchfield, 1954, p. 309).

the temporal field, the spatial field and causal relations, and the totality of the affective development of the infant. Only when this work has been completed can we write the psychology of the first eighteen months of life.

CHAPTER I

GENERAL SURVEY OF PIAGET'S THEORY

RANGE OF THE PRESENTATION

We accept as a starting point Jean Piaget's theory concerning the object concept. This is our first assumption. Thus we are not concerned with a defense of that theory, but merely with a presentation of it, if possible without misrepresentation; furthermore, we shall constantly keep in mind the specific aim of this investigation.

The core of Piaget's theory appears in the second volume of his trilogy, namely in *The Construction of Reality in the Child*.[1] The author frequently comes back to his observations and their interpretations in other works (Piaget, 1945, 1947, 1954, 1957, 1960), but never in such a precise and detailed manner. Hence, the said work will serve us as a kind of textbook to which we shall refer again and again.

From a chronological viewpoint, *The Construction of Reality in the Child* (1937) stands almost midway between the works of his youth, *The Language and Thought of the Child* (1926b), *Judgment and Reasoning in the Child* (1924), and the synthesis of his

[1] "Together these three works (i.e., *The Origins of Intelligence in Children, The Construction of Reality in the Child,* and *Play Dreams and Imitation in Childhood*) form one entity..." (Piaget, 1948, p. IX).

work represented by *Psychology of Intelligence* (1947). It was determined to a large extent by the birth of Piaget's three children. The specific area of investigation covered in the book is the mental development of the infant before the appearance of articulate language.

This is, according to Piaget, the period of the development of sensorimotor intelligence, that is, "that aspect of intelligence which is a preparation in the field of elementary activity for what will much later become the operations of reflective thought" (1945, p.1). But while *The Origins of Intelligence in Children* follows the functional development of this intelligence starting with the behavior of the child, *The Construction of Reality in the Child* tries to maintain not the viewpoint of the observer but rather that of the awareness of the subject. When studying the concepts of object, time, space, and causality "the description of behavior no longer suffices to account for these new products of intellectual activity; it is the subject's own interpretation of things which we must now try to analyze" (Piaget, 1937, p. xii).

This analysis is carried out by Piaget with constant reference to the great themes of his genetic theory. We cannot follow him therefore, not even in the limited zone of the object concept, without good knowledge of the principal statements of his system. [2] This necessary minimum in itself creates a problem: Piaget's theory has such coherence that each of its elements dovetails with the next one, and taking hold of one link of this wonderful chain

[2] This outline will no doubt seem tedious and superfluous to the reader who is familiar with Piaget's work. We have included it here for the easier understanding of our work by child psychoanalysts who are as yet poorly acquainted with the main findings of the Geneva school (if one consults the references of some 130 authors who have contributed to *The Psychoanalytic Study of the Child* from 1945 to 1959, one finds that Piaget is rarely quoted). There are summaries of Piaget's theory (Inhelder, 1943; Aebli, 1950; Anthony, 1956b), but these are comprehensive views which are much too wide for our purpose. Peter Wolff's (1960, pp. 3ff.) theoretical model which is limited to the six stages of sensorimotor intelligence is better for our needs. However, he dwells little upon the concepts of stages and periods—essential elements for the present research —and we therefore thought it necessary to include here a functional survey of Piaget's theory.

one's thoughts glide imperceptibly toward the next link; we would not wish thus to be carried away through the 256 ternary operations and the 16 binary operations! A developmental period can therefore really be understood only if one knows the preceding and the following periods: a stage is meaningful only to the extent that we are familiar with the characteristics of the preceding and subsequent stages.

Does it follow, therefore, that we must describe the three great periods which, according to Piaget, characterize mental development? We do not think so, but rather believe that the aim of this research can be achieved by analyzing only the *first* period of mental development—"This first period extends from birth to the appearance of language, that is, approximately through the first two years of life" (Piaget, 1956, p. 37).

In this case we need not be concerned with anything preceding birth, since the intrauterine development, as far as we know, has never been studied systematically by Piaget. He does, on occasion, speak of the fetus in connection with a particular problem, such as the conditioned reflex (cf. Piaget, 1948, p. 57f.), but such comments are rare. In his monumental work, we have found nothing comparable to the work of Gesell (1945, 1946) on the embryology of behavior. Neither do we need to concern ourselves about the second great period of mental development, i.e., the period of "preparation and organization of concrete operational classes, relations, and numbers." This second period is distinguishable from the period of sensorimotor intelligence by the appearance of language and symbolic function which both presuppose the systematic use of representation. Now, we need neither language nor symbolic function to delineate the terminal stage of the object concept. For this, it will suffice to analyze the beginning of representation. Therefore, it seems justified to limit Piaget's theory to a certain extent within a chronological frame which extends through the first two years of life, and to use as examples only those phenomena which are typical of the first period of the development of intelligence.

TWO DEFINITIONS OF INTELLIGENCE

Piaget is a biologist by training and a logician "by aspiration." His concept of intelligence is influenced by those two disciplines.[3] Indeed, he writes that "intelligence is an adaptation" (1948, p. 3) but also that "it is an ultimate goal" (1947, p. 7).

No doubt we have here only two of Piaget's definitions of intelligence, whereas there are numerous others. Nevertheless, we consider these two particularly significant, and we have therefore chosen them as logical instruments in this attempt to outline his theory. We shall first discuss the definition "intelligence—ultimate goal" even though it is much less frequent than "intelligence—adaptation" and forces us temporarily outside of our chronological boundary; but this will facilitate our survey by enabling us to introduce immediately the concepts of periods and stages.

Intelligence is an ultimate goal: this is a "generic term to indicate the superior forms of organization or equilibrium of cognitive structurings" (Piaget, 1947, p. 7). Therefore, considering *functional* aspect, one can say "that behaviour becomes more 'intelligent' as the pathways between the subject and the objects on which it acts cease to be simple and become progressively more complex" (*ibid.*, p. 10). However, from the *structural* point of view, it is possible "to define intelligence in terms of the progressive reversibility of the mobile structures which it elaborates" (*ibid.*, p. 11). This means that, for Piaget, the adult (not any adult, however, but the civilized adult) is more "intelligent" than the six-year-old child dominated by egocentrism. He constantly compares this child, even at three months, with the adult. The perfect reversibility of the mental operations of the mathematician constitutes for Piaget not only the final point of intellectual development, but also its norm and measure. This has brought him the accusation of adultomorphism, and it is true that the

[3] "During our studies of zoology, our twofold interest in problems of variations and adaptations and in logical and epistemological questions caused us to dream of constructing a biological epistemology based exclusively upon the concept of development" (Piaget, 1949, Vol. I, p. 5).

child described by Piaget sometimes impresses us as a "diminished" adult (Anthony, 1957).

The child, in progressive development, will go from a primitive, subjective, egocentric mode of thought to a complex, objective, socialized mode. This development, however, is not linear but rather a spiral one, constantly subject to shifts and divisible into general periods and particular stages.

We find here a discontinuity which is not found in the development of perception or of language, so that

"... in the area of intellectual operations, we witness the dual phenomenon of seeing the formation of the structures, being able to follow the first features step by step, and yet witnessing also their conclusion, that is, the formation of levels of equilibrium [Piaget, 1956, p.33]."

Periods and stages form such plateaus where the equilibrium is more or less stable. This is a far cry from arbitrary segmentation such as that of chronological ages (Osterrieth, 1955). The stages, in order to deserve their name, must satisfy a number of criteria.

THE STAGES

We shall briefly summarize five characteristics[4] of developmental stages on the basis of Piaget's paper "Les Stades du Développement intellectuel de l'Enfant et de l'Adolescent" (1956, pp. 33ff.).

1. There can only be stages if *the order of the acquisitions is a constant one,* i.e., the sequence of most of the phenomena observed by Piaget constitutes an essential part of his theory. In any population studied, any item considered as typical of a stage must never appear *before* a second item in one group of individuals and *after* that same item in a second group of subjects. This rigidity is similar to that of the development of fine motor co-ordination: certain stages of prehension cannot be reversed, and one does not as-

---

[4] We shall present here the maximum requirements developed by Piaget for the definition of stages in the different areas of the child's development. The minimal requirements consist of three criteria only (Piaget, 1960, pp. 13-14).

sume that in some subjects the thumb-index grasp could appear before the cubito-palmar grasp (Koupernick, 1954, pp. 117ff.).

2. A stage necessarily has an *integrative character*, "that is, the structures which are constructed at a given age become integrated parts of the structures of the following age" (Piaget, 1956, p. 34). For example, the permanent object, which develops on the level of sensorimotor intelligence, will be an integral element of the concept of conservation of matter which belongs to the phase of concrete mental operations.

We are dealing here not with a simple juxtaposition, but with a real construction by the child himself. It is this integration of multiple mental acquisitions from which Piaget's system derives its genetic character.

3. A stage is characterized by *structural properties* which in turn form an integrated whole: "once such a structure has been attained one can determine all the operations which it covers" (*ibid.*, p. 35). Thus the use of representation which characterizes the last stage in the development of the object concept will also cover deferred imitations on the level of language and of gestural signs (Piaget, 1945, pp. 62ff.).

4. A stage consists of *a level of preparation* and *a level of completion*. Each stage can therefore be divided in such a manner that, from a chronological point of view, one can speak of a beginning and an end.

5. Within a sequence of stages, one must distinguish (a) *the process of formation* or origin and (b) *the forms of final equilibrium* (in a relative sense)—it might be better to speak here of plateaus of equilibrium.... The processes of formation appear as successive differentiations of a specific structure and almost always contain an additive element relative to the preceding structure and a restrictive element relative to the following structure. The (relatively) final forms of equilibrium alone constitute the structural whole discussed above.

This important concept of "stages" must not lead us to the assumption that mental development is an uneven, discontinuous process. Though Piaget emphasizes the necessity of the concept of "stages" and of its correspondence to reality, he stresses the continuity of intellectual development from the primitive behavior of sensorimotor intelligence to the integrated structures of lattices and groups which characterize formal thought (Piaget and Inhelder, 1955). He maintains, however, that this continuity is a functional and not a structural one:

"It must be understood that if intelligence is not a faculty this denial involves a *radical functional continuity*[5] between the higher forms of thought and the whole mass of lower types of cognitive and motor adaptation; so intelligence can only be the form of equilibrium toward which these tend [Piaget, 1947, p. 6]."

This functional continuity excludes neither diversity nor even heterogeneity of the integrated structures; these structures will differ to such a degree that one can assert the unity and coherence of childhood mentality as "differing essentially in nature, not only in degree, from adult thought" (Inhelder, 1943, p. 40).

Therefore, Piaget divides mental development into three large periods, each comprising stages and substages. These divisions and the approximately corresponding ages are reproduced in Table 1. This is the summary of a summary: for an initial understanding and a better grasp of the crucial moments of mental development, we refer the reader to *Psychology of Intelligence* (Piaget, 1947) and to the brief survey by Bärbel Inhelder (1956b); it must be remembered, however, that this skeleton can be animated only by a study of the fundamental works of the master.

Nevertheless, concerning Table 1 and the definition of intelligence as "ultimate goal," it is important to stress, in conclusion, that:

"... these three great periods, with their particular stages, constitute successive equilibration processes, steps toward equilibrium. As soon as equilibrium has been achieved at one point, the structure is integrated into a newly developing system, until a new equilibrium of wider reach is achieved.

[5] Italics added (T.G.D.).

TABLE 1

Intelligence is an Ultimate Goal

Periods	Subperiods	Stages	*Approximate Chronological Age*
I. *Sensorimotor Intelligence*		1. Use of reflexes	0 to 1 month
		2. First habits and "primary" circular reactions	1 to 4½ months
		3. Co-ordination of vision and prehension, "secondary" circular reactions	4½ to 8-9 months
		4. Co-ordination of secondary schemas and their application to new situations	8-9 to 11-12 months
		5. Differentiation of action schemas through "tertiary" circular reactions, discovery of new means	11-12 to 18 months
		6. First internalization of schemas and solution of some problems by deduction	18 to 24 months
II. *Representative Intelligence* and the period of concrete operations	A. Preoperational representations	1. Appearance of symbolic function and the beginning of internalized actions accompanied by representation	2 to 3½-4 years
		2. Representational organizations based on either static configurations or on assimilation to one's own action	4 to 5½ years
		3. Articulated representational regulations	5½ to 7-8 years
	B. Concrete operations	1. Simple operations (classifications, seriations, term-by-term correspondences, etc.)	8 to 9-10 years
		2. Whole systems (Euclidian co-ordinates, projective concepts, simultaneity)	9 to 10-11 years
III. *Representative Intelligence* and formal operations		1. Hypothetico-deductive logic and combinatorial operations	11-12 to 13-14 years
		2. Structure of "lattice" and the group of 4 transformations (INRC)	13-14 years

This table is based on Piaget's paper "Les Stades du Développement intellectuel de l'Enfant et de l'Adolescent" (1956, pp. 37ff.).

"It is advisable to remember that equilibrium is defined by reversibility. To say that there are steps toward equilibrium indicates that the intellectual development is characterized by increasing reversibility. Reversibility is the most obvious characteristic of the act of intelligence, which is capable of detours and reversals [Piaget, 1956, p. 41]."

Piaget carefully distinguishes between "reversibility" and "revertibility"; in the latter case there is only an empirical return to the point of departure without awareness on the part of the subject of the identity of the action. "Reversibility" is essentially the "capacity to carry out the same action in both directions while being aware that it is the same action" (Piaget, 1957, p. 44). To some extent the reversibility of the intellectual act corresponds therefore to the physical definition of reversibility (movement from A to B and from B to A, passing through the same states), but the awareness of the identity of this action (despite the difference of direction) endows reversibility with a special psychological meaning "corresponding to the involutional character of a logico-mathematical transformation" *(ibid.)*.

We shall have to discuss in greater detail the reversibility which is characteristic for the final stage of sensorimotor intelligence. For the time being this brief outline will have to suffice for an understanding of the essential elements which constitute a stage.

Intelligence is adaptation

Piaget writes without differentiation that intelligence is "adaptation" (1947, p. 7) or "an adaptation" (1948, p. 3) or "a readaptation" (1947, p. 4). In any case this term must be taken in a biological sense; one cannot be more explicit concerning this point: "intelligence is a particular instance of organic activity" (1948, p. 4); it is not a faculty but a biological process. From this definition, which returns constantly in the writings of Piaget, one can develop schematically the major statements of his genetic system.

We shall attempt to do this on the following pages, and keep very close to Piaget's own outline in *The Origins of Intelligence in Children*. Piaget (1948) states:

"To say that intelligence is a particular instance of biological adaptation is thus to suppose that it is essentially an organization and that its function is to structure the universe just as the organism structures its immediate environment. In order to describe the functional mechanism of thought in true biological terms it will suffice to determine the invariants common to all structuring of which life is capable [pp. 3-4]."

The common invariants or functional invariants or invariant functions (*ibid.,* p. 4) belong in the framework of the two most basic biological processes: adaptation and organization. Furthermore, from the biological viewpoint these are but two complementary processes of a single function, for "organization is the internal aspect of adaptation when the interdependence of already adapted elements and not the adaptational process in action is under consideration" (*ibid.,* p. 12).

Piaget also stresses that intelligence is organization, after having written that it is adaptation. These two concepts will serve us from here on as points of reference.

We shall analyze first the concept of *intelligence-adaptation.* Adaptation as such (or the act of intelligence, which is the same) is essentially characterized by an equilibrium between accommodation and assimilation. Intelligence-adaptation, in Piaget's sense, can therefore be understood only if one knows the role of these two great mechanisms which govern mental development.

Assimilation is an integral part of life; there is assimilation in every living being. Basically, "assimilation is an incorporation of the structure of actions which the subject judges to be equivalent objects into the action schemas of the subject (that is into among themselves), in such a way that an object is perceived and conceived as a function of the actions which utilize it" (Piaget, 1959, p. 42). More precisely, from our viewpoint assimilation is a process through which a sensorimotor schema (visual, auditory, kinesthetic, gustative, etc.) gradually integrates itself and also an external object. Its "hunger" is so great that it has a tendency not only to incorporate external objects but also all other schemas so that this incorporation is limited only by the restrictions of the environment or by inconsistencies due to conditions of the subject's activities. [6]

Since any schema tends to assimilate any object, it follows that any schema also tends to *accommodate* to any object: in order to function in terms of objects other than the original one, the schema must adapt itself to those new objects. Essentially, accommodation is the differentiation of an assimilatory schema. [7] At the level of development we are discussing, it is the modification of a sensorimotor schema in terms of external reality.

At first, this accommodation takes place within a closed system as when the 6-7-day-old infant learns to turn his head in the direction of the breast: the accommodatory movement of his head and his mouth is an integral part of the over-all sucking schema. Later, accommodation will lead to new results: the 11-12-month-old child who shakes a bell more and more violently to make it ring louder and louder and then swings it very gently, uses the experience to *accommodate* his movements to the desired goal. This goal is included neither in the schema of prehension nor in the schema of audition, but is an immediate function of external reality. The child, when he wants the bell to ring loudly, cannot permit himself to swing it gently. Therefore, in accommodation the movement can be conceived, in a sense, as going from the object toward the subject and compelling the subject to adapt to the object; whereas in assimilation the movement proceeds from the subject toward the objects.

[6] The assumption of a tendency to assimilate inherent in all schemas makes it unnecessary for Piaget to resort to a "need" as an intervening variable (Apostel, 1959, p. 66) or to tension reduction as a cause for activity (Wolff, 1960, pp. 60, 78-79; cf. Piaget, 1959, pp. 46ff.).

[7] Since accommodation is an activity which tends to differentiate an assimilatory schema, and since the former is therefore only derived from or secondary to assimilation, one cannot merely say that "any schema tends to accommodate to any object. . . . It tends to *assimilate* any object, but, not succeeding in doing so because of external resistance, it either does not go into operation because it cannot accommodate, or it becomes more differentiated at the price of a compensation in relation to the initially unforeseen resistance" (Piaget, 1959, pp. 44-45).

In the beginning, assimilation and accommodation act primarily as antagonists:

"In effect, in the beginning the child only accommodates himself to things when he is in some way forced by them, whereas at the outset he tries to assimilate the real, impelled by an invincible and vital tendency [Piaget, 1948, p. 275]."

Later, as the behavior becomes less primitive, accommodation and assimilation become correlates and make an equilibrium possible: "One can speak of adaptation when the object does not offer much resistance, to such a point that it cannot be assimilated, but resists enough to require accommodation" (Piaget, 1954, p. 4).

An understanding of the practical implications of these concepts is essential to fully comprehend our conclusions. We shall illustrate with examples the three forms of assimilation and the structuring of reality which normally results from it.

SELECTION OF EXAMPLES

We shall borrow all our examples from the second stage of sensorimotor intelligence, i.e., the stage of the "first acquired adaptations and the primary circular reactions." These do not show the complexity of the observations used to illustrate the first stage (stage of "the use of reflexes"). On that level, almost all of the observed facts can be explained by physiology alone, and Piaget is the first one to admit this. Nevertheless, he sees there a sort of "preshaping" of the later stages of representational thought (Piaget, 1956, p. 38), and he is careful to distinguish between a reflex like sucking and such reflexes as yawning and sneezing, which are not modifiable by learning. Furthermore, it is more difficult to delineate the truly psychological aspect of behavior in the first stage than in the second. On the first level, it is the schema of sucking which is the dominating schema; it will play a *relatively* small part in the elaboration of the object concept. The schema of vision, which will be of great importance, pervades the second stage. In limiting ourselves to characteristic examples from the second stage we remain close to the operational criteria which we have used for the development of the object concept and which are primarily visual ones. Finally, if we want the following examples to be understood we must explain the term "schema" which has been used various times.

Concept of schema

"The conception of mental development as it appears in the works of M. Piaget is somewhat disconcerting, not because of the facts but because of the terminology" (Inhelder, 1956, p. 75). Since this remark by Inhelder many clarifications of terminology have been added to Piaget's theory (cf. especially the volumes of the *Études d'épistémologie génétique*); but even according to Apostel (1959) the concept of schema in the context of Piaget's theory remains not "definable other than by postulates which define it implicitly" (p. 65). In *Les Liaisons analytiques et synthétiques dans les Comportements du sujet* (1957, pp. 45ff.) Piaget introduces a whole series of definitions of elements which constitute the schemas, their extension, comprehension, meaning, etc. But these definitions, while very valuable for anyone who has already studied Piaget, hardly seem to suffice for the novice. We have chosen, in preference, an older definition which covers the sensorimtor schemas which are our sole concern here:

"... the 'schema' whose existence we have always acknowledged can be compared to a 'form' or 'Gestalt.' The system, composed of determined and completed movements and perceptions, reveals the dual character of being structured (hence of itself structuring the field of perception or comprehension) and of constituting itself from the outset inasmuch as it is a totality without resulting from an association or synthesis between elements separated earlier [Piaget, 1948, p. 378]."[8]

[8] I agree with Piaget's remark, in his preface, that my analysis of the concept "schema" is somewhat brief. I should have added at least that if a schema can be compared with a "Gestalt," it also differs radically from it, because it is a "Gestalt" with a history. Flavell whose outstanding work, *The Developmental Psychology of Jean Piaget,* was not yet edited at the time of the publication of my own book, admits that "Piaget does not give a careful and exhaustive defini-

The schemas which we shall use are specific: they are all originally schemas of elementary activities which are based on heredi-
tary substructures and steeped in physiology. The most important
ones are: sucking, vision, grasping, olfaction, audition, phona-
tion and kinesthesia.

THREE FORMS OF ASSIMILATION

Assimilation can be functional, generalizing, or recognitory.
Functional (or reproductive) assimilation appears as an increasing need for repetition and as use of a function for its own sake.
For example, toward the end of the first month, the child becomes
capable of visual attention and of following a moving object visually—two forms of behavior which transform the vague and absent
stare of the first weeks. The infant can, from now on, stop his crying to look in front of him for several minutes, without manifesting sucking-like movements. According to Charlotte Bühler, this
behavior reaches its peak at three months: ". . . staring at a single
spot is one of the most beloved occupations of a three months old
child" (Bühler, 1930, p. 48). Gesell notes that a colored piece of
material, placed within the visual field of a four-week-old baby, is
sufficient to pacify him (Gesell and Ilg, 1943, p. 96).

In an effort to analyze this behavior, Piaget asks first to what it
could correspond:

"If the child looks constantly, and more each day, at the objects
surrounding him, this is not, at the beginning, because he is interested in them as objects nor as signals devoid of external meaning, nor even (at the very beginning) as sensorial images capable
of being recognized, but simply because these moving, luminous
spots are an aliment for his glance and permit it to develop while
functioning. Objects are therefore first assimilated to the very ac-

---

tion of the term in any single place. . . ." He gives the following definition: "A
schema is a cognitive structure which has reference to a class of similar action
sequences, these sequences of necessity being strong, bounded totalities in which
the constituent behavioral elements are tightly interrelated" (Flavell, 1963, pp.
52-53).

tivity of looking; their only interest lies in being objects of vision [Piaget, 1948, p. 67]."

This is the time of "looking for the sake of looking," and it is very representative of the operation of functional assimilation. However, the infant does not remain there; from this reproductive assimilation, he will progress, through pure repetition, to a solidifying of the world of external objects and to a more and more objective outlook. How will this happen? "Three steps must be considered here: generalizing assimilation, recognitory assimilation, and the co-ordination of the schemata of visual assimilation with the other schemata of mental assimilation" (*ibid.*).

We shall briefly consider the three stages. Through *generalized* (or transpositive) assimilation (Piaget, 1947, p. 100) a schema incorporates into itself every object which can serve as a stimulus. For example, at about 2-3 months of age, the baby becomes able to look at things. Gesell places true ocular fixation at the beginning of the third month (1940, p. 76) and Koupernick writes: "Ocular control is usually accomplished between the second and third month" (1954, p. 132).

By minutely detailed observations one can evaluate the spontaneous visual interests of the infant and this has enabled Piaget to state:

"The bassinet hood, having at first only been the object of 'looking for the sake of looking,' arouses growing interest through its particularities as well as through its successive modifications (the objects hanging from it). Interest in certain faces adduces interest in all others and in everything which complicates the original appearance of the former. New perspectives, due to positions fortuitously discovered, arouse immediate interest through comparison with habitual perspectives, etc. In short, practice of looking brings with it the generalization of its activity [1948, p. 70]."

And so the infant, progressing in concentric waves, will look at an increasing number of things, while these things finally become detached from a uniform background to the point of arousing different sensorimotor and affective reactions in the infant. This is recognitive assimilation, or "looking for the sake of seeing," for it is *recognitive* assimilation by which a global schema is differentiated into particular schemas, and this in itself leads to diversified behavior.

For instance, some of the things at which the child gazes constantly are immobile: the spot of light of the window, the hood of the bassinet, the ceiling which can be distinguished in the distance. Other things move slightly: the curtains at the window, the fringes of the bassinet hood, the objects which hang down from it. Still other things move constantly, appear and disappear; these remain for a time in the perceptual field, then suddenly dissolve into nothing, such as human faces. And so the child, by and by, reacts differently according to the perceived picture: he cries at the disappearance of the human face, but smiles when it appears. This smile is a sure indication of visual recognition.

This, however, is not a recognition of objects; the infant recognizes at first only his own subjective state relative to such a sensory picture. *Here, actually, enters the problem of the object concept.* Suffice it to say for the time being that the visual pictures of the 2-3-month-old baby are not yet solidified or, in other words, that they are not yet "cut up into objects." For the objectification of such pictures,

"It seems to us essential that the visual schemas be coördinated with other schemata of assimilation such as those of prehension, hearing, or sucking. They must, in other words, be organized in a universe. It is their insertion in a totality which is to confer upon them an incipient objectivity [Piaget, 1948, pp. 74-75]."

We have now reached the third step mentioned above and the *organizational* aspect of intelligence.

STRUCTURING OF THE EXTERNAL WORLD THROUGH INTEGRATION OF SCHEMAS

In the context of our examples, the organizational function of intelligence at this stage consists essentially in the integration of visual schemas with each other and in co-ordinating them with the other schemas of mental assimilation.

First there is a kind of "intra-integration." The visual pictures which confront the child are capable of mutual co-ordination. Thus, the co-ordinations of position, of distance, of size, etc. lead to the construction of visual space. There are also the entirely qualitative co-ordinations of color and light, whose interplay is expressed precisely in generalizing and recognitive assimilation. Independently of all co-ordination with the other schemas, the visual schemas are partially co-ordinated with each other at this level. But of prime importance for the objectification of the external world is the co-ordination of the visual schemas with the other heterogeneous and independent schemas. This is what we call "inter-integration."

Co-ordination between vision and hearing begins in the second month: the infant searches with his eyes for the source of a sound. Around the fourth month there are clear co-ordinations between sucking and vision: the sight of the bottle initiates suckinglike movements. At about 5-6 months, co-ordination between vision and grasping (which will transform the whole universe of the infant) enables the baby to grasp what he sees.

We must point out two genetic principles concerning this co-ordination of heterogeneous and independent schemas. In the first place, the different sensorimotor schemas have their periods of hegemony; at the beginning of his existence the infant is dominated by the sucking schema: he will try to suck everything which comes into contact with his mouth, the sheet, the ears of his teddy bear, his mother's fingers. From the pleasure he experiences in sucking his thumb he will learn to co-ordinate the movements of his hands and his mouth. As soon as prehension is established he will suck everything his hands will grasp.

"Concerning what he sees or hears, if the nursling does not try to suck this from the outset it is perhaps less because these realms have no connection with sucking (it often happens that he makes sucking-like movements as soon as he hears a sound) than because it is difficult for the child to do two things at once (looking attentively and making sucking-like movements, etc.) [Piaget, 1948, pp. 84-85]."

One can, moreover, notice attempts at oral grasping as the infant opens and closes his mouth in front of an object which he cannot yet grasp.[9] This period of hegemony will occur similarly for the other sensorimotor schemas (visual, auditory, tactile): there will be a time when the baby will try to see everything, then to grasp everything, etc. By generalization and reciprocal assimilation, the schemas will finally penetrate each other and at one point one can say that "the child tries, in a sense, to listen to the face and to look at the voice" (*ibid.,* p. 87).

A second genetic principle must be remembered concerning the above-mentioned co-ordination of heterogeneous and independent schemas:[10] a sensory picture which occurs at the intersection of several of these schemas will necessarily be among the first to be solidified and "projected into a universe where coherence makes its first appearance" (*ibid.,* p. 143).

Let us suppose two things in the familiar world of the infant: the mother (by which we mean the mothering one) and the bottle. The first of these two things to be externalized relative to the subject, the first to be solidified and cut out as an object will be the mother. Why? Because she is at the intersection of the largest number of schemas.

The mother can be sucked (sucking schema) and heard (auditory schema). She smells (olfactory schema) and even tastes some-

[9] "The first pattern of grasping is manifested by the infant in prone position, when it turns its head towards an object, makes crawling motions towards this object opening its mouth at the same time. This activity is more like eating than grasping. It is an oral approach to the world . . ." (Spitz, 1951a, p. 143).

[10] As in the case of assimilation-accommodation, we shall leave aside the details of the reciprocal processes of integration and assimilation of schemas. The interested reader need only consult Piaget's trilogy; we believe that only the detailed analysis of Piaget can account for the *order* of appearance of many phenomena. Only when one observes how the schemas take shape can one understand why language remains impossible before 12-15 months, why symbolic games unfold at 2 years, etc.

thing (gustative schema). She can be grasped (prehensive schema) and she can take and rock (kinesthetic schema) and caress (tactile schema). Finally, she is one of the things which enter the visual field of the baby most frequently (visual schema) and in many contexts: sometimes she is far away and cannot be grasped, sometimes she can be seen but not heard, sometimes she can be heard without being seen, she changes in color, form (with or without hat) and even in size (near or far).

The assimilation among schemas frequently comes into play with regard to a specific object and thereby leads faster toward accommodation and recognition. On the visual level, the sensory picture, "human being" will therefore be recognized earlier than the picture, "bottle." Even though the bottle is sucked, grasped, often felt, it is neither a source of sounds, nor a means for the integration of kinesthetic schemas. This makes clear why the mother, according to Piaget, is not only the principal source of affective stimulations, but also the most important object of the external world from the viewpoint of mental acquisitions. Concerning precisely this point, Piaget criticizes certain psychoanalytic conclusions as being very incomplete (1954, pp. 66ff.).

SUMMARY

Starting from the dual concept of *intelligence-ultimate goal* and *intelligence-adaptation,* we have attempted to delineate the theory of Jean Piaget concerning the origins of mental development.

We have seen the meaning of the particular stages and the general periods in this genetic system; it will now be easy to insert the six stages of the development of the object concept. We indicated how the interplay of assimilation and accommodation leads to the specific integration of the sensorimotor schemas and to their co-ordination, and how this integration and co-ordination eventually result in the organization of the world of external objects.

In this functional outline we have not touched upon the organization of the internal world. We shall now approach this problem by assuming the viewpoint of the subject's awareness and by analyzing one of the "categories" of intelligence: the object concept.

In concluding we note that in Piaget's theory these two organizations go side by side, and that they are in fact inseparable, since "it is by adapting to things that thought organizes itself and it is by organizing itself that it structures things" (Piaget, 1948, p. 8).

CHAPTER II

DEVELOPMENT OF THE OBJECT CONCEPT AND ITEMS OF THE PIAGET SERIES

The preceding outline of Piaget's general theory enables us to use his terminology without further explanations; we can now speak of assimilation, accommodation, schema, stage, etc. and assume that these concepts are familiar to the reader.

As we have already indicated above, the essence of the theory concerning the elaboration of the object appeared in *The Construction of Reality in the Child* (Piaget, 1937), particularly in the first chapter; the other chapters discuss the construction of the spatial field, the temporal field, and the development of causality. In fact, these four "real" categories of thought[1] are inseparable in their elaboration, and Piaget separates them arbitrarily in order to facilitate their presentation.

When considering these concepts singly, there is good justification for first abstracting the object concept, isolating it from the questions of time, space and causality:

[1] Following Hoeffding's thought, Piaget distinguishes between more "real" categories of thought and those which are more "formal." Among the categories which are more real are "those which, besides the activity of reason, imply a *hic* and a *nunc* inherent in experience such as causality, substance or object, space and time, each of which operates an indissoluble synthesis of 'datum' and deduction" (Piaget, 1948, p. 11). Cf. Piaget's comment concerning integral relativism and the methodology of genetic psychology (Piaget, 1957b, p. 45).

"A question of this sort conditions all other questions. A world composed of permanent objects constitutes not only a spatial universe but also a world obeying the principle of causality in the form of relationships between things, and regulated in time, without continuous annihilations or resurrections [Piaget, 1937, p. 3]."

In Piaget's view, the initial universe of the child is radically different from that of the adult. It is a universe of things or of "perceptual pictures,"[2] which are mobile, plastic, and entirely centered on the action itself; it is a universe which has no permanent objects, no objective space, no time which establishes a relationship between events *qua* events, no causality outside of the activity of the subject.

In what way is a universe of *things*[3] different from a universe of *objects*? What is an object in Piaget's context?

"What I call an object is a polysensory complex, i.e., something one can at the same time see, hear, touch, etc.; but a polysensory complex which in the eyes of the subject continues to have a durable existence beyond all perceptual contact [Piaget, 1954, p. 59]."

In other words, we can speak of "objects" when things are "conceived as permanent, substantial, external to the self, and firm in existence even though they do not directly affect perception" (Piaget, 1937, p. 5). One ought to add here "and maintain their own identity whatever the changes of position"; this is emphasized by Piaget in the same work (*ibid.*, p. 7). To have recognized that the universe of the infant does not consist of the same entities as those which occupy our adult world and which seem obvious to us, is Piaget's deeply intuitive contribution. He retraced the origin of this insight to a very simple observation which he made on a child who was, however, already 13 months old (*ibid.*, p. 59). It must be admitted that nothing in the infant's behavior

[2] Piaget does not speak of an "image" in order to avoid confusion with the mental image (1954, p. 59).
[3] We use "things" in the most general meaning of percepts before the constitution of "permanent objects" (Piaget, 1957, p. 74n.).

before the age of 5-6 months makes it possible to decide for or against the existence of a universe of distinct objects. On the other hand, in order to account for the infant's primitive behavior, nothing obliges us to resort to anything but the existence of simple perceptual pictures. As we shall see, the presence of sensorimotor recognition from the first weeks on does not in itself require a world of objects. However, as soon as the habits of grasping are acquired, observation and experimentation combined seem to show the plausibility of Piaget's hypotheses concerning the formation of the object concept. We shall now spell out these hypotheses.

According to Piaget, it is one of the main characteristics of the object that it is conceived as remaining in existence even when it has left the immediate field of perception. One can therefore infer the presence of permanent objects in the infant's thought when the baby searches actively for something which he no longer sees, touches, hears, or smells, etc., for it is obvious that if he continues to search for an absent thing, he believes that it continues to exist somewhere in the external world. *The different steps in the active search for the vanished object* will therefore serve us as criteria for the development of the object concept. Moreover, the special study of this aspect of the object's *permanence* will not hinder us from considering also the other characteristics of the object, namely identity and externalization which are based on this permanence. We shall, however, study these aspects less systematically as they are more difficult to control experimentally.

We shall use Piaget's own technique in going over the different steps in the search for the vanished object, namely, by illustrating each step with observations and their interpretations in terms of our problem. We shall, however, take the liberty of combining and condensing these observations into a single one which is outstanding and representative of each level. We shall systematically leave aside the numerous refutations given by Piaget when he considers all possible interpretations of these observations. These controversies would lead us too far afield, and we have already accepted as basic assumption the value of Piaget's hypothesis.[4] We shall attach to this outline the constituent items of our first research instrument: the Piaget Scale or the Piaget Series. We want to explain here that we are using the terms "item, series, scale, score," etc. in their widest meaning and outside of a rigorous statistical context, as it was never our intention to construct a test. Indeed, it was sufficient that our first working tool, in order to be adequate, meet the following conditions: (a) that the constituent items reveal the different stages of the development of the object concept, according to Piaget's criteria; (b) that these items can be administered in a standardized way by a number of competent experimenters; (c) that passing or failure on these items makes it possible to rank the subject along a scale, or in other words, that these items can be scored objectively.

Fundamentally, the problem consists in the transformation of certain observations by Piaget into operational criteria. At the end of our pilot study five, mainly visual,[5] items were isolated from the 66 observations by Piaget which give evidence of the development of the object concept. We have described elsewhere in detail (Décarie, 1960) the manner of administration and the material utilized.

STAGES OF DEVELOPMENT OF THE OBJECT CONCEPT

The elaboration of the object concept takes place in five steps from the beginning of life to the age of 18-20 months. Piaget inserts these steps into the six stages of sensorimotor intelligence (see Chapter I, Table 1) so that stages 1 and 2 are included in the first step, since during these first two stages (which extend

---

[4] We are making an exception concerning the problem of the first recognition which will prove to be very important in the context of psychoanalytic theory.

[5] By choosing all items from the visual field we insured a greater homogeneity for the scale and by splitting two items in half (items 3 and 4) we achieved some measure of fluidity of procedure. In this way none of the trials was repeated.

chronologically from 0 to approximately 4½ months) there appears no behavior in relation to vanished objects.[6]

THE FIRST TWO STAGES: NO ACTIVE SEARCH FOR THE VANISHED OBJECT

Two kinds of behavior must be analyzed here: (a) the recognition of sensory pictures and (b) anticipatory behavior. Both give evidence of some solidity and coherence of the external world, but to such an infinitesimal degree that we are still far from a universe of organized objects.

A. *The recognition of sensory pictures*

We have already seen how smiling can serve as an index for visual recognition at the age of 2-3 months (and even earlier in a good many subjects). The baby who smiles consistently at the picture human being thereby evidences that he has become capable of extracting this picture from among other perceptual pictures in his universe and of associating a pleasurable affect with it. However, this is not the first form of recognition of which the infant is capable; another one appears within the first weeks of life and belongs to the first stage of the use of reflexes. We shall analyze this form of recognition in terms of our problem since it has led a number of researchers to conclusions which differ greatly from those of Piaget.

---

[6] There is no perfect synchronization between the stages of sensorimotor intelligence which affect the general development of intelligence and the developmental stages of the various categories of this intelligence (object, space, time, and causality) (Piaget, 1937, pp. 25-26n.). Necessarily, there occurs a shift, and the elaboration of the object concept, among others, "naturally lags behind the progress of the intellectual functioning in general, since it results from this progress instead of engendering it by itself" (*ibid.*, p. 46).

This created a problem concerning the chronological position of the stages as there is some lack of correspondence between the chronological distances given as characteristic for a stage of sensorimotor intelligence and for the same stage in the development of the object concept. We stayed with the chronological suggestions given by Piaget in *The Construction of Reality in the Child* so that when we speak of the chronological position of a stage it is always in the limited frame of the development of the object concept.

Observations. From the first weeks on, the infant who is hungry but not hungry enough to be furious or to cry will happen to suck by generalized assimilation (and depending upon accidental encounter) his fingers, the fingers of the adult, his sheet, his fists, etc. But if the infant is very hungry, he will reject—sometimes violently with his tongue—all these substitutes.[7] Placed in the arms of his mother,[8] he will succeed in finding the nipple by a co-ordinated search and thereby show that he differentiates it from the surrounding tissues.

We have here a first recognition. When one refers back to the basic assumption of the object theory, questions arise immediately. Doesn't this recognition require the permanence of the recognized thing? How can there be a recognition of an external object without evoking the image of this object at the moment of recognition? Is it not the very association between the image and the prevailing sensations which constitutes recognition? If this is the case (and this is the reasoning of associationism and of a number of psychoanalysts) then the conserved image can arise in the mind in the absence of the thing and suggest thereby the idea of its conservation. Recognition should consequently imply permanence of the object.

For Piaget, recognition as it exists in the infant of a few weeks does not at all require the evocation of the mental image. "For recognition to begin, it is enough that the attitude previously adopted with regard to the thing be again set in motion and that nothing in the new perception thwart that process" (Piaget, 1937, p. 6).

The Origins of Intelligence in Children contains a passage of paramount importance concerning this subject, wherein Piaget considers a multitude of problems to which we shall have to return frequently:

---

[7] According to Jensen (1932) the not too hungry baby discriminates better than the very hungry one.

[8] Piaget's three children were breast-fed. In a later context, Piaget uses the reaction to the bottle as a criterion for the construction of the spatial field (Piaget, 1937, pp. 130ff.).

"How is this kind of recognition to be explained? Of course there could be no question either here or in connection with generalizing assimilation, of the recognition of an 'object' for the obvious reason that there is nothing in the states of consciousness of a newborn child which could enable him to contrast an external universe with an internal universe. Supposing that there are given simultaneously visual sensations (simple vision of lights without forms or depth), acoustic sensations and a tactile-gustatory and kinesthetic sensibility connected with the sucking reflex, it is evident that such a complexus would in no way be sufficient to constitute awareness of objects: the latter implies, as we shall see, characteristically intellectual operations, necessary to secure the permanence of form and substance. Neither could there be a question of purely perceptive recognition or recognition of sensorial images presented by the external world, although such recognition considerably precedes the elaboration of objects (recognizing a person, a toy or a linen cloth simply on 'presentation' and before having a permanent concept of it). If, to the observer, the breast which the nursling is about to take is external to the child and constitutes an image separate from him, to the newborn child, on the contrary, there can only exist awareness of attitudes, of emotions, or sensations of hunger and satisfaction. Neither sight nor hearing yet gives rise to perceptions independent of these general reactions. As H. Wallon has effectively demonstrated, external influences only have meaning in connection with the attitudes they arouse. When the nursling differentiates between the nipple and the rest of the breast, fingers, or other objects, he does not recognize either an object or a sensorial picture but simply rediscovers a sensorimotor and particular postural complex (sucking and swallowing combined) among several analogous complexes which constitute his universe and reveal a total lack of differentiation between subject and object. In other words, this elementary recognition consists, in the strictest sense of the word, of 'assimilation' of the whole of the data present in a definite organization which has already functioned and only gives rise to real discrimination due to its past functioning [Piaget, 1948, pp. 36-37]."

In an effort to find a very concrete illustration for this primitive recognition we were reminded of certain toys which are said to facilitate the learning of geometric forms (Holgate letter box,

Playskool box, etc.). These consist of boxes with slots of various shapes and sizes (square, triangle, circle, etc.) and of wooden pieces which correspond exactly to these openings. The child has to put the wooden pieces back into the box but the circular piece will obviously enter only if put into the round slot, the triangular piece through the triangular slot, etc. At first the small child succeeds in this game by groping around: he recognizes the circular slot merely because it is the only one which fits when he has the round piece in his hand and tries to push it through the various slots. This is recognition by action. During the first weeks of life, the infant is a little like this box and a little like that child. When he is hungry, he presents a certain sensorimotor complex, a Gestalt, let us say, one which corresponds to the circular form (when he is wet, the whole of the sensations differs and corresponds, let us say, to the triangular form): the breast corresponds to the first sensorimotor complex; it possesses a combination of data which "give" to it a circular shape; in other words, it alone functions regarding the hunger complex. When the baby feels the running milk and the lessening of the stomach contractions, he "recognizes" the breast. Little by little (past functioning intervenes here) everything that leads to grasping of the breast will be integrated into the sensorimotor complex (for example the kinesthetic sensations) and "recognized" also; this explains why the baby begins to search for the breast as soon as he is placed in the nursing position.[9]

B. Anticipatory behavior

Recognition presages the constitution of the object without however requiring it. The same is true for anticipatory behavior

[9] From Piaget's point of view this search only extends the earlier act of accommodation and, if a given reflex mechanism thus enables the child to grope until he encounters his objective, it is due to the fact that the objective is in the direct extension of the act. "It is as though the child did not dissociate one from the other and considered the goal to be attained as depending on the action alone . . ." (Piaget, 1937, p. 12). It is evident that we are still far from an object which is external to the subject.

which reveals a universe on the way toward solidification, where the perceptual pictures begin to be differentiated without yet constituting a universe of distinct objects.

Observations. From the third month on, the infant can follow a human being with his eyes and it happens frequently that he continues to look in the direction where a person disappeared from his visual field until the picture reappears. One can observe analogous behavior concerning hearing, the child trying to hear again an interesting sound which has stopped; concerning prehension one can see that the baby, long before he can grasp what he sees, frequently seems to be convinced that he can find again with his hand what he had just let go. A little later, around 4 months (Spitz, 1947), he is even able to reveal with facial expressions (tears, grimaces, staring) his eagerness to see the picture which had left him reappear.

The emphasis here is on the fact that in all these cases the infant gives evidence of an expectation, therefore apparently of a sort of belief in the permanence of the vanished object; but this is purely *passive* expectation: as yet there is no active search for the vanished sensory picture.

During this period while the human being keeps the infant's attention longer than any other thing does, when a person withdraws from his perceptual field, the baby can be observed to be content to look at the spot where the figure disappeared. His expectation rests in the direct extension of the immediately preceding posture put on during the earlier perception. If he had an object concept, it would be difficult to understand why he did not attempt to see where the picture human being might have moved. Though he cannot yet grasp what he sees[10] he can nevertheless search with his eyes, alter his perspective, etc., but he does not do so; and if the human being does not return soon, the infant gives up even this passive expectation.

[10] "... if motor unskillfulness of these initial stages suffices to explain the child's passivity, in other words, if the child, while not knowing how to search for the absent object, nevertheless believes in its permanence, we should state that search for the vanished object begins as soon as the habits of prehension have been acquired. But we shall now see that this is not the case" (Piaget, 1937, p. 18).

When this expectation lasts and is accompanied by emotional discharge, must one assume the continued existence of the object? Piaget denies this, for in order to explain such behavior it suffices to attribute affective permanence to the vanished object. This distinction which Piaget makes between affective permanence and "objective" permanence is of prime importance in terms of the libidinal object which we shall have to consider later. Speaking of the baby who cries whenever the human being disappears, Piaget emphasizes that we do not need a world of external objects to explain this behavior:

"... because it suffices, for the child to hope for the return of the interesting image (of his mother, etc.), that he attribute to it a sort of affective or subjective permanence without localization or substantiation; the vanished image remains, so to speak, 'at disposal' without being found anywhere from a spatial point of view. It remains what an occult spirit is to the magician; ready to return if one catches it successfully but obeying no objective law. How does the child go about bringing to himself the image of his desires? Merely by crying at random or by looking at the place where it disappeared or where it was last seen. It is here that the hypothesis of an object situated in space is contrary to the findings of observation. The child's initial search is not at all an effort to understand the displacements of the vanished image; it is only an extension or repetition of the most recent acts of accommodation [Piaget, 1937, p. 13]."

Affective permanence can thus precede objective permanence. Only in the following stage (which chronologically falls between $4\frac{1}{2}$ and 8-9 months) behavior appears which indicates the beginning of true permanence of objects in Piaget's sense.

THE THIRD STAGE: BEGINNINGS OF PERMANENCE EXTENDING THE MOVEMENTS OF ACCOMMODATION

At this stage we find a whole series of intermediary behavior patterns which lie between total absence of active search for the vanished object and the beginnings of active search. These behavior patterns reveal that an initial permanence has been given to the perceptual pictures (this is the *additive* element relative to the preceding stage). However, this permanence shows up only in so far as it refers to the act of accommodation itself (this is the *restrictive* element relative to the following stage).

There are five such behavior patterns. The first one, "visual accommodation to rapid movements," does nothing more than extend the behavior of the stages which we have analyzed above, while the fifth, "removal of obstacles preventing perception," presages behavior of the fourth stage.

The first two behavior patterns mentioned by Piaget are analogous but one is in the visual and the other in the tactile field. We shall discuss them together.

Observations

1. Visual accommodation to rapid movements. During the first 3-4 months of life no visual reaction to falling objects is noticeable: when objects are dropped under the child's eyes he will not look for them on the coverlet or on the floor. A few months later (between 5 and 9 months) one can note a first reaction, if the child has observed the initial movement of the falling object. But this reaction is most frequently so limited that the subject abandons the pursuit as soon as the object leaves his visual field and his glance then returns to the point of departure (for instance to the now empty hand of the adult who held the object). A concomitant sound or a slowing down of the movement can facilitate the search. In the following phase the reaction is positive when the object is bulky enough to have been followed with the eyes for some time, but the reaction remains negative in the case of a tiny object. In the last phase the child systematically looks on the floor for everything which one drops from above him, whether or not he has touched the object, has noticed the beginning of the fall or has heard a sound accompanying the disappearance of the object.

2. Interrupted prehension. Between 4 and 9 months the baby does not look for an object, which drops *abruptly* from his hand, where it could have fallen. But the infant will search for an object which escapes him while his hand is touching, removing, or grasping it. This search, however, does not consist of realistic explorations: ordinarily, the child will be satisfied to lower his arm and, if the object does not happen to be in this trajectory, he will give up. Yet, if the dropped object touches the subject's cheek, his chin, or his abdomen, he knows how to find it.[11]

A fundamentally new factor was added to these two behavior patterns (visual accommodation to rapid movements and interrupted prehension) as compared to the behavior of our preceding stage: "the child no longer seeks the object only where he has recently seen it but hunts for it in a new place" (Piaget, 1937, p. 18). This visual or tactilo-manual anticipation of future positions of the object certainly makes it possible to invest it with some permanence; but the very specific conditions under which this search for the vanished object takes place reveal that if there is progress "it is a progress in degree and not in quality; the object still exists only in connection with the action itself" (*ibid*, p. 20).

Nothing in the given observations allows us to believe that the infant at this stage has succeeded in conceiving of the displacements of sensory pictures as autonomous and outside of him; on the contrary, the fact that he frequently happens to return to the point from where they left reveals that for him these pictures remain available or "at disposal," even if this availability from now on is a function of an appropriate action which can be effective (in certain absolute situations). This, certainly, is a beginning of permanence but this permanence remains subjective:

"The child cannot conceive of just any displacements or just any objective permanence. He is limited to pursuing, more or less correctly, with his eyes or with his hand the trajectory delineated by the movements of accommodation peculiar to the immediately preceding perception; and it is only in the measure in which, in the absence of the objects, he continues the process begun in their presence that he is able to endow them with a certain permanence [Piaget, 1937, p. 18]."

3. Deferred circular reaction. This is the third behavioral pat-

---

[11] This last fact indicates clearly that the absence of objective searching is not due to a lack of motor ability.

tern characteristic of this stage. Here we find again the dependency of the object upon the appropriate action. In *The Origins of Intelligence in Children* Piaget analyzes the various circular reactions (primary, secondary, and tertiary). Basically, circular reactions consist of functional exercises leading to the maintenance or to the rediscovery of a new and interesting result.[12]

Observations. Between 6 and 9 months Piaget notices certain behavior patterns which all tend in the same direction: the child who is busy looking at someone or playing with something returns after a brief interruption and, on his own initiative, resumes the position and the necessary gestures for the interrupted activity. For example, Jacqueline, about 9 months old, tries to reach behind her head for a coverlet which she likes to swing. Piaget distracts his daughter by showing her a plastic duck. She looks at it, tries to take it, but interrupts herself abruptly to hunt for the coverlet which, at that moment, is outside her field of vision.

We have here, undoubtedly, a permanence analogous to that analyzed in visual accommodation to rapid movements and in interrupted prehension. But in so far as the recovered action is more complex, the permanence attributed to the vanished pictures is probably more developed. In any case, according to Piaget, the accumulation and systematization of such behavior patterns lead gradually to the solidification of the external world and to the belief in its permanence. Yet at this stage permanence remains global and pragmatic; actual identity of the object is not implied in deferred circular reactions; of this the child is capable if the situation as a whole remains the same for some time: "It is not the object which constitutes the permanent element (for example the coverlet), but the act itself (swinging the coverlet), hence the whole of the situation; the child merely returns to his action" (Piaget, 1937, p. 27).

[12] "Circular reaction is, therefore, an acquired functional exercise which prolongs the reflex exercise and has the effect of fortifying and maintaining, no more only a completely assembled mechanism, but a sensorimotor whole with new results pursued for their own sake" (Piaget, 1948, p. 66).

4. Reconstructions of an invisible whole from a visible fraction. The following behavior patterns are especially revealing for the development of the object concept. They appear only when the schemas of vision and grasping are co-ordinated. Theoretically a child in the first stages could try to look at an object which he sees in part only. In fact, reconstructions of an invisible whole from a visible fraction are not observed until between the ages of 6 and 9 months.

Observations. At this period it suffices to show to the child a part of a desired object (but not any part, as not every presentation of a part is equally favorable), and the child will hunt for it behind the screen which hides it almost completely.

A partially hidden pencil will be grasped if 3 cm. or more are visible. There is no search if the visible fraction is reduced to 1cm. or 2 cm. Any toy, such as the stork in observation 22 (Piaget, 1937, pp. 28-29), will cause immediate searching when head or tail appear, and the child will lift the whole sheet which covers the toy. But the sight of the feet alone will arouse great interest without leading to an attempt at grasping the total object.

Objects hidden *entirely* at no time give rise to an active search.

This last restriction shows that, despite such behavior patterns, the child at this stage has not yet reached the idea of a substantial object which retains its identity under another object which hides it. The very complex concepts of "in front of" and "behind" are not yet mastered by the subject. To explain his behavior it suffices if, from the visible fraction, the integrity of the object can be conceived of as being *virtual:*

"Everything occurs as though the child believed that the object is alternately made and unmade: ... When the child sees a part of the object emerge from the screen and he assumes the existence of the totality of that object, he does not yet consider this totality as being formed 'behind' the screen; he simply admits that it is in the process of being formed at the moment of leaving the screen [Piaget, 1937, p. 31]."

5. Removal of obstacles preventing perception. This behavior is very similar to the active search for the vanished object which

is characteristic of the following stage, and only attention to minute details makes a distinction possible.

Observations. Around 5-7 months it happens frequently that
the child plays a kind of hide-and-seek game with the adult which
consists of removing from in front of his face the screens which
block his view. Several psychologists have made use of this spontaneous desire of the child to free his perception: this behavior is
used as item 4 of the 7-months level by Bühler and Hetzer (1935),
and Griffiths (1954) distinguishes five steps which extend from
the first to the ninth month.

Apparently the child who is capable of pushing a screen aside
to see what is hidden behind it believes in a substantial and permanent object. But one must note that "the child is trying less to
free the object masked by a screen than to free his own perception ..." (Piaget, 1937, p. 34). This is proven by the facts that
he will act in the same way in the absence of any object and that
the removal of the obstacle remains very limited: the child does
not achieve a displacement of the screen *in terms of* the hidden
object (and at this level it could not be due to a lack of motor
control). Hence there is indeed removal of an obstacle but of an
obstacle "in relation to the subject and not in relation to the object; there is, indeed, differentiation of the action but the obsta-
cle-screen and the object as such are not yet related. From this
point of view, the object is still only the extension of the action
in progress [*ibid.,* p. 36]."

This last restriction constitutes the essential characteristic of
the third stage. It supplies a meaningful explanation for all the
intermediary behavior patterns which we have just described.
Undoubtedly, these five behavior patterns presuppose an embryonic permanence, but only in so far as this permanence simply
extends the movements of accommodation.

At this level what the child cannot do still reveals more of his
interpretation of the world than those few new acquisitions.
There is as yet no true search for the vanished object as the child
remains unable to find an object which is *entirely* hidden: in this

case he either gives up his search or he tries to find the object elsewhere rather than behind the screen. This observation is decisive and allows the conclusion that the universe of the infant of the third stage remains:

"a totality of pictures emerging from nothingness at the moment of the action, to return to nothingness at the moment when the action is finished. There is added to it only the circumstance that the images subsist longer than before, because the child tries to make these actions last longer than in the past; in extending them either he rediscovers the vanished images or else he supposes them to be at disposal in the very situation in which the act in progress began [*ibid.*, p. 43]."

The first item of the Piaget series

The first item is founded on the behavior pattern, "visual accommodation to rapid movements." Since, in some respects, it only extends the "anticipatory behavior" characteristic of the first two stages, visual accommodation belongs to the very beginning of the third stage, called by us IIIa. Nevertheless, it indicates basic progress beyond stages I and II (there is an anticipation of future positions of the object and active search in the extension of the movements of accommodation). It can therefore serve as point of demarcation between the first step in the object development, where there is no search for the vanished object, and the second step, where an infinitesimal degree of permanence is conferred upon the object. The first item reads as follows:

Item 1—Visual accommodation to rapid movements. The subject (S) is lying or sitting up. The experimenter (E) has S touch a red rubber ball. E stands in front of S, makes sure that S looks at the ball, slowly lowers it over a distance of about 15 cm., and then drops it abruptly into a net outside S's visual field. E repeats this experiment once to the right and once to the left of S.

+: S searches for the ball in the new place. We score a plus considering the item passed if the subject immediately searches with his eyes for the ball *at least once* where it fell. If the child upon not seeing it (and here the experimenter must show it to

him as soon as the behavior is evoked) returns to the empty hand
which stayed immobile in his visual field, the item is nevertheless
scored positively as the initial reaction evidences that a beginning of permanence is granted to the object. We are therefore at
stage IIIa (see Table 2 at the end of this chapter for correspond-
ences between scores and stages).

—: S's response is limited to a visual fixation of the empty hand
of E. There is no active search: the ball is simply perceived as
being "at the disposal" of the subject. He has not passed the first
stage.

—: No active search. Expressions of disappointment at the object's disappearance (grimaces, tears, etc.), disorganized agita-
tion, a turning of the head from side to side and even more specific demands for the return of the object (in the case of an older
child a hand stretched out toward the experimenter). These behavior patterns cannot be considered as active search in the exact
sense of Piaget's theory. We are here confronted with affective
permanence; but from the viewpoint of object development this
is not yet objective permanence.

The second item

Since visual accommodation to rapid movements is characteristic of the beginning of the third stage, the second item must be a
behavior pattern representative of the end of the third stage as
well as somehow presaging the more advanced behavior patterns
of the fourth stage.[13]

The fifth and last of these intermediate behavior patterns, the
removal of obstacles preventing perception, fulfills these conditions but is somewhat ambiguous; the fourth of these behavior
patterns, reconstruction of an invisible whole from a visible fraction, belongs almost to the same level[14] and has the advantage of

[13] As we saw earlier (Chapter I) the stages contain a level of preparation and a
level of completion so that they can almost always be split in half. We have
attempted to do this in order to increase the number of items and thereby
make the Piaget Series more discriminative.

[14] "However, it is self-evident that these latter two groups of behavior pat-

being easily structured as an experiment. Hence we have chosen this behavior pattern for our second item and limited ourselves to a slight modification of observation 21 (Piaget, 1937, p. 28).

Item 2—Reconstruction of an invisible whole from a visible fraction. S is lying or sitting. E shows him a red pencil and, at the moment when S is ready to grasp it,[15] E gradually lowers it behind a piece of cardboard (parallel to the pencil and of neutral color) until it disappears completely. E then raises the pencil until 4 cm. of it show. E repeats the experiment twice (a single attempt at grasping is sufficient for a positive score).

+: S immediately grasps (or tries to grasp) the protruding end of the pencil. Piaget writes: "When I raise the pencil one to two centimeters he grasps it *at once*" (1937, p. 28). The speed of the reaction is evidence for the reconstruction of the object from a visible fraction as, ordinarily, the child at this level does not reach at once for an entirely new object.

—: No attempt at grasping when the pencil reappears. That the subject stops his movement toward grasping indicates that he has not reached the reconstruction of an invisible whole from a visible fraction, or, in other words, that he has not yet reached stage IIIb.

FOURTH STAGE: ACTIVE SEARCH FOR THE VANISHED OBJECT BUT WITHOUT ACCOUNTING FOR THE SEQUENCE OF VISIBLE DISPLACEMENTS

The fourth stage (chronologically, between 8 and 10 months) is characterized by the search for the vanished object even if it does not lie in the extension of the act of accommodation (this is

---

terns and particularly the fifth (Obs. 26 & 27) are those which bring us closest to the true taking of possession of the object, that is to say, to the advent of active search for the vanished object" (Piaget, 1937, p. 35). The fourth behavior pattern can therefore be considered to be representative of the end of the third stage.

[15] One must, however, not allow actual grasping as this could belong to the slightly lower level, interrupted prehension, and the behavior pattern would be primarily tactile.

the *additive* element relative to the preceding stage); but this search remains a conditional one: the child does not yet take into account successive displacements of the object, although they are visible (this is the *restrictive* element relative to the following stage), and endows it with a kind of absolute position.

It is necessary to distinguish, within this stage, a first behavior pattern, which lies at its very beginning and merely extends the intermediate behavior analyzed above, from a second pattern which is characteristic of the fourth stage, and to which the "typical reaction" which illustrates the limits of this stage is grafted.

Finally, we must mention a residual reaction, a residue of this period, which is especially interesting because Piaget's hypothesis of the development of the object concept originated from it.

Thus, at this level, there are three kinds of behavior patterns which represent different periods of development.

Observations

(a) At about 8-9 months the baby begins to show a behavior pattern which consists essentially in the removal of some kind of screen to find an entirely hidden object. Bühler (Bühler and Hetzer, 1935) placed an item which is analogous to this behavior pattern at the level of 9-10 months (item 7: *Uncovering a hidden toy*) and Griffiths (1954), in her performance scale, places a slightly different item at the ninth month (E 23: *lifts inverted box in search of toy*). At first the search for the hidden object is maintained only if the movement of prehension had already been initiated at the very moment of the visual disappearance of the object; but the object need not have been manipulated as in the case of tactilo-manual permanence indicated earlier.

(b) In the following step, however, the child hunts for the object which was slipped under the screen, even without an immediately preceding attempt at prehension. But despite this acquisition, the child does not yet succeed at finding the object under *no matter which* screen; it suffices to somewhat complicate the initial situation to observe the "typical reaction" of this period.

Let us assume two screens, A and B, which are placed in front of the baby. At A one hides under his eyes a toy which he evidently desires: the baby hunts for it and finds it. This experiment is repeated once or twice and then, still under the eyes of the child, one hides the toy under screen B. The child who saw the coveted toy disappear at B will immediately search for it under A.

(c) Still later, when the child has become able to search for an object at B which he had found previously at A, he returns abruptly to A if he encounters difficulties in finding the object hidden at B (e.g., because it is buried too deeply). The same behavior occurs if the problem is complicated by the addition of a third displacement to C. This "residual reaction" will, because of a law of shifting (*loi de décalage;* cf. footnote 19, this chapter), appear in later stages, but it gives evidence of an elaboration of the object which belongs to the present level.

Here Piaget's original observation fits in. We shall quote it in full and add an observation of our own which consists also of a residual reaction.

1. "Gérard, at 13 months, knows how to walk, and is playing ball in a large room. He throws the ball, or rather lets it drop in front of him and, either on his feet or on all fours, hurries to pick it up. At a given moment the ball rolls under an armchair. Gérard sees it and, not without some difficulty, takes it out in order to resume the game. Then the ball rolls under a sofa at the other end of the room. Gérard has seen it pass under the fringe of the sofa; he bends down to recover it. But as the sofa is deeper than the armchair and the fringe does prevent a clear view, Gérard gives up after a moment; he gets up, crosses the room, goes right under the armchair and carefully explores the place where the ball was before [Piaget, 1937, p. 59]."

2. Pascale at 16 months is sitting in her carriage which is pushed by her father. On arriving home where she has recognized the stairs for quite some time, she calls "papa, papa." This habit dates back a month, for her father can see her from the office window and usually comes to get her and carry the carriage inside. This time he indicates to her that he is behind her. Pascale turns around, looks at her father, and then calls "papa" again, obviously surprised at not seeing him appear at the top of the stairs.—This observation is almost identical with observation 51 by Piaget (*ibid.*).

How are these behavior patterns to be interpreted? Some of them (especially the last ones) give the impression of being schizoid. Where is the child of the fourth stage in the elaboration of the object concept? Are we not finally witnessing a universe cut up into objects, since vanished objects are now actively searched for? But if this is the case, how can one explain the typical reaction which shows up occasionally, even much later?

Piaget attributes these behavior patterns to memory difficulties as well as to difficulties of spatial localization, but he considers these difficulties as *fundamentally* due to the as yet incomplete object concept. We shall restrict ourselves to this characteristic of the fourth stage. At this level the essential acquisition arises from the fact that the child from now on searches for the vanished picture outside his visual field even if it does not happen to be in the extension of movements of accommodation.

The child distinguishes between an obstacle-object which he eliminates and a goal-object which he pursues. Furthermore, he searches *with his hand* for an object which he has *seen* only. Thus, we are sure that tactile and visual permanences are now co-ordinated. Does this mean that the child's action, from now on, pertains to organized objects?

The answer seems to be "no," since the subject's search ceases to be reality-adapted when the object disappears in two or more different places. In that case the child does not take into account the *visible* successive displacements of the object. Investing the object with a kind of absolute position, the child seems to reason: "The object is not where I saw it disappear the last time but where I have already found it once. If the first place has already 'given' me the object before, it can do so again; the object 'comes' from there." The existence of this "privileged position" reveals that there is as yet no truly objective spatial localization and that the externalization of the object is far from being completed. Undoubtedly the infant's search no longer depends exclusively on the act outlined during the preceding perception (as in the third stage), but it remains a function of the success of the subject's activity.

At this level there does not yet exist any awareness of position and displacement relations or the concept of "groups"[16]; the "how" of the objects' disappearances and appearances remains a mystery for the child. In this sense the vanished object still remains a thing "at the disposal" of the infant, but it does so *in a specific context which itself depends upon a specific action.*

"Thus the object is, perhaps, to the child, only a particularly striking aspect of the total picture[17] in which it is contained; at least it would not manifest so many 'moments of freedom' as do our images. ... Certainly the same object reappearing in different practical positions or contexts is recognized, identified, and endowed with permanence as such. In this sense it is relatively independent. But, without being truly conceived as having several copies, the object may manifest itself to the child as assuming a limited number of distinct forms of a nature intermediate between unity and plurality, and in this sense it remains a part of its context [Piaget, 1937, pp. 62-63]."

Obviously the adult cannot conceive of an object concept as phenomenal as that of children of the fourth stage; without being aware of it the adult constantly conceives of an object as potentially occupying an infinity of different positions. Consequently he can abstract this object from all these positions.

The third item

Items 1 and 2 covered the first two steps of object development, that is, stages I and II, characterized by the absence of permanence granted to the object, and stage III where one notes some more or less pronounced degree of permanence depending on whether one deals with the beginning (IIIa) or the end (IIIb) of the stage. With the third item we elicit experimentally behavior patterns representative of stage IV, where we have an active search for the completely vanished object (IVa), but without taking into account the sequence of visible displacements (IVb).

---

[16] According to Piaget true "groups" could not exist without the possibility of a reversible action.

[17] Object-under-screen-A, ball-under-the-armchair, father-at-his-window, etc.

Such mastery of visible displacements characterizes the beginning of the fifth stage.

Item 3 is divided into two steps: one experiment (item 3a, below) shows whether the subject has attained the lower limits of the fourth stage; the other (item 3b, below) enables us to determine whether the upper limits of the stage are just reached or already passed.

Item 3a—Presence or absence of active search for the vanished object with previous prehension outlined. S is sitting. E draws S's attention to the stop watch, then places it at approximately 15 cm. from S and as soon as S tries to grasp it, E covers it abruptly with screen I.[18]

+: S lifts the screen, throws it aside and manipulates the stop watch. Under these conditions an active search for the vanished object is clearly evident: the fourth stage has been reached.

—: S arrests his gesture of grasping or is satisfied with manipulating the screen. Nothing in his behavior enables us to conclude that he has progressed to the fourth stage.

Item 3b—Active search for the vanished object, with or without making use of the sequence of visible displacements. E, while holding S's attention on the stopwatch, quickly places in front of him screens I and II. Twice, in front of S's eyes, E hides the stop watch behind screen I and allows the child each time to search for and find it there. Then, still in front of S's eyes, E hides the stop watch under screen II.

++: S immediately looks for the stop watch where it is. If the search takes place immediately, we can conclude that now the subject takes into account the sequence of visible displacements or, in other words, that the restrictive element characteristic of the fourth stage no longer exists. Consequently, this stage is passed and stage V is attained, as we shall see later.

---

[18] The equipment consisted of six screens (first series: screens I, II, III; second series: screens A, B, C). They were made of squares of material sufficiently heavy to mask the shape of the object hidden underneath. We varied the screens in order to avoid every possibility of perseveration.

+: S searches only under I (or even under II but after some groping). In both cases we are still in the fourth stage although the behavior is clearly more advanced than merely in the success of item 3a.

—: No search for the vanished object. This indicates that the child is not capable of active search without an outlined grasping movement, and in this case we are still at the beginning of stage IV.

FIFTH STAGE: THE CHILD TAKES INTO ACCOUNT THE SEQUENCE OF VISIBLE OBJECT DISPLACEMENTS BUT DISREGARDS THE SEQUENCE OF INVISIBLE DISPLACEMENTS

The fifth and next to the last stage extends chronologically from the end of the first year to about the middle of the second year. The child, in this period, becomes able to search for the vanished object whatever the number and complexity of screens which hide it, *provided that he can watch all the successive displacements of the object.* This abrogation of the "privileged position" constitutes the *additive* element relative to the preceding stage.

The subjective object has therefore lost ground; nevertheless it has not disappeared entirely: As soon as one introduces the simplest of *invisible* displacements the child is again helpless in the face of the problem. He may even master this step and empirically find the object which disappeared in a for him "invisible" manner, but with a slight complication of the situation his behavior will reveal that he does not yet use deduction. This is the *restrictive* element relative to the last stage.

Thus we have at this level, as in the fourth stage, three behavior patterns whose complexity is a function of the forementioned "law of shifting." We shall now explain this concept. Even Piaget agrees that the introduction of this law makes the description of the behavior patterns of the fifth stage anything but easy; this explains our difficulty in trying to condense into a few lines a whole series of minutely differentiated observations.

Observations

(a) Around 11-12 months the child masters the situation of the two screens: if one first hides an object under screen (A) where the child looks for and finds it and then hides the same object (always before the child's eyes) under a second screen (B), this is where the child, from then on, will begin his search. This search remains effectual even if a third screen (C) is added. But this will not be the case if a single *invisible* displacement is introduced.

(b) The adult places a desired toy in a box (or in his closed hand which can here play the same role). Then, watched by the child, he slips the box under some screen, turns it upside down, and brings it out empty. At first, though the toy may have made some noise in falling out (as in the case of the celluloid fish containing a rattle in observation 56 [Piaget, 1937, p. 69]), the child searches for the object in the box and gives up when he does not find it. He does not try to lift the screen which obviously is the only other place where the object can be! After some time, the subject (by empirical learning) succeds in solving this problem without however mastering the *sequences* of invisible displacements.

(c) Placed in the above situation, the child will from now on find, for instance, a toy which without his seeing it was slipped under the carpet (screen A) from a box. But if the adult adds a second screen (B) and repeats the procedure with it, the child will immediately look for his toy at A.

These meandering behavior patterns do not surprise us after the observations of the preceding stage. It is easy to understand that an ever-closer contact with reality (which comes primarily from constant manipulation of inanimate things) enables the year-old baby to endow the object with such permanence that he can from now on find it where it is, *provided that all its displacements* have been visible. "On this point phenomenalism has certainly yielded to awareness of relation; the child takes account of all the visible displacements he has observed and dissociates the object from its practical context" (Piaget, 1937, p. 68).

How is it then to be explained that the child does not succeed in finding the object which underwent the simplest of invisible displacements? Here we have an instance of "shifting." Piaget had used this concept fruitfully in his first works (1924, 1926b) and later circumscribed it in "Les stades du développement intellectuel de l'enfant et de l'adolescent." We quote the basic passage:

"Shifting characterizes the repetition or the reproduction of the same formative process at different ages. We shall distinguish between horizontal shifting and vertical shifting. We shall speak of horizontal shifting when the same operation applies to different contents [Piaget, 1956, p. 36]."

As example Piaget offers the case of the 6-7-year-old child who can serialize, classify, measure, etc. amounts and dimensions; having arrived at the concept of conservation in relation to these qualities, the child still remains incapable of these operations when applied to weight. This, therefore, is a shift within the same period. "A vertical shift, on the contrary, is the restoration of a structure by means of other operations" (*ibid.*).

The example used here is that of the young child who moves from a practical "group of displacements"—which makes a physical orientation in a room with reversals and detours possible—to a representative "group" where these same displacements can be merely imagined. We have here analogous steps of formation, but on a different plane, and therefore, in fact, different operations.

These last behavior patterns refer to the spatial field, but they are analogous to those actually observable in the development of the object concept. This is therefore a case of vertical shifting: the child must solve, on a higher plane, a problem already mastered on the action level.[19]

---

[19] In *The Construction of Reality in the Child* Piaget (1937, pp. 376ff.) speaks of "shifting in extension" (*décalage en extension*) which corresponds to the horizontal shift (*décalage horizontal*), and of "shifting in comprehension" (*décalage en compréhension*) which corresponds to the vertical shift (*décalage vertical*).

Translators' note. The above-mentioned English translation of this book uses "temporal displacement in extension" and "temporal displacement in comprehension" for the two concepts. "Displacement" is, however, the standard trans-

"In particular, the group of displacements of the object which, at the beginning of this fifth stage, had been constituted on the plane of direct perception of relationships of position, must be formed anew as soon as it has been transferred to the plane of representation of these relationships. In effect, when an invisible displacement of the object intervenes, the child relapses into the same difficulties which he has already overcome when visible displacements were involved [Piaget, 1937, p. 77]."

The clinician will be reminded of the regression which may precede the attainment of increased maturity. These behavior patterns not only illustrate a phenomenon of shifting, they also reveal the place reached by the child of the fifth stage in his elaboration of the object: as soon as it disappears, *invisibly* for the subject, the object remains attached to a whole context and the child's search becomes ineffectual because it does not go beyond a practical schema. At this level, therefore, the object has a kind of twofold nature: the child will regard an object as having permanence and identity if it has been subjected to visible displacements, but he will remain doubtful concerning an object submitted to invisible displacements. For Piaget there is no contradiction involved. He reminds us that "the child who speaks, or even the adult, may alike bestow the quality of object on the things which surround them and yet find themselves incapable of so doing with regard to the stars or other distant bodies" (Piaget, 1937, p. 78).

Could we claim without further qualifications to be on the plane of the representation of positional relations when the 18-month-old succeeds in finding the object which vanished without his seeing it? Piaget does not reach this conclusion which his preceding interpretations seem to call for; he denies that the child of the fifth stage has access to the plane of representation. He invokes the restrictive behavior pattern indicated earlier (observa-

---

lation for *déplacement,* a word here used frequently for a very different important idea. We have therefore chosen the more specific English word "shift" or "shifting" to translate *décalage* (cf. translator's note in Piaget, 1924, p. 209).

tion c) and sees in the mastery of invisible displacements an instance of *practical learning* rather than the result of a representation of the relationship of positions.

Only Piaget's detailed observations (1937, pp. 70ff., observations 58-59) make it possible to understand this interpretation. We shall return, later, to the analysis of the behavior patterns which are characteristic for the end of this fifth stage. But we wish to mention, before studying the sixth and last stage, that, even preceding any experimentation, this interpretation by Piaget seemed to us theoretically less satisfactory than others.

The fourth item

If the subject completely passes the third item (3b++), he can be placed at the beginning of the fifth stage: "In other words, the child learns to take account of the sequential displacements perceived in the visual field; he no longer searches for the object in a special position but only in the position resulting from the last visible displacement. This discovery we consider *the beginning*[20] of the fifth stage" (Piaget, 1937, p. 66). Item 4 must therefore make use of a behavior pattern which is both representative of the completion of stage V and clearly different from the characteristic behavior of the sixth and last stage. Item 4, like the preceding one, is also divided into two subitems.

Item 4a—Active search for the vanished object with or without making use of the sequence of invisible displacements. S is sitting. E shows him two large safety pins linked together and then hides them in front of S in a small box. E places the box under screen III, gently turns it upside down leaving the safety pins under screen III, without S being able to observe this action. E brings the empty box out and places it within S's reach. E asks: "Where are the safety pins?"

+: S searches for the safety pins under screen III. In this case the subject takes the invisible displacements into account and shows thereby that he has certainly reached the end of the fifth stage.

[20] Italics added (T.G.D.).

—: S does not search for the safety pins under screen III. Failure of item 4a permits the conclusion that the subject has not yet completed the fifth stage.

THE SIXTH STAGE: REPRESENTATION OF INVISIBLE DISPLACEMENTS

With the sixth stage (which is found around 18 months) we reach the last step in the elaboration of the object concept. Henceforth the child is capable of conceptualizing the things which inhabit his universe (not all things, as we have seen: even the four-year-old may not believe in the uniqueness of the sun or in the identity of the moon during its various phases).[21] He leaves the level of sensorimotor intelligence and advances to that of representative intelligence.

But what is representation? It is impossible to give an immediate and satisfactory answer to this basic question which underlies all our work. We shall achieve one of our aims if we succeed in supplying an answer at the end of our research. For the time being, we must be satisfied with the definition of representation as an internalized action schema (Piaget, 1945, pp. 77-78); this internalization makes a new mode of thought possible, namely deduction. The following three kinds of observations give evidence of this new acquisition.

Observations

(a) The 18- to 20-month-old child is seated in front of two screens (A and B), one to his right and one to his left. He watches the adult who has hidden an attractive object in a box, and who slips the box under screen A and takes it out empty. For some months this experiment has ceased to present any difficulty for the child, and he immediately hunts for the object under the first screen. Even if the adult repeats this invisible displacement at B, the subject's search remains effective, and he henceforth pursues

---

[21] Jean-Claude, at the age of 2½, thought of the full moon as being the mother of the moon crescents which he called the "baby moons" (cf. also Piaget, 1926a, Chap. VIII).

the object at B. This behavior is new but nevertheless very stable, as even a third invisible displacement at C will not interfere with the objectivity of the subject's search.

(b) The search for an object which is hidden under a series of superimposed or encasing screens presents a behavior pattern which differs from those which we have discussed so far, but which also reveals the degree of elaboration of the object. The child in the sixth stage is able, for example, to find a pencil hidden under three superimposed screens: an overturned strainer covered by a beret which in turn was covered by a blanket (Piaget, 1937, p. 81, obs. 66). Even multiple complications of this initial situation do not succeed in diminishing the effectiveness of the searching. At the end of the sixth stage the child can solve problems as complex as the following:

(c) "[At 1 year, 7 months, 23 days] Jacqueline is seated opposite three object-screens, A, B, and C (a beret, a handkerchief, and her jacket) aligned equidistant from each other. I hide a small pencil in my hand, saying 'Concou, the pencil.' I hold out my closed hand to her, put it under A, then under B, then under C (leaving the pencil under C); at each step I again extend my closed hand, repeating, 'Coucou, the pencil.' Jacqueline then searches for the pencil directly under C, finds it and laughs.

"I repeat the experiment nine times in succession, always taking the following precautions: (1) I show the child my closed hand every time I withdraw it from under one of the three object-screens, and especially after having brought it out of the third one. (2) I vary the order in each experiment, taking care to begin by putting my hand under the object-screen under which the child found the pencil during the preceding test. For example, the first attempt having been made in the order A, B, C, the second test will follow the order C, A, B (the pencil being in B), the third, B, C, A, etc. (3) Each time I move the object-screens; sometimes the beret is on the left, sometimes in the middle, sometimes on the right, etc. (4) Each time the pencil is left under the last screen under which I passed my hand.

"During the first eight experiments Jacqueline constantly searches for and finds the pencil under the last object-screen under which I put my hand [Piaget, 1937, pp. 79-80, obs. 65]."

At this point in our account one cannot but be surprised by the distance which separates these last behavior patterns from the

primitive patterns typical for the third stage, regarding both interrupted prehension and visual accommodation to rapid movements. In the sixth stage, the child has become capable of conceiving and consciously following a system. Undoubtedly it remains a
rudimentary system, but nevertheless it gives definite evidence of
representation. The child cannot perceive the invisible displacements of the object to find it; he must deduce its route mentally.

"True representation therefore begins only when no perceived
sign commands belief in permanency, that is to say, from the
moment when the vanished object is displaced according to an
itinerary which the subject may deduce but not perceive [*ibid.*, p.
85]."

Permanence of the object has been accomplished and no longer
depends upon the action itself, "but obeys a totality of spatial and
kinematic laws which are independent of the self" (*ibid.*, p. 83).

In the case of the superimposed screens (much more difficult to
analyze) the child must remain aware of the double nature of the
object: the containers are both objects to be found and screens to
be discarded in order to obtain the coveted toy. This is a complex
or "indirect" relation and we have here a precursor of the "multi-
plication of relations" which the child will have to master on the
level of operational thought. All these observations lead to the
same conclusion:

"The object is no longer, as it was during the first four stages,
merely the extension of various accommodations, nor is it, as in the
fifth stage, merely a permanent body in motion whose movements
have become independent of the self but solely to the extent to
which they have been perceived; instead, the object is now definitely freed from perception and action alike and obeys entirely
autonomous laws of displacement [*ibid.*, p. 84]."

Item 4b and the fifth item

The second part of the fourth item shows whether or not the
subject has reached the beginning of the last stage.

Item 4b. After S has succeeded in finding the safety pins under a first screen (III), E adds any one of the other screens and repeats the item but uses only this last screen.

+: S searches for the safety pins where they are. In this case the child takes the sequence of invisible displacements into account; he behaves like the subject in observation "a" (this chapter, stage six) and therefore has reached the beginning of the sixth stage.

"... up to the fifth stage *inclusively*,[22] as soon as the displacements are not all visible, the child searches for objects in the place where they were found the first time, as though they were always at the subject's disposal, whereas from this sixth stage he takes account of all possible displacements, even if they are invisible [Piaget, 1937, p. 85]."

—: S returns to the first screen (III). This indicates that the subject is still within the fifth stage. It is equivalent to the simple passing of item 4a.

Doubtless the sixth stage has been reached when item 4b is passed successfully, and we can therefore be sure that representation is beginning to be used. But to what extent is it used systematically? To what extent has the period of completion of the sixth stage been attained? To what extent has the object reached "a new and final degree of liberty"? To what extent is it "conceived as remaining identical to itself whatever may be its invisible displacements or the complexity of the screens which mask it"? (*ibid.*, p. 84). All these questions are equivalent. The child's mastery of the fifth item will enable us to answer each of them positively.

Item 5. Intervention of deduction. S is seated facing screens A, B, and C. E shows his closed hand to S, then opens it quickly revealing a doll he is holding and says: "Here is the baby!" While S watches, E immediately slips his closed hand under A, under B, then under C where he leaves the doll. At each step E opens his hand containing the doll and says: "Here is the baby!"[23] but at

[22] Italics added (T.G.D.).
[23] In his experiments, Piaget kept his hands closed at all times (1937, pp. 79ff.). During our pretesting experiments we ascertained that for our subjects it

the last step (i.e., after C) he does not open his hand and asks: "Where is the baby? Find it."

E repeats this experiment three times (four times if there is a failure at the first trial) and always leaves the doll under the last screen under which he placed his hand. Each time the screens are moved around according to the following pattern:

1st trial:	1	2	3
	A	B	(C)
2nd trial:	1	3	2
	C	(A)	B
3rd trial:	3	2	1
	(B)	C	A
4th trial:	2	1	3
	A	B	(C)
5th trial	1	3	2
(if needed):	C	(A)	B

N.B. The arabic numerals indicate the sequence of the move and the encircled screen is the one under which the object is left.

+: S gets the doll all four times where it is. To obtain a positive score there must be no tentative groping whatsoever. Obviously, the subject may first search in E's closed hand before turning to the last screen under which the hand passed: this logical search ought not to be considered groping.

---

was meaningless to indicate verbally the presence of an object in the closed hand ("Here is the pencil."). This observation is very probably a result of the fact that in our country adults like to tease small children by making them believe that an object is in a place when it is not really there. However that may be, we could verify that normal 2-3-year-olds (who obviously had reached the sixth stage) failed the test as Piaget presented it. We have therefore enabled our subjects to ascertain *visually* that the doll remains in the experimenter's hand during the first two displacements: It is not a matter of guessing, but of deducing that if the doll is no longer in E's hand after the third displacement, it can be only under screen C.

There may be a failure at the first trial due to the newness of the situation and/or because the subject expects the adult to play a trick rather than to present a problem. In such a case the experimenter himself shall discover the doll and show the subject that this is not an attempt to deceive him. E then repeats the initial experiment four times. Success in four out of four trials seems to us to give sufficient assurance of a systematic use of representation.

—: Less than four trials are passed. In this case we are not justified in concluding decisively that the last stage has been completed.

CONCLUSION

The first cycle in the development of the object concept ends with the sixth stage of sensorimotor intelligence; from now on the child is faced with the problems of the conservation of matter, weight, and volume (Piaget and Inhelder, 1941). The distance traveled in these 18 months is immense: to become aware of this, it suffices to compare the child's universe at the beginning of this development with his universe at the end of this period. At the beginning we found a world without objects, a chaotic world with moving pictures which appear and vanish magically, with the subject's activity as the first and almost exclusive mover. These pictures remained centered on the undifferentiated I.

At the end of this period, thanks to representation and deduction (which is nothing but the systematic utilization of this representation) we have a world of objects whose permanence, substantiality, identity, and externality are no longer a function of the subject. The solidification and objectification of this universe reach from now on into regions outside the realm of perception and immediate action. As a final and important consequence, the body of the child himself now becomes an object among other objects.

Indeed, due to imitation which is more and more internalized, the child becomes able to have a representation of his own body in analogy to the bodies of others and to conceive of his body as having permanence, substance, identity with itself, etc.

Therefore the 4-week-old baby differs from the 20-month-old child not only because of a series of tightly interwoven new acquisitions, but also by some kind of remodeling of his primitive *Weltanschauung,* since at the end of the elaboration of the object concept, "the child ends by completely reversing his initial universe, whose moving pictures were centered on an activity unconscious of itself, and by transforming it into a solid universe of co-ordinated objects including the body itself in the capacity of an element" (Piaget, 1937, p. 86).

In this sample case (Table 2, below) the subject has reached the beginning of the fourth stage and is placed at 3 on the scale.

TABLE 2
The Piaget Series

Stages	*Items*		*Score Scale*	
I & II		no search	.....	0
IIIa	1	visual accommodation	..V..	1
IIIb	2	reconstitution of the whole	..V..	2
IVa	3a	active search with grasping move	..V:.	③
IVb	3b	without sequence of visible displacements	.....	4
Va	3b++	with sequence of visible displacements	.....	5
Vb	4a	without sequence of invisible displacements	.....	6
VIa	4b	with sequence of invisible displacements	.....	7
VIb	5	systematic use of representation	.....	8

CHAPTER III

OBJECT RELATIONS IN CONTEMPORARY PSYCHOANALYTIC THEORY

> *"Psychoanalysts are at one in recognizing the child's first object relations as the foundation stone of his personality: yet there is no agreement on the nature and dynamics of this relationship"* (Bowlby, 1958, p. 350).

The difficulties inherent in a presentation of Piaget's theory of the object concept appear slight indeed, compared to the difficulties inherent in a presentation of the theory of object relations!

Without a doubt Piaget's thoughts are very compact and sometimes weighted down by terminology unfamiliar to us, but this does not diminish their rigor or their extreme coherence. On the other hand, that today even publicity agents use the terms "libido," "aggression," and "narcissism" does not in the least diminish the complexity of these concepts or the terminological confusion which pertains to them; and psychoanalysts themselves are the first to deplore this confusion (Hartmann, 1950b, 1955, 1956). When we add to this an abundance of ill-assorted documentation which extends over half a century, we can see that an exhaustive study of the theory of object relations could in itself easily fill a whole book. Fortunately, the aims of our research do not require as much: we will attain them if this study is sufficiently documented to permit the construction of operational criteria which are representative of the development of object relations. This limitation of our objectives explains the scope of this study which consists essentially in extracting from contemporary psychoanalytic works the theory of object relations seen from a genetic viewpoint and in its most coherent aspects.

SCOPE OF THIS STUDY

1. IT IS NONHISTORICAL

It would have been fascinating to attempt to trace the vicissitudes of the theory of object relations all the way back to Freud, but this did not prove necessary. It seemed more judicious, in the framework of a study such as ours, to consider only contemporary psychoanalytic thinking as it is truly representative of psychoanalysis as a science.

With this in mind we have limited ourselves to the ten years which immediately preceded this study, i.e., to works which appeared between 1945 and 1955. We chose 1945 as a point of departure because it was then that the deep influence of genetic research (whose authors were oriented either toward classical psychology or toward psychoanalysis) began to make itself felt in the development of the major Freudian hypotheses (Hartmann and Kris, 1945; Glover, 1945).

Obviously, papers dated as far back as 1945 required the consideration of still earlier writings, while we attempted as well to include works written after 1955.

2. IT IS ONLY GENETIC

To this first limitation concerning time a second one must be added relative to the specific aspect under which the development of object relations was studied. We considered it only from the genetic viewpoint and to the degree that the development is (a) normal and (b) limited to the first years of life. We have therefore omitted the study of developing object relations in the adult and in the child past the age of two. We have deliberately left aside the innumerable clinical problems connected therewith unless a syndrome or a particular pathological symptom clarified the normal development of object relations.

3. THIS STUDY IS LIMITED TO CERTAIN WORKS OF ORTHODOX FREUDIAN PSYCHOANALYSIS

This is a twofold restriction. First, we have chosen a single school of psychoanalytic thought, i.e., the Freudian or orthodox. Following the classification of G. S. Blum (1953, p. ix) we have disregarded the neo-Freudians (Horney, Fromm, Sullivan, etc.), the English school (M. Klein, Rivière, Winnicott, Isaacs, Fairbairn, etc.) and the "unclassified" (Erikson, Alexander, etc.). We refer almost exclusively to the works of researchers whom Anna Freud (1954b, p. 26) considers as theorists or practitioners in the field of early childhood development, and who belong to the psychoanalytic school of which she is one of the greatest representatives.

The second restriction is due to the existence of three distinguishable categories of researchers within this relatively homogeneous group: (1) the practitioners whose primary source of knowledge is the direct and systematic observation of infants; (2) those theorists who base their interpretations of early childhood development neither on their own observations nor on data from psychoanalysis, but rather on data from biology, neurology, ethology, or psychology; (3) the clinicians whose primary source of information is the verbalizations of children and of neurotic or psychotic adults.

Fifteen years ago only a very small number of psychoanalysts used direct observations of infants for a better understanding of the psychological processes of the first months and years. Today one can add to the names of such pioneers as Margaret Ribble, René A. Spitz, Käthe Wolf, Anna Freud, and Thérèse Benedek those of Fries, Escalona, Mittelmann, Bowlby, Mahler, Dolto-

Marette, Brody, Heider, etc. Nevertheless, considering the mass of psychoanalytic works dealing with preverbal stages, one is forced to admit that the need for such an approach is far from being generally accepted (Kris, 1950; Spitz, 1950e; A. Freud, 1953, 1958; Hartmann, 1958).

The need to integrate into psychoanalysis the data accumulated by general psychology and especially by genetic psychology is more often recognized: "Psychoanalysts ... have failed in many respects to take into account the data that child psychology has assembled; an omission that has led to many incongruities" (Hartmann and Kris, 1945, p. 13).

Several writers have tried to fill this gap: Odier (1947a, 1947b) bases his work on Piaget, Lacan (1949) on Wallon, Hoffer (1949, 1950a) uses Gesell, while Spitz (1945a, Spitz and Wolf, 1946) refers to Charlotte Bühler. Hilgard (1952) attempts a synthesis, and in more recent works Brody (1956), Bowlby (1958), and Spitz (1957, 1959) endeavor to take the numerous discoveries of comparative psychology into consideration.[1]

Hartmann, Kris, Loewenstein and Rapaport pick up Freud's central hypotheses from various viewpoints and thereby also weaken the splendid isolation of psychoanalysis. The writings of these great theorists, who are aware of the data of general psychology and respect Freud's thoughts, form an invaluable scientific contribution.[2]

----

[1] On this particular point and for definite reasons, Nacht raises a dissident voice: "The wish expressed by Hartmann, Odier, and Saussure, among others, to push psychoanalysis toward the heights of general psychology and thereby introduce a different methodology seems to me, to say the least, an inhibiting and regressive step" (1951, p. 571).

[2] We want to mention, in passing, that the endeavors of these authors are quite different from those of researchers such as Sears (1936, 1947, 1950), Sewell and Mussen (1952), Davis et al. (1948), or Maslow and Szilagyi-Kessler (1946) who tried somehow to "test" the psychoanalytic hypotheses with more or less rigorous experimental display. In several of these studies it seems that the authors had no grasp whatsoever of the profound significance of Freudian concepts. We do not know if these authors had any psychoanalytic training. One may wonder if the psychoanalytic experience, at the very least, is not a necessary precaution for anyone who dares to venture into the delicate area of validation of Freudian hypotheses.

As to the third category of works, it is certainly no exaggeration to state that, even today, the large majority of psychoanalysts reconstruct the mental life of the infant from the verbalizations of adults. It is not incumbent upon us to discuss here whether this procedure gives valid results concerning the child who has arrived at the stage of articulate language. We all know that this was the procedure used by Freud and that unparalleled progress in our understanding of early childhood resulted from his discoveries.

However, the fact that the memories of adults in psychoanalysis have enabled us to penetrate the emotional world of the young child of 3-4 years does not mean that memory can render the same service concerning infants. Nothing in the present state of our science supports the belief that human beings can remember what happened during the first 12-18 months of life. Here, we fully endorse the comments of Waelder (1937) who writes:

"Our impression is that the earliest recollections which human beings retain or which emerge in analysis go back to the second year. At any rate I know of no case in which it was possible to *prove* that an individual consciously remembered what happened in his first year, though I know of many instances of ostensible memories which were discovered to be phantasies produced at a later period [p. 414]."

An analogous problem is the reconstruction of the infant's psychic life from certain symptoms noted in neurotics or psychotics. Clinical inferences of this type are innumerable (Jones, 1923; Greenacre, 1952; Marty and Fain, 1955; Bouvet, 1956) and almost always gratuitous (Seitz, 1950, may serve as paradigm). The lack of agreement, the absence of experimental controls, the small degree of concern for genetic data explain undoubtedly the precariousness of the conclusions reached by these clinicians (within the restricted area of very early childhood) and also their relatively slight influence upon contemporary psychoanalytic thinking.

For the sake of coherence we have therefore systematically neglected authors whose hypotheses are primarily based upon "the untenable assumption that the unconscious mental life of the adult (or the post infantile child) is the replica of the infant's experience" (Hendrick, 1942, p. 33). We have used only the first two categories of works.

4. THIS STUDY DEALS PRIMARILY WITH CRITERIA FOR THE DEVELOPMENT OF OBJECT RELATIONS

As it was the aim of our study to construct an object relation scale analogous to the Piaget series, we paid very special attention to concrete critera which psychoanalytic investigators had clearly indicated or simply suggested as evidence of the development of object relations. Our study is in no way speculative, and the following pages will contain few theoretical controversies. We accept a priori the theory of object relations in the psychoanalytic context, as we have also accepted a priori the theory of the object concept in the context of Piaget's work.

Our study is therefore quite restricted: mechanisms such as introjection and projection will not be mentioned. These are certainly very important in the psychoanalytic tradition, but in the present state of research they cannot easily be translated into operational criteria, at least not for the first two years of life.

In conclusion, we add that this study follows a descriptive plan. We did not attempt to analyze the underlying dynamics of object relationships—the why and how of their development—yet we believe that an investigation like ours may eventually throw some light on the very nature of the tie which binds the child to its first love objects.

DEFINITION OF OBJECT RELATIONS

When we undertook this study the term *objectal* was rarely used in French psychoanalytic literature. In the *Vocabulaire de la psychologie* (1951), Lagache defines *objectal* as follows: "In psychoanalysis the quality of a tendency or form of behavior directed at an object as opposed to a tendency or form of behavior directed at the self," and he contrasts *objectal* with *narcissisme*.

Objectal thus has here rather a clinical than a genetic meaning. This is not the case in French contemporary psychoanalytic writing where the term is used so commonly that many authors do not take the trouble to define it. They speak of *rapports objectaux* (Servadio, 1954), of *relation objectale* (Lebovici and Diatkine, 1954), of *relations objectales* (Spitz, 1954; Bernassy, 1956); these various expressions cover slightly different concepts but have in common the same general meaning: *the affective tie which a subject establishes with an object.*[3] This is after all the usual meaning of the German term *Objektbeziehung* as used by Freud and his disciples, of the English term "object relationship" as used by Anglo-Saxon psychoanalysts,[4] and of *la relation d'objet* as used by some French psychoanalysts (Marty and Fain, 1955; Bouvet, 1956). The extension and complexity of this concept explain, without doubt, why in numerous psychoanalytic papers the objectal relation (or object relationship) has become a kind of omnibus concept which may stand for almost anything. In order to avoid ambiguities we found it necessary to limit this concept in terms of our experimental plan. Within our framework "objectal relation" means "the libidinous (and/or aggressive) tie which the subject establishes with any object." We shall briefly analyse this definition:

(a) "The libidinous tie . . .": This term seems more precise and more exact than the terms "emotional" or "affective."[5] By "libidinous" we mean the specific quality of psychic drive energy, partic-

---

[3] *Translators' note.* Spitz uses the adjective "objectal" in his English papers as well (cf. 1950e, pp. 68, 70). We are following his lead in this translation in order to maintain the author's clear distinction between Piaget's "object" (*objectif* = "objective") and the Freudian "object" (*objectal* = "objectal"). "Objective development" is therefore the development of the object concept, while "objectal development" refers to the development of the affective ties with objects.

[4] The dictionary by English and English (1958) does not contain a definition of "object relationship."

[5] Some writers try to make a distinction between "affects" and "emotions," but the majority of psychoanalytic writers do not adhere to such a distinction although they may admit it in principle (cf. Jacobson, 1953, pp. 38ff. and Rapaport, 1942, Chapt. II). "The term affect will be used in this paper to stand for the terms 'emotion' and 'feeling' also, since there is no clear distinc-

ularly of sexual energy in Freud's sense.[6] We shall see that libidinal cathexis can precede the ability to experience a positive emotion. Thus a given situation (e. g., nursing) can be cathected with
libido before the infant is capable of an emotional relationship
with any object.

At this stage we are undoubtedly still far from a true object
relationship or the objectal relation as such, but one of the essential elements of this relation—the libidinal tie—is present nevertheless. We are thus, from a genetic point of view, at the very beginning of objectal development. The objectal tie is, however,
not exclusively libidinous; it can also be of aggressive nature or
even (and this is most frequently the case) aggressive and libidinous at the same time.

"Aggressive" must here be understood in its wider sense. Present-
day writers considerably diminish the old connotation of hostility and speak of aggression even in reference to simple mastery of
postures.[7] We recognize that this distinction between libidinal and
aggressive cathexis is necessary, but in the context of our work it
will be largely disregarded because it is extremely difficult to distinguish *operationally* between libidinous and aggressive manifestations in the infant.

Even if the connotation of hostility (and eventually of sadism)
is added to aggressive behavior, it remains difficult for the first
two years of life (1) to clearly determine that a given activity of
the infant (e.g., biting) is aggressively cathected; (2) experimentally to evoke aggressive behavior which may be considered representative for the development of objectal relations.

Hoffer (1950b) stated categorically: "No doubt exists as to the
aggressive and destructive character and aim of the infant's oral

---

tion in the literature in the use of these terms" (Rapaport, 1954c, p. 274). We
shall follow Rapaport and use the terms "affects" and "emotions" interchangeably.

[6] This is the usual meaning found in technical dictionaries (Fodor and
Gaynor, eds., 1950, p. 105; Drever, 1953, p. 153).

[7] Cf. *The Psychoanalytic Study of the Child* (Eissler et al., eds., 1949) and
Spitz, 1953, as well as Hendrick, 1942.

attack on the mother's breast or its substitute" (p. 159).[8] But we prefer the guarded approach of Leitch and Escalona (1949): "There is, as yet, a wide gap between concepts such as 'primary narcissism' or 'oral aggression' and what we see when regarding a squirming, smiling, babbling, sucking and crying baby" (p. 121). Consequently, we did not deal with the aggressive objectal tie, but merely attempted to evoke experimentally behavior which leaves no doubt as to *libidinal* cathexis. Certainly, aggression plays a part when objectal criteria contain an element of frustration, but we shall see that its presence or absence does not enable us to determine the objectal level.

(b) "... which the subject establishes ...": Throughout this work, the objectal relation is seen only from the subject's point of view. We are concerned here with a dynamic relation which presupposes at least some minimal activity on the part of the subject. In other words, we disregard the "inter-reaction" aspect of the objectal tie which, in recent years, has been emphasized by many psychoanalysts.

"Since the advent of ego psychology the libidinal object occupies the center of interest for psychoanalytic research. However, as early as 1905 Freud had introduced the concept of object choice in his *Three Essays on Sexuality*. This is actually the only place in his entire work where he deals in detail with the mutual relations between mother and child, between object and subject. He did not revert to this topic. In the many later passages in which he dealt with the libidinal object he did so from the subject's viewpoint. He wrote about object cathexes, object choice, discovery of the object but not about object relations [Spitz, 1954, p. 480]."

"It [the specificity of the phase] is characterized by the developmental process of the ego and at the same time by the objectal re-

---

[8] It is true that Hoffer speaks of true oral aggression only during the oral-sadistic phase which he characterizes by the appearance of teeth and the imperfect formation of the breast as object, whereas Hartmann, Kris, and Loewenstein clearly distinguish between sadism and aggression: ". . . in the oral sadistic stage, the breast has already become an object, it is not 'me' for the baby any more" (Hoffer, 1950b, p. 159). "Sadism therefore can be viewed only in the context of an already developed and complex object relation" (Hartmann, Kris, and Loewenstein, 1949, p. 27).

lations, reactions, and interactions of child and mother. Following Baldwin we shall speak of a mother-child circular reaction [Bernassy, 1956, p. 782]."

We are well aware that by considering the child solely we divided the objectal relation arbitrarily; but the reader will understand that in view of our aims we could not analyze the mother's affective relationship toward her child experimentally. Our study concerns itself with the subject-object tie and not with the reverse. Within the context of our research the 3- to 20-month-old infant, including the institutionalized infant who has no true mother substitute, is the subject of the objectal relation, and the object may be other than the mother.

(c) "... *with any object*": By "object" we mean everything which is not the self. In this context the object corresponds to Willie Hoffer's (1950a) "not-self" ("... the outer world which in the most primitive language is the 'not-self' " [p. 18]), and up to a certain point to the "non-I" of Spitz (1957): "Genetically, the self can be traced to the 'I,' while the 'I' originates from the infant's emotionally cathected physical relations with the 'non-I' " (p. 120). This distinction is, however, a recent one in Spitz's works and in the majority of his papers he uses "I" and "self" interchangeably (Spitz, 1953, p. 129n.).

The object may encompass: (1) global experiences such as certain mothering situations whose cathexis seems to be the basis for the objectal relation; (2) the infant's body itself or some parts of it, e.g., the thumb (around 3 months), the hand for some atypical children, the excrement, etc.; (3) live objects (animals, humans) and inanimate objects; care must be taken not to identify the libidinal object with only people because:

"... a large part of the human environment will never attain the dignity of a libidinal object for a given individual; and in the individual's history a number of his contemporaries will run their course as 'things.' On the other hand, it is altogether possible (and it regularly occurs at one time or another in the development of the individual) that an inanimate object is by a particular constellation of events enabled to fulfill needs which correspond to the drive structure directed toward the libidinal object [Spitz and Wolf, 1949, p. 108f.]."

According to our definition the object is not equivalent with the libidinal object (true object) which presupposes an objectal relation in the true sense. We define it broadly so as to include both this final libidinal object and its precursors which characterize the preobjectal phases. We proceed within a genetic context, and thus our definition is valid for the beginning as well as for the end of the objectal relation.

DISTINCTION BETWEEN OBJECTAL RELATIONS AND LIBIDINAL PHASES

Unfortunately our definition disregards an essential distinction which must be emphasized at this point, namely the distinction between psychosexual development and objectal development. A generation ago the terms "psychosexual development," "libidinal phases," "development of the instincts" (or better, "drives")[9] were unambiguous. Psychoanalysts used these terms to refer to Freud's (1905) phases of psychosexual development: oral, anal, phallic, and genital. The development of infantile sexuality was then described mainly in terms of successive priority of erogenous zones and of their specific mode of object cathexis: an object could be "loved" orally, anal-sadistically, etc.

Moreover, the first objectal relations were characterized almost exclusively in terms of cathexis distribution (narcissistic object, autoerotic object, object choice, etc.), of need satisfactions (transitory, anaclitic, permanent), or of nonsatisfaction of these needs (from which the two archaic dangers arise: fear of loss of the love object and fear of loss of the object's love).

Obviously, id psychology remained in the forefront. Of course, drives and their vicissitudes could not be described without considering their dynamics, source, aim, and *object,* but from that

[9] Cf. Odier, 1947a, p. 25n. (*Translators' note:* see also Brandt, 1961).

perspective the object represented only one of several aspects of the drive. Ego psychology, now in the center of psychoanalytic interest, is focused on this second part of the psychic apparatus and on one of its essential characteristics: object relations.

These relations can be described in different ways. Their development can be broken down into various periods in terms of psychic structures, or of the formation of objects, or of the mode of libidinal and/or aggressive cathexes. The evolution of the drives and that of the object have this last criterion in common, which easily causes confusion. Furthermore, while object relations remain in some ways an aspect of libido development, the latter is not sufficient for their explanation. At any given point in ego development, object relations seem to encompass phenomena which—in consideration of the autonomous functions of the ego (cf. Hartmann, 1958b)—cannot be reduced to mere drives.

From a strictly experimental viewpoint, we disregarded the development of the drives, but from a theoretical viewpoint we sometimes allude to it because in Freud's (and his commentators') thinking, as well as in reality, objectal and psychosexual development frequently interact. Thus, a concept borrowed from the libidinal phases may occasionally enable us better to delineate a given objectal stage.[10]

THE VARIOUS STEPS OF OBJECTAL DEVELOPMENT

Piaget's basic assumption concerning the object concept is found in a transposed form in the psychoanalytic theory of objectal development. Piaget assumes the existence of a chaotic, moving initial universe without independent objects and in which the subject remains focused on an activity of which he is unaware. He

---

[10] Regarding the libidinal phases, half of our subjects were in the oral phase (age levels 3, 6, and 9 months) and half were entering or already in the anal phase (age levels 12, 15, and 20 months), if one takes a chronological point of view and places *the transition* from the oral to the anal phase around the end of the first year (Spitz, 1959, p. 45; Lampl-de Groot, 1950, p. 160; A. Freud, 1951b, p. 22).

speaks of a "narcissism without Narcissus." A development which consists of clearly defined stages completely transforms the initial universe over a period of 18-20 months. The 2-year-old child finds himself thus as one element within a world consisting of objects which are substantial, permanent, independent of the subject's activity, and which retain their identity.

The psychoanalyst conceives of a primitive universe in which the subject has no self-awareness or awareness of an external world. In this universe only states of tension and discomfort are felt (the satisfied neonate drops off into sleep), the reality principle does not yet intervene, and attachment to someone or something remains impossible. This loveless, objectless universe over a period of 12-15 months passes through a certain number of phases and becomes transformed into a world within which the subject clearly distinguishes himself from the environment, and a "person-object" in the environment. Toward the end of the first year, the child has learned to understand the communicative signs of that object (and to respond to them adequately) and he will remain deeply attached to it, even if it occasionally becomes a source of frustration due to interventions of the reality principle.

Thus both theories describe some kind of object development extending over the first 18 months, beginning with practically nothing and ending with a universe of extremely diversified objects. However, the same term has entirely different meanings in the two theories. "Object" when it applies to the development of object relations and as defined by Piaget are far from synonymous. In the following, we shall attempt to specify the essential characteristics of the libidinal object. The objectal development does not proceed in as clearly defined steps as the development of the object concept. We shall have to discover the former in the writings of various authors. We shall be confronted constantly with differing interpretations of the concrete manifestations of these steps, with different criteria for their distinction and for their chronological appearance. We shall highlight points of agreement rather than divergences of viewpoints among psychoanalysts. Such a perspective enables us to extract from contemporary psychoanalytic writings, even on the basis of a quick survey, three general periods in the objectal development: (1) a "narcissistic" period, (2) an intermediary period which remains "preobjectal," (3) a final period which constitutes the truly objectal phase.[11]

In our analysis of these three periods of objectal development we shall attempt to remain faithful to our previously adopted framework. Even within these limits, our path will be long and sometimes arduous since, on the one hand, the theory of the development of object relations is still in its infancy and, on the other, a simple description of this theory requires that we touch upon all the important problems of genetic psychoanalysis.

The object relationship can be expressed in terms of (a) psychic structures and particularly ego development, (b) distribution and mode of libidinal and/or aggressive cathexis, (c) formation of the object.

THE OBJECTAL RELATION IN TERMS OF
THE PSYCHIC STRUCTURES

A few quotations will demonstrate to what degree contemporary psychoanalysis regards objectal development as interrelated with the development of the psychic structures (id, ego, and superego[12]) and particularly with that of the ego.

"Every step in the formation of the object corresponds to a phase in psychic differentiation. That differentiation itself is determined by the maturation of the apparatus, which later comes under the control of the ego, and by the experiences that structure the psychic apparatus. Hence both processes, differentiation of psychic structure and relation of the self to external objects are interdependent; the nature of this interdependence can

---

[11] "I found that the first year of life can be distinguished into three distinct periods or stages. From the psychological point of view, these are as different from each other as adolescence is from latency and latency from the preoedipal stage" (Spitz, 1959, p. 10).

[12] *Translators' note:* cf. Brandt, 1961.

be characterized as dialectical [Hartmann, Kris, and Loewenstein, 1949, pp. 26-27]."

And in relation to a systematic study of the ego we find:

". . . here is the closest relation with object relations: while the development of object relations is codetermined by ego development, the former is also one of the main factors that determine the latter [Hartmann, 1950b, p. 11]."

Glover (1950, p. 128) suggests "a study of object relations and boundaries" as one way to analyze the functional aspects of the psychic apparatus, while Spitz (1957, p. 131) writes: "These object relations produce reverberations in the child's endopsychic processes leading to shifts of cathexis, *to the formation of psychic structures*,[13] which in their turn interact in a circular process with the force field of ever-changing objectal relations." We should add that not only the structural but also the *topographical viewpoint*, i.e., the division of the psyche into unconscious, preconscious, and conscious systems (Ucs, Pcs, Cs), is often put forward by psychoanalytic writers as an index of objectal development.

THE OBJECTAL RELATION IN TERMS OF THE DISTRIBUTION AND MODE OF LIBIDINAL AND AGGRESSIVE CATHEXIS

We have already seen how difficult it is at times to distinguish between psychosexual and objectal development. We drew attention to the fact that what these two developments have in common must be found in the distribution and kind of libidinal and/ or aggressive cathexis. In the relevant literature, this twofold aspect (quantitative and qualitative) of psychic energy serves to describe both the phases of drive development and the steps of object relations.

Quantitatively, the distribution of cathexis determines the distinction between self and environment. This distinction is a prerequisite for any object relation.

---

[13] Italics added (T.G.D.).

"Moreover, psychoanalysis works with the hypothesis of another necessary condition,[14] which concerns the distribution of psychic energy. Freud assumed that with the newborn, psychic energy is concentrated upon the self (primary narcissism). When we state that an object in the external world is experienced as part of the self, we imply that the object partakes in its narcissistic cathexis. When we speak of a distinction between the self and the external object, we assume that the object which is experienced as independent from the self has retained cathexis in spite of the separation; we infer that primary narcissistic cathexis has been transformed into object cathexis [Hartmann, Kris, and Loewenstein, 1946, pp. 20-21]."

Qualitatively, the kind of cathexis (libidinal, aggressive, desexualized, diffuse, neutralized, etc.) and the corresponding affect (unpleasure, pleasure, pain, etc.) make it possible to specify the various periods of objectal development.

"And yet the development and socialization of both groups of instinctual impulses[15] can, as we know, not be separated from each other. They cannot be separated from the study of the development of the ego functions of the child. Freud's conception of the role and the transformation of psychic energy provides the link between these areas of problems, i.e., in the assumptions that the love object is cathexed with libido and aggression, that the early identification with the love object leads to the cathexis of the ego with energy, neutralized, or at least in part neutralized. As a consequence of these assumptions one might expect that the permanent cathexis of the ego with neutralized energy—one of the surmised conditions of ego autonomy—is dependent on the quality of the preceding object relation [Kris, 1951a, pp. 13-14]."

Anna Freud wrote in less theoretical and simpler terms:

"When the child's awareness develops sufficiently to discern other qualities besides those of pain and pleasure, the libido cathexis progresses from the pleasurable experience of feeding to the food which is the source of pleasure. The infant in this second

---

[14] Besides frustration, for the distinction between the self and the environment.

[15] This obviously concerns libido and aggression.

stage 'loves' the milk, breast, or bottle [A. Freud, 1946, pp. 124-125]."

This *qualitative* aspect of psychic energy extends, moreover, beyond the problem of affects to the complementary one of the genesis of emotions. The specificity of emotions (which in itself is closely interrelated with the psychic structures) will supply us with a valid index for a subject's objectal level.

THE OBJECTAL RELATION IN TERMS OF THE FORMATION OF THE OBJECT

This is obviously one of the most common descriptions of objectal development, which does not prevent the authors from disagreeing in their terminology. They speak of an "anaclitic," a "situational," a "precursor," a "partial," a "psychological" or "constituted" object, and no agreement exists concerning the definition of each of these terms.

On the basis of a certain number of writings, we have attempted to decide to which phase a given object generally corresponds. We hope that this endeavor at a schematic synthesis will not distort too much the ideas which inspired it.

I. THE NARCISSISTIC PERIOD

The first period of object relations, which we have called the narcissistic period, begins with birth. It can quite easily be distinguished from the following phase by a series of negative characteristics. Most writers consider this phase as a period of undifferentiation from a structural viewpoint, either in the absolute sense of an absence of a distinct ego and a distinct id, or in the more restricted sense of the absence of a structured ego. This undifferentiation is, moreover, not limited to the structural aspect and includes the problem of consciousness. There is said to be no clear distinction at this level between the systems Ucs, Pcs, and Cs.

In terms of cathexis, this first period is characterized quantitatively by a concentration of cathexis inside an as yet undifferentiated psyche and by a concomitant lack of distinction between self and environment. From the point of view of the mode rather than the distribution of cathexis, certain authors acknowledge a single affect in the newborn, namely unpleasure, a kind of vague, undifferentiated emotion of a negative nature. Others consider the newborn to be already subject to the pleasure principle and view him as oscillating between the two states of tension-pain and satisfaction-pleasure. They speak immediately of a positive emotion ("love"). Be that as it may, the authors agree in acknowledging that certain experiences are very early libidinally cathected and that, consequently, the total undifferentiation which characterizes the beginning of the narcissistic period is (within the first few days or weeks) replaced by another distribution of cathexis. The cathexis is now distributed between a subject who is as yet unaware of himself and an object which he does not perceive as being in the environment. Thus, within this first period, we already can distinguish two steps (phases A and B, below) to indicate this first modification of the objectal relation.

From the point of view of object formation, there is obviously no true libidinal object and the great majority of authors distinguish the narcissistic period from all other periods precisely by the fact that there is no object.[16] Nevertheless, some elements of this period foreshadow the pre-object or precursor of an object of the following period. Thus, the libidinal cathexes of certain experiences (which the first specific reactions of the infant reveal) indicate the beginning of "objectalization" of the environment and make it possible to predict the functional nature of the pre-object. In any event, there is still only a libidinal tonality between a subject and an "object" which remain fused.

[16] Balint (1953, pp. 63ff., 103ff.) does not accept the existence of a phase of primary narcissism as we describe it. Compare also the interesting hypotheses of Greene (1958) who considers the physiological activities of the mother as the primary object and who analyzes the objectal relation during intrauterine life.

While this brief description of the first period of objectal development sketches the outlines of our presentation, it cannot replace a systematic analysis of the various characteristics of that period in the light of contemporary psychoanalytic writings.

A. THE NARCISSISTIC PERIOD IN TERMS OF PSYCHIC STRUCTURE

Most present-day psychoanalysts, theoreticians and practitioners alike, who concern themselves with early childhood, accept Heinz Hartmann's theory of ego autonomy and of the existence of a conflict-free sphere. They agree with him on an initial phase of structural undifferentiation. According to Hartmann (1958b) there is not, at birth, an id from which the ego gradually emerges, but an undifferentiated core from which both are progressively formed. Kris and Loewenstein joined Hartmann and declared: "We start from the assumption of the existence of an undifferentiated phase of psychic structure" (Hartmann, Kris, and Loewenstein, 1949, p. 25).

Loewenstein (1950, pp. 51-52), expresses himself most categorically in another paper: "More recent studies of the ego, however, have shown the ego and the id as developing from a common, undifferentiated phase—the ego functions following an independent development and soon acquiring their independent characteristics."

Anna Freud (1952, p. 46) and Willie Hoffer (1952, p. 31) accept this hypothesis as is, while Spitz enlarges upon Hartmann's concept:

"The period prior to the crystallization of this first visual percept[17] has been described by Hartmann [1958b] and Anna Freud [1952] as the period of *undifferentiation,* by myself as that of *nondifferentiation.* The term nondifferentiation should be understood in a global, total sense ... [Spitz, 1955c, p. 217; see also p. 235, footnote 8]."

[17] This refers to the period preceding the first smile, i.e., from birth to 2-3 months. We shall see shortly what Spitz means by "percept."

Indeed, Spitz's "nondifferentiation" has three aspects: not only is the psychic apparatus at birth not yet structured into an ego and an id, but there is also no distinction between the systems Ucs, Pcs, and Cs, and there exists as yet no clear separation between psychic and somatic systems:

"The emergence of consciousness in the human being has never been investigated by psychoanalysts. A number of psychologists, however, have done so. They were able to prove rather conclusively that consciousness, conscious perception and memory traces connected with these do not exist at birth and in the four weeks following birth . . . [Spitz, 1950e, p. 67]."

". . . the psychic system is not yet differentiated from the somatic system in the infant. What we might call psyche at this stage is so completely merged with the physical person that I would like to coin for it the term *somato-psyche* [Spitz, 1951c, p. 256]."

Many authors avoid this problem of an undifferentiated system. They emphasize a correlative aspect of structural development, namely the absence of an actual ego[18] during the first period of object relations.

"We are used to assuming that a functioning ego does not exist at the neonatal period, and we generally see what we regard as its first traces—delay in response to stimuli—only at a much later period [Bergman and Escalona, 1949, p. 345]."

"The ego development has not yet begun in the newborn child even though an innate nucleus of the ego exists. It still takes a rather long time before the infant develops his ego functions and before he is able to achieve an even primitive co-ordination of some of these functions. However, only after such an achievement

---

[18] Throughout this book, the ego is defined in terms of its *functions*. Thus, within the context of early childhood development and in agreement with Hartmann, Glover, Kris, Loewenstein, Anna Freud, Spitz, Hoffer, etc., we ascertain its existence from the appearance of certain functions. These functions can be reduced to the following five: (1) a genuine perceptual activity, (2) a certain degree of motor control, (3) the use of memory, (4) reality testing, (5) a special synthetic function (Hoffer, 1950a, pp. 20-21).

is one justified in speaking of a primitive ego [Lampl-de Groot, 1950, p. 159]."

Spitz is just as emphatic; indeed, in almost all his works he underlines the nonexistence at the beginning of life of an ego and its functions. He clearly places himself in opposition to those who believe that they perceive in the small infant psychic processes as complex as those found in adults (particularly in psychotics), and he specifically rejects the Kleinian propositions.

". . . there exists no thought at birth. Similarly, representation, sensation, perception and volition do not exist in any form or shape. At birth the infant is in a nondifferentiated state. All his functions including his drives become differentiated later on via a process which originates in either maturation or development.[19]

Consequently, I do not concede the presence of an ego at birth. For this reason, a certain number of psychoanalytic theorems cannot be applied to early infancy. For example, the questions of an Oedipus complex and of a superego do not even arise. Similarly there exists no symbolism and consequently no symbolic interpretation [Spitz, 1954, p. 481]."

With a background different from that of the authors considered so far and in the context of an intervention relating to motricity and object relations, J. de Ajuriaguerra too insists upon the absence of a true ego in the newborn child:

"We do not believe that one can pass abruptly from a phase of 'non-I' to a phase of the 'I'; but we do not believe that what is called the 'I' from birth on is equivalent with what is called the ego after the appearance of objectal relations. Hence it would be better to speak of a structured ego only after the subject has become aware of a world of objects [Ajuriaguerra, 1955, p. 296]."

He suggests the term *Pré-Moi*.[20]

[19] Spitz distinguished, in a footnote, between maturation and development.
[20] *Translators' note:* Ajuriaguerra uses *Moi* and *Non-Moi* which seem to refer at one time to the I and at another to the ego as translated by us. *Pré-Moi* could thus be translated by "pre-ego" (cf. Brandt, 1961, p. 333, particularly footnote 1).

B. THE NARCISSISTIC PERIOD FROM THE DYNAMIC AND ECONOMIC VIEWPOINTS

There cannot be any true object relation without distinction between the self and the environment. This distinction is based on the interaction between distribution and kind of drive cathexis.[21] Only when psychic energy ceases to be totally stored in its original reservoir and becomes cathected to an outside something (cf. Fenichel, 1945) can we consider an advance from primary narcissism and speak of the *possibility* of differentiation between the self and the external world.[22] Moreover, it is important to know of what this first cathexis may consist. Is it mere escape from pain? A vague libidinization? Or could a positive affect already exist and possibly be accompanied by a pleasurable feeling? These questions are far from sterile, since, as we have pointed out earlier, the nature of the libidinal cathexis is one of the earmarks of objectal development. Unfortunately present-day psychoanalytic ideas on this issue are not always easy to understand. Two criteria served us as guides in our selection of texts: the clarity of the writings and the suggestions they contained regarding a chronological order.

1. The quantitative aspect

(a) No distribution of psychic energy during the first phase of the narcissistic period.

[21] We remind the reader of Freud's threefold hypothesis: (a) of a storage of libido within the psychic apparatus until this accumulation becomes so intense that it becomes painful and leads to a first distribution of energy; (b) of the relaxation-satisfaction which is experienced as emanating from the body itself and contributes to the formation of the first representations of the self; and (c) of the frustration-pain which is projected onto the environment: this original discernment of the quality of stimuli soon leads to a first distinction between self and environment. Cf. the theoretical outline by E. Jacobson, *The Self and the Object World* (1954), and the careful analysis by Mahler and Gosliner (1955).

[22] Theoretically, a distinction between self and environment is inconceivable without distribution of cathexis (as the former reflects the imperceptible processes of the latter), *but* the reverse is not true. One can actually conceive of an initial distinction of cathexis without true differentiation between self and the external world: in this case, the infant does not perceive whatever is cathected as external to him, although, in reality, it is outside himself.

The absence of distinction between self and environment is one of the most commonly used criteria for the narcissistic period, i.e., psychoanalytic theory claims the absence of a distribution of psychic energy during this period and assumes that the entire energy available is directed toward the subject himself. Agreement on this point is such that it seems superfluous to quote too many sources. We shall mention only a few.

"The pre-objectal stage coincides more or less with the stage of primary narcissism. I have described this state by the term "nondifferentiation" which was recently picked up by Hartmann [1958b] (and Hartmann, Kris, and Loewenstein, 1946) and which designates a state of primitive organization in the newborn child. In this state the latter is unable to distinguish one object from another one and even his environment from himself [Spitz, 1954, pp. 488-489]."

Speaking also of the beginnings of life, Hoffer associates primary narcissism with primary identification and compares these states to sleep:

"What happens in deep sleep we conjecture to be an almost complete withdrawal of cathexes. In it primary narcissism and identification, the lack of all qualities discriminating between self and not-self, inside and outside, is temporarily achieved [Hoffer, 1952, p. 33]."

Spitz, however, emphasizes that despite their similarity the narcissism of the sleeper and that of the newborn infant cannot be equated. He notes that the cathexis could not be exactly the same in the two instances:

"The newborn is incapable of perceiving the outer world. This has been shown in numerous findings of experimental psychologists as well as in our own. The sensorium is not yet functioning because, in terms of the dynamic viewpoint, the newborn has not yet cathected it [Spitz, 1955c. p. 234]. The basic difference between the adult and the newborn lies in the fact that while the adult cathects a body ego, an organized structure of body representations in the psyche, there is no such thing in the newborn. The newborn has still to develop the body ego, and what we witness in the newborn is not a withdrawal of cathexis but a non-existence of cathexis [Spitz, 1954, p. 235]."

Hartmann, Kris and Loewenstein (1946, pp. 20ff.; 1949, pp. 25ff.) pick up Freud's basic assumption concerning total absence of any distinction between self and outer world as long as the infant is in a state of total gratification[23] and they introduce slight modifications (see Hartmann, 1956, p. 34). Speaking of this initial absence of any distribution of drive energy, Hartmann (1950b) points at the frequent error in psychoanalytic writings of identifying narcissism with libidinal ego cathexis. He sees this error as resulting from the ambiguous usage of "narcissism" which covers two conflicting conceptualizations. One of these pertains to the self (one's own person) as opposed to the object, i.e., in exactly the sense in which we defined it; the other refers to the ego as a psychic structure in opposition to the other psychic structures.

"... the opposite of object cathexis is not ego cathexis, but cathexis of one's own person, that is self-cathexis; in speaking of self-cathexis we do not imply whether this cathexis is situated in the id, in the ego, or in the superego. This formulation takes into account that we actually do find 'narcissism' in all three psychic systems; but in all of these cases there is opposition to (and reciprocity with) object cathexis. It therefore will be clarifying if we define narcissism as the libidinal cathexis not of the ego but of the self [Hartmann, 1950b, pp. 84-85]."

While Escalona (1953, p. 12) agrees with the other writers—"Like every one else, I assume that the new-born and very young child lives in a peculiarly fluid, unbounded, twilight sort of world"—she contributes a hypothesis which seems especially stim-

---

[23] Freud conceives of frustration as the origin of the first contacts with the environment. Thus, as long as the infant is perfectly satisfied, there is no possibility of differentiation between self and environment. Experimentally, this state of absolute gratification does not exist (Pratt, 1946): from birth on the newborn experiences states of tension and discomfort. Yet, if one considers only hunger—the classic example—the newborn can obviously be in a state of complete satisfaction as long as he does not experience visceral contractions, i.e., during the first few hours of life.

ulating and which she supports by observations.[24] She suggests that the distinction between self and environment is by no means a clear-cut one even with respect to the waking state. Eight years of experimentation with infants lead her to believe that:

"... during the first half year of life, and likely beyond, the awareness of an outer world in which things happen can rise and submerge, so that at one moment the baby may engage in purposive directed action, the next moment the boundary between self and nonself may disappear [Escalona, 1953, p. 22]."

(b) Initial distribution of psychic energy during the second phase of the narcissistic period but without distinction between self and environment.

Complete absence of psychic energy distribution seems to characterize only the beginning of the narcissistic period: in fact, many authors indicate that at a very early age certain global situations become positively cathected.

"The newborn infant is self-centered and self-sufficient as a being when it is not in a state of tension. When it is under the pressure of urgent bodily needs, as for instance hunger,[25] it periodically establishes connections with the environment which are withdrawn again after the needs have been satisfied and the tension is relieved. These occasions are the child's first introduction to experiences of wish-fulfillment and pleasure. They establish centres of interest to which libidinal energy becomes attached. An infant who feeds successfully 'loves' the experience of feeding (narcissistic love) [A. Freud, 1946, p. 124]."

[24] "I feel confident that I have seen babies use their foot in kicking against a surface with awareness and purpose, and a second later, when their foot is raised into their visual field, reached for it exactly as for a toy, momentarily experiencing the reaching hand as part of the self, and the reached-for foot as part of the outer world" (Escalona, 1953, p. 22).

[25] Spitz emphasizes that the first tension states are connected with thirst rather than with hunger: "I have stressed again and again in the last twenty years that speaking of hunger in the newborn and infant is a misnomer. The sufferings of hunger are not comparable to thirst, nor do they occur in response to as brief a deprivation as those of thirst .... Thirst, or rather dryness of this area [i.e. the mucosa of the mouth, throat, nasal passages, etc.] will therefore be one of the first experiences of discomfort in the infant" (Spitz, 1955c, p. 221).

Rather than of centers of interest, Escalona speaks of "islands of consistency" (1953, p. 25). She attributes to these global situations (which normally recur in similar manners) an important role in the distinction between self and environment.

Spitz (1947) is one of the few psychoanalysts who specify age levels: ". . . after about a week, when the mother takes up the baby to give him the breast, he will turn toward her. This is the first active sign the infant gives that anything pleasurable is happening" (p. 69).

Several other investigators (Hartmann, Kris, and Loewenstein, 1946; Benedek, 1938) also mention this first specific reaction of the human being which gives evidence of an advance to the second phase of the narcissistic period. Be that as it may, this first distribution of cathexis does not permit the conclusion that there is also a differentiation between the self and the outer world. As stated earlier, whatever is cathected remains confused with the subject himself. Even during the second phase of the narcissistic period there is at best a libidinous attachment and a subject-object.

2. *The qualitative aspect*: *not more than two primary emotions*

On the basis of certain observable facts some authors push the hypothesis of undifferentiation to its logical limits and declare that the newborn experiences two states: tension (or excitation) and quiescence. Excitation constitutes the original core from which the various emotions subsequently arise, first of all a vague, undifferentiated negative emotion which these authors refuse to call pain but name "unpleasure." Its counterpart, quiescence, is not so much the absence, as the relative decrease of tension accompanied by neither emotional attachment nor affect.[26] Thus, accord-

---

[26] Katherine Bridges, an author to be admired for her distinction of nuances and for her caution, placed excitement at the origin of all emotions in her genetic system of emotions: "It is a moot question whether 'distress' is an original emotion or whether it is a very early differentiated reaction to disagreeably painful stimuli. It may be that it is a part of the general emotional response of excitement which copes more satisfactorily with obnoxious stimuli. Tense

ing to these authors, the child is at first not subject to the pleasure, but rather to the Nirvana principle, and his earliest motivation is tension reduction and not pleasure seeking.

"Since a hungry baby, when unfed, will cry and fail to sleep and as a rule will show an increase in restless motility, as well as mottling of the skin, changes in respiration, and changes in tonus, we infer that hunger corresponds to a heightened tension state. Most of us are willing to assume that, beyond a certain degree, this hunger state is accompanied by displeasure. The relaxation of muscles, the equalization of skin color, the change toward less shallow and labored respiration, the decrease in motility and the tendency to go to sleep toward the end of a feeding period we correlate with a discharge of tension leading to a relative state of quiescence and the cessation of displeasure [Escalona, 1953, p. 13]."

This reduction of pleasure to quiescence and of pain to simple displeasure is one of Spitz's preferred conceptualizations. He already submitted it as a hypothesis in his monograph on "The Smiling Response" (Spitz and Wolf, 1946) and offered it as the indisputable conclusion of systematic observations in his more recent works:

"We therefore feel justified in assuming, provisionally, that in the new-born there exist only two primal undifferentiated emotional attitudes: that of accepting and that of rejecting a stimulus. Even this statement should probably be qualified, since there is some doubt whether acceptance of a stimulus is really a positive attitude. It might be also assumed that when a stimulus like food

---

muscles resist or remove pressure; activity warms a chilled body and reduces tension; and cries, at first, a reflex due to the rush of air in and out of the lungs, bring comfort and aid. These responses become differentiated from excitement, associated together and conditioned to the disagreeable stimuli as a result of experience. If such differentiation actually takes place, it must begin immediately after birth. For the two emotions of excitement and distress are already distinguishable in a three-weeks old infant . . . . Delight is much later in becoming differentiated from general excitement than distress. The baby under a month old is either excited or quiescent. Gentle striking, swaying and patting soothe him and make him sleepy. When satisfied after a meal, he is no longer excited nor even distressed by hunger. And yet he is not positively delighted. He is just unemotionally content, and either tranquil or busy" (Bridges, 1932, pp. 327, 334).

or warmth is accepted it does not create emotional reaction, but is rather incorporated into the child's system of psychic equilibrium without disturbing his state of quiescence. Conversely, when a negative emotional manifestation is stopped by 'positive' stimulation (such as food, warmth, etc.), then it might be that the removal of the negative stimulus merely re-instates the previous situation of quiescence, without creating a positive emotion at all [Spitz and Wolf, 1946, p. 61]."

Eight years later Spitz specified: ". . . during the first hours and days of life unpleasure is the only observable affect. Its counterpart is not pleasure but quiescence. This is a mode of functioning along strictly physiological lines" (Spitz, 1954, p. 489). The great majority of contemporary writers disregard this distinction. Although they use "unpleasure" instead of "pain" with increasing frequency, they still speak of pleasure as appearing right after birth.

"During this phase manifestations of both libido and aggression are frequently indistinguishable or difficult to distinguish. However, observation of the neonate and infant invariably enables us to differentiate between manifestations of pleasure and unpleasure of various degrees [Hartmann, Kris, and Loewenstein, 1949, p. 25]."

As we have already seen, Anna Freud (1946), in the first papers she published in *The Psychoanalytic Study of the Child,* spoke of "love" even in the narcissistic period. However, by placing the word in quotation marks, she indicated the particular sense in which she used it. Before the objectal period true love is out of the question; yet Anna Freud seems to believe in a precocious pleasure affect.

"With the step from intrauterine to extrauterine life, need satisfaction becomes incomplete; there is never as much as the infant demands, and it never arrives quite as quickly as expected. Wish fulfillment is delayed, and *pleasure* is rationed and curtailed[27] [Kris, 1954, p. 60]."

[27] Italics added (T.G.D.).

Anna Freud also uses the terms "tension" and "relief," but the latter never seems to be identical with mere quiescence. Relief is apparently accompanied by ineffable emotions. "The libidinal cathexis at this time [the beginning of life] is shown to be attached, not to the image of the object, but to the *blissful experience of satisfaction* and relief . . ."[28] (A. Freud, 1954, p. 12).

C. THE NARCISSISTIC PERIOD IN TERMS OF OBJECT FORMATION

When we attempt to describe the typical object of the narcissistic period we encounter a problem of terminology: here, the influence of Kleinian concepts is particularly marked and results in variations of the meaning of such terms as "part object," from one author to another. In order to remain faithful to our aim of simplification we shall refer only to the most explicit texts. This considerably reduces our source material.

Most authors concur in acknowledging that in a strict sense there are no objects in the narcissistic period.

"Psycho-analytical theory claims that the first part of infancy is characterized by the narcissistic stage. Phenomenological and experimental observations confirm and limit this statement to the first three months. During this period environmental perception takes place only in function of the presence of a need-configuration directed towards this perception. The object, which at this period is to be considered a part object, is perceived only in function of the internal need. Therefore this period has to be considered objectless [Spitz, 1950d, p. 140]."

Spitz's part object seems to correspond to a large extent to the object of the anaclitic relation which, according to Anna Freud, constitutes the specific object relation of the beginning of life:

"The concept of an anaclitic relationship has never been fully utilized in analytic writings. It means, shortly, that the relationship to the mother, although the first to another human being, is

---

[28] Italics added (T.G.D.).

not the infant's first relationship to the environment. What precedes it, is an earlier phase in which not the object world but the body needs and their satisfaction or frustration play the decisive part [A. Freud, 1954, p. 11]."

In the ensuing discussion of this idea, Anna Freud established a parallel between the "anaclitic" object and the concepts of Melanie Klein, Hartmann, and Hoffer:

"What leaves me dissatisfied with these formulations is the fact that in their very terminology they stress the importance of the *object* whereas the child is dominated by the *need*. It is true that the mother's breast, or the bottle, have to be present so that the child can drink. But what is cathected with libidinal interest at that stage is the moment of blissful satiation, not the object which enables satiation to be obtained [A. Freud, 1954, p. 58]."

Hoffer took this aspect into consideration when he wrote:

"At first the mother has meaning for the infant only in so far as she can serve the need for tension reduction. Indeed, we can say that the object at the early stages of childhood has for some time no independent existence for the child, but is treated as part of the 'milieu interne,' serving the satisfaction of the child's inner needs in the same manner in which these needs are served by his own body [Hoffer, 1955, p. 88]."

As mentioned above, for Spitz too the "object" of the narcissistic period characteristically exists only in its function as something that satisfies physiological needs. However, he includes the breast and the mother (or any mother substitute) in this particular category of objects. Thus, from the first month on, the breast becomes the first partial or anaclitic[28] object because of the oral, tactile, and kinesthetic (but not visual) sensations: "It is correct that the breast is the first object; it is probable that the breast, or rather the nipple, forms a part of the first percept..." (Spitz, 1955c, p. 223). Spitz defines "percept"[29] and indicates how this first object differs from the true libidinal object.

[28] We prefer this term which avoids all possible confusion with Melanie Klein's "part-object."
[29] "Percept, the thing perceived (Hinsie and Shatsky) should be clearly dis-

The infant's response to human beings as early as during the narcissistic period is due to a precocious integration of the human being into the experience of nursing. On this level the human partner is not at all perceived as such; he merely plays the role of a signal announcing the drive gratification through kinesthetic and cutaneous cues.

There seems to be no major disagreement among authors regarding object formation during the narcissistic period; they all agree that life in its initial stages is devoid of true objects.

We conclude this brief analysis with a beautiful passage by Escalona wherein she hypothesizes what the infant experiences in the narcissistic period:

"At first, the world is a succession of different sensations and feeling states. What varies is the quality and distribution and intensity of sensations. Except for the difference in the nature of the sensations involved, hunger, which we say originates from within, and a sharp sound or cold breeze, which we cannot imagine except as something that reaches us from the outside, are indistinguishable. There is no awareness of such things as approach, withdrawal, or direction of any sort. Even if the baby turns his head toward the nipple and grasps it, his sensation is that the nipple comes or is; no other state with which to contrast this exists. Light and darkness; harshness and softness; cold and warmth; sleep and waking; the contours of mother's face as seen from below, vis-à-vis, or even from above; being grasped and released; being moved and moving; the sight of moving people, curtains, blankets, toys; all these recede and approach and comprise the totality of experience in whatever constellation they occur at each split second in time. With recurrence, there develop islands of consistency [Escalona, 1953, p. 25]."

II. THE INTERMEDIATE PERIOD

The second period of objectal development is essentially a transitional phase. It still contains elements of the narcissistic period

---

tinguished from object (libidinal); the latter originates through the focussing of a constellation of drives into a percept. Perception of the percept is the prerequisite of object formation" (Spitz, 1955c, p. 223).

while it presages through some of its characteristics the final period of objectal development. Like any intermediary stage, it is particularly difficult to delineate and can be understood only with reference to the preceding and following periods. Hence our analysis will be brief. Moreover, some authors do not even acknowledge this second period; others merely suggest its existence; others, finally, among them Spitz, describe it explicitly. The latter, a specialist on objectal relations, will serve as our guide through this period.

A. THE INTERMEDIATE PERIOD FROM THE STRUCTURAL VIEWPOINT

The narcissistic period was characterized by undifferentiation of the psychic apparatus and nonexistence of the ego. During the period under discussion certain restricted ego functions appear which make it possible, at best, to speak of a primitive ego. Yet, differentiation within the psyche and first reality testing are revealed. Kris, who prefers the term "gradient" to "phase" or "period," indicates the existence of such a gradient at about the third month, when certain phenomena seem to imply a new forward step in ego development.

"However hesitant we may have become in our endeavor at setting such gradients, it seems that at the age of twelve weeks or three months previously imperceptible or less well perceptible functions become on the average integrated and can be established by observation. The most spectacular of these developments concerns a definite change in the relation to need satisfaction, a step in ego development. The infant learns to anticipate the imminent feeding situation and under optimal conditions to wait for it [Kris, 1951b, p. 97]."

Anna Freud too uses the ability to wait as an indication of ego formation. She places this ability somewhere after the sixth month:

"The rudiments of the ego, as they emerge gradually in the first half of the first year of life, take their pattern from the environmental conditions which have left their imprint on the infant's mind by way of his early pleasure-pain experiences, the conditions themselves becoming internalized in the ego structure. Although the ego as an agency furthers wish fulfillment, it does so accepting the principles of delay and rationing which govern infant care. This acceptance can be shown to be significant from various aspects: (a) it represents the beginning of what will later become the reality principle; (b) it creates in the ego a lasting, cautious, curtailing attitude toward the id drives; and thereby (c) introduces into the personality a first break, id and ego serving different aims from then onwards, governed in their functioning by different principles[30] [A. Freud, 1954, pp. 13-14]."

In his paper, "Development of the Body Ego," Hoffer (1950a) resumes the hypothesis already put forward in "Mouth, Hand, and Ego-Integration" (Hoffer, 1949) according to which voluntary thumb-sucking is an indication of the emergence of the ego and thereby of a first differentiation within the psychic apparatus. He places such sucking between the twelfth and sixteenth week and takes it as a sign for the appearance of specific ego functions. Hoffer (1950a, pp. 19ff.) speaks of the existence of a "mouth-ego" as the first element of the body ego at this level.

"Our clue to this differentiation of psychic structure is to be found in the voluntary intended use of one part of the body to allay tension arising in another part. I am thinking here of the situation, which does not usually arise before the twelfth week, when, no longer reflexively, quite intentionally, the hand is put into the mouth in order to relieve oral tension[31] [Hoffer, 1955, p. 77]."

Spitz attributes paramount importance to the appearance of smiling. Considered in its entirety, he regards this phenomenon

[30] The reader is reminded of the importance given to this concept of waiting and postponement by David Rapaport in the construction of his primary conceptual model (cf. Rapaport, 1951, pp. 599ff.).

[31] In the course of the initial construction of our objectal scale we had thought of using thumb-sucking as an operational criterion. We had to give up this thought because this manifestation of the emergence of the ego is not sufficiently generalized.

as an index of the elaboration of the first pre-object (Spitz, 1950e, p. 68) and of the infant's having reached the pre-objectal phase: "the transition point from the primary narcissistic to the libidinal object stage" (Spitz, 1954, p. 500). He analyzes ten aspects of this problem: the first six concern directly the development of psychic structures and ego formation. Spitz writes:

"1. This stage marks the point at which the infant turns away from what I have called internal *reception* of experience toward external *perception* of stimuli coming from the environment. 2. This development presupposes the establishment of conscious memory traces in the infant's psyche. 3. At the same time it presupposes a division between conscious and preconscious and the separation of both from the unconscious. 4. This establishment of memory traces and the separation of Cs, Pcs and Ucs make the beginning of thought possible. 5. The arrival of thought introduces at the same time the emergence of the reality principle which is a detour function. 6. This very development during the third month marks the rudimentary beginning of the ego, if we define it as the central steering mechanism [Spitz, 1954, pp. 499-500]."

B. THE INTERMEDIATE PERIOD FROM THE DYNAMIC AND ECONOMIC VIEWPOINTS

1. The quantitative aspect

We saw that the total absence of psychic energy distribution was of short duration; however, undifferentiation between self and outer world runs through the entire narcissistic period. Will it still be so during the period under scrutiny, or will the infant of the intermediary period begin to distinguish between himself and his environment?

The parallel between the emergence of ego functions and the appearance of the first formative elements of the self seems obvious. Thus, the authors consulted agree in pointing at the first differentiation between self and external reality as an index for the initiation of the intermediate period. Yet, this differentiation remains limited, fragmentary and vague.

"When using the term 'self-regard' for an infant from about three to four months onwards we mean, no doubt, a psychological stage in which primary narcissism has already been modified but the world of objects has not necessarily yet taken on definite shape. The boundaries of a supposed self, to follow Paul Federn, are still on the move towards the body and its surface and by no means defined [Hoffer, 1950b, p. 159]."

In one of his most recent works, Spitz clearly distinguishes between "ego," "I," and "self."[32] He regards the self as an extremely complex process whose relatively late appearance he locates around 15 months. This hypothesis is, however, his own; most psychoanalysts describe as the self of early infancy what Spitz calls the "I." The following excerpt has to be understood in this light:

"Another way of expressing the significance of the smiling reaction is that its onset designates that level of the infant's development at which it becomes able to differentiate 'I' from 'You,' the subject from the object, his own person from other persons (and incidentally from objects without emotional significance) [Spitz and Wolf, 1946, p. 89]."

For Benedek, smiling and the ability to postpone gratification (she places the latter at 5 months) reveal an initial security, a confidence which represents an essential turning point in objectal development and indicates a first differentiation between self and environment: "This confidence[33] is a stage of object relationship

[32] "In the previous chapters it has become evident that we make a rather rigorous distinction between the 'ego,' the 'I,' and the 'self.' The definition of the ego was given by Freud when he introduced the concept of psychic structure. Among the ego's functions is that of a central steering organization, mediating between the outside and the rest of the psyche. The 'I' and the 'non-I' are nonanalytic concepts. They were introduced by us to describe phenomena normally occurring and empirically observed in infants. These terms denote the incipient awareness of there being 'something separate' from him. At this stage this 'something separate' is the surround. This awareness arises through a progressive restriction of the new-born primary narcissism by the onset of rudimentary ego functions, foremost among which is perception" (Spitz, 1957, p. 115).

[33] "What I call 'trust,' Thérèse Benedek has called 'confidence.' I like the word 'trust' better because confidence is a more mature and conscious attitude" (Erikson, 1950, p. 19).

which precedes the positive object love. It has on one hand connection with the primary narcissism, on the other hand it already reaches out for the object" (Benedek, 1938, p. 203).

Escalona speaks of differentiation between self and environment in terms of time and space, the two complementary aspects of the ability to wait. She emphasizes that:

". . . when we speak of a separation between the self and the nonself, it is equivalent to saying that some experience of distance emerges; separation implies distance. It seems more than chance, therefore, that early forms of reality oriented behavior and intentional action become observable at that time in development when distant receptors (vision and sound) have reached relative functional maturity. Very roughly speaking, the phenomena in question become overtly manifest during the three to five months' period, though if our observational powers were more subtle we could probably see the same sort of thing at an earlier age[34] [Escalona, 1953, p. 23]."

Hoffer sees in the infant's ability to intentionally suck his thumb one of the causal factors for the distinction between self and outer world. "Coming in touch with its own body elicits two sensations of the same quality and these lead to the distinction between the self and the non-self, between the body and what subsequently becomes environment" (Hoffer, 1950a, p. 19).

If we speak no longer in terms of differentiation between self and environment, but attempt to specify the hypotheses concerning libidinal energy distribution during the intermediate period (this distribution being a prerequisite for said differentiation), in other words, if we limit ourselves to the shift of cathexis, we now become aware of the increasing difficulty of distinguishing between the quantitative and qualitative aspects of psychic energy. This must explain why there are so few texts on this point and why they raise so many problems.

For example, two of Anna Freud's papers dealing explicitly with this subject refer to only two steps in the energy distribu-

---

[34] Concerning this point, see Chambers, 1957, pp. 85ff.

tion: (1) the satisfying experience is cathected. This characterizes the anaclitic relationship discussed above as being typical of the beginning of life; (2) the intermediary (or its image) through which the satisfying experience is obtained is cathected. This step represents the dawn of true object relations and takes place—probably—at about the sixth month. The cathected intermediary may be a thing or a person. "Libidinal cathexis shifts gradually from the experience of satisfaction to the image of the object without whom satisfaction would not have come about. With this step forward in development, the infant enters into the stage of object love" (A. Freud, 1954, p. 13). In the ensuing discussion she goes into further detail:

"I believe that we neglect the difference which exists between the object of a need, or a drive, and a love object. We should speak of the latter only after libido cathexis has been transferred from the experience of wish fulfillment to the (material or human) object by means of which satisfaction comes about. ... On the other hand, there is no doubt that the object of the need (or drive) becomes the first love object. I do not know when this happens. I should imagine that it occurs toward the middle of the first year, and that it happens very gradually, so that we are not able to say at what particular moment in time the shift of cathexis has occurred. It may be wrong altogether to use chronological terms here instead of terms designating psychic structure [A. Freud, in Kris, 1954, p. 59]."

There is no mention here of an image of the object except, perhaps, by implication. Be that as it may, Anna Freud speaks explicitly of object love as soon as cathexis of a particular thing or person appears. In an earlier paper she seemed to see in that material object cathexis only an intermediary stage of objectal development and reserved the term *object love* for the time when a person is libidinally cathected:

"When the child's awareness develops sufficiently to discern other qualities besides those of pain-and pleasure, the libido cathexis progresses from the pleasurable experience of feeding to the food which is the source of pleasure. The infant in this second

stage 'loves' the milk, breast or bottle. (Since on this level of development, no certain distinctions are made between the child's
self and the environment, this libido attachment forms a transitional stage between narcissism and object love.) When its powers
of perception permit the child to form a conception of the person through whose agency it is fed, its 'love' is transferred to the
provider of food, that is to the mother or mother-substitute (ob-
ject-love) [A. Freud, 1946, pp. 124-125]."

This passage is certainly not easy to understand. Yet, we do
not believe that we distort the ideas of its author too much when
we interpret it as follows.

Object cathexis and *object love* are not equivalent. Cathexis of
a specific object can be conceived of in the absence of a true object relation. Here, development of perception plays an important
part, i.e., the attachment to the mother follows actually an "attachment" (in the preceding quotation, *love* certainly has a very
relative meaning) to the breast or the bottle, and appears at the .
time that the infant becomes capable of conceiving of the mother as
agent. This conceptualization requires a certain perceptual development.

This initial hypothesis of a first object cathexis preceding a
true object relation fits well into current psychoanalytic thinking,
more so than Anna Freud's later hypothesis which obliterates the
distinction between "cathexis of the object" and "objectal cathexis." Furthermore, it seems paradoxical to speak of object love
when the differentiation between self and outer world has hardly begun. Anna Freud acknowledges that when the child forms an
attachment to the breast, the milk, or the bottle, he does not yet
clearly distinguish himself from his environment. It is to be noted
also that most investigators interpret the role of perceptual processes differently from the way Anna Freud does. For example,
Spitz and Benedek insist that, from the viewpoint of *visual* perception alone, the person is associated to the satisfying experience
long before the breast or the bottle, and that the first manifestations of "love" (such as smiling) appear in a sustained fashion

when the child sees a human face and not when he perceives the direct source of food.

2. *The qualitative aspect*

According to Spitz (who is one of the few psychoanalytic writers interested in the genesis of emotions) the intermediate period is characterized by the progressive differentiation of the affect of unpleasure on the one hand and by the appearance of smiling, the first indisputable indication of positive emotion, on the other.

"During the same period the unpleasure responses become more specific. The stimuli which provoke them are not connected any longer nearly exclusively to inner sensations. Neither are these unpleasure responses any more the fleeting and short-lasting discharge phenomena of the first days. . . .

"Therefore, in the third month, the infant is not only able to manifest pleasure when beholding its human partner, but also to produce long-lasting unpleasure reactions when deprived of him. These two responses are the greatest advance in discriminatory development at this age. No such discrimination can be demonstrated in respect to toys or even to food at the same period [Spitz, 1950d, p. 2]."

Spitz, (1954, 1959) borrows from embryology the term "organizer" and part of its theoretical implications and further analyzes the smiling of the three-month-old. He sees in its appearance a crucial moment in the evolution of pleasurable affects.

". . . the smiling reaction is an indicator of the emotional maturation of the child during its first half year. It informs us that the child is not only achieving mastery of perceptive discrimination and neuromuscular coördination of its mimic musculature, but that it is also progressing toward a finer differentiation of emotional reaction. It has become capable of distinguishing, within the chaos of its reactions, *some* which produce something different in the way of experience than did either the unpleasure reaction or the attitude of quiescence in the neo-nate. It has become capable of relating such experiences to external factors. These external factors are in some way connected with a human partner. The coloring of the child's reaction to them appears to be similar to what we call pleasure in the grown-up. We may, therefore, say that the child has acquired the capacity to distinguish and to experience positive emotions [Spitz and Wolf, 1946, p. 90]."

At this period the infant's smile is, however, nothing but a response to a signal: he smiles, similarly at a mask and at a human face, at a sardonic and at a smiling expression, and he stops smiling when he sees the face or the mask only in profile.[35] It has, however, from the intermediate period on an undeniable, objectal meaning since:

". . . this signal belongs to and is derived from the mother's face. It is tied up with a situation of food, protection and sense of security. It will develop later on and finally transform the mother as a whole into an actual object. I have therefore called this restricted response to part of a human face a pre-object relation whereas I have called the signal by which the recognition takes place a precursor of the object [Spitz, 1954, p. 496]."

C. THE INTERMEDIATE PERIOD IN TERMS OF OBJECT FORMATION

The above quotations make it easier for us to describe the specific object of the intermediary period. We saw that, for Anna Freud, after the anaclitic relation the object may be material (milk, breast, bottle) or human (usually the mother). Be that as it may (and even if the primitive attitude which consists in considering the love object solely as a means of gratification persists well beyond the narcissistic period), as of the third or fourth month the movement is clearly toward "personification" of that object. Normally the cathexis of a thing constitutes only a step in that evolution.

". . . I stressed that all the early, 'impersonal' experiences of the need-satisfying phase are translated gradually into the per-

---

[35] We remain here within the context and limitations of Spitz's experiences; we shall return to this problem of the stimuli for the smiling response when we construct our objectal scale.

sonal terms of relations with the mother. In an increasing degree the mother is recognized as the source of pleasure and unpleasure and cathected as such [A. Freud, in Kris, 1954, p. 59]."

To our knowledge Anna Freud does not offer other characteristics of the object at this level. Yet we shall attempt to explain what she may mean by this personification of the object, when we study the last period of objectal development.

Spitz is more precise: the object of the intermediate period is the smiling human face, the natural stimulus for the smiling response in the infant, and it forms a precursor of the true libidinal object. Spitz (1950d) writes about the "pre-object": "The second quarter is a transitional period in which a slow emergence takes place from a narcissistic to a pre-objectal stage. The part-objects are organized into pre-objects in the shape of the human partner's face" (p. 140). What, then, are the characteristics of this particular object?

". . . the pre-objects are interchangeable, for they are lacking in object attributes. Their characteristics are not objective. They are characterized by the capacity to fulfill the exact requisites of a given need-configuration. The objects at this period do not have a face, they have a function [Spitz, 1950d, p. 141]."

Spitz comes to this apparently paradoxical conclusion on the basis of the fact that the child of this stage does not smile at a human profile, whereas he smiles without distinction at anybody slowly shaking his head in front view. It has been demonstrated experimentally that the 3-month-old does not visually recognize the human partner as such; all he recognizes is the gestalt forehead-eyes-nose. If this gestalt is altered only slightly (e.g., by hiding one eye), the alleged object is not recognized.

"It is for this reason that we called this gestalt a pre-object. What the child recognizes in this sign-Gestalt are not the essential qualities of the object (i.e., the qualities which enable the object to provide for wants, protect and satisfy) but its superficial attributes. The libidinal object differs from 'things' precisely in the fact that its essential qualities are anchored in its genesis.

These qualities remain unalterable through all the vicissitudes which transform the outer attributes of the libidinal object. 'Things' are, in contrast, characterized by their superficial attributes and any change in these attributes would hamper the recognition of the 'thing.' The sign-Gestalt thus forms an attribute which belongs rather to 'things' than to the libidinal object and is consequently ephemeral. Yet, from its elaboration through the genesis of objectal relations this sign receives a quality which exceeds that of 'things' and assures it of a place in the consequent genealogy of the libidinal object [Spitz, 1954, p. 495]."

We see that the pre-object foreshadows the libidinal object which is the goal of the object relation, but it still differs from the libidinal object on the basis of the elements which it has as yet in common with things and with the anaclitic object of the preceding period. For this reason we called this a transitional period.

III. THE TRUE OBJECTAL PERIOD

The further we follow the objectal development, the more fluidity we encounter in psychoanalytic hypotheses. When we reach the last step, the criteria of development become more and more tenuous, the lines of demarcation less and less clear, and the significant texts increasingly meager.[36] The writings remain, however, explicit enough to enable us to speak of an objectal period within the first eighteen months of life. This period has a terminal character; it marks the end of a cycle and extends over a period which spreads from about 6 to 12-15 months.[37] It seems

[36] The most significant are again those by Spitz who remains the psychoanalyst who wrote the most (and in our opinion the best) about the genesis of objectal relations.

[37] As far as we know, Spitz (1957) is the only one who speaks of a third organizer around the fifteenth month. He attributes to the "No" gesture an objectal meaning (the child identifies with the prohibiting adult) and a topological one (the gesture is a precursor of the superego) (1958). We terminated our experiments before the publication of these latter hypotheses and, therefore, could not take them into consideration. We did make use of them, nevertheless, in subsequent research.

superfluous to emphasize the extreme importance of this first cycle: all psychoanalytic writers see in it a decisive moment in the psychological development of man and analyze all social relationships of adults in the light of those first years.

The main characteristic of that period is the blossoming of all the elements which are contained in a germinal state in the previous step. From now on one can speak of an ego which has reached a certain functional maturity and of neutralized and even "socialized" libido attached to true libidinal objects. At the same time, a multitude of emotions (tenderness, rage, anxiety, jealousy, etc.) are encountered at this level, giving evidence of the extraordinary complexity of the psychic apparatus.

Two steps seem distinguishable within the objectal period, marking its beginning and its peak respectively.[38] In the sphere of normality, gradual disappearance of undifferentiated smiling, the first active manifestations of affection, and the appearance of anxiety are said to belong to the beginning of the objectal period, while the first possibility of an anaclitic depression at the time of loss of the love object is considered to be its pathological correlate.[39]

The essential characteristic of the end of the objectal period is a permanent object whose objectivity is recognized; the status of libidinal object is finally reached. Theoretically, the line between the two phases of the objectal period can be drawn with relative ease. Experimentally, this is not so, since the phenomena flow imperceptibly into one another, which makes an objective evaluation of these two levels almost impossible.

---

[38] Spitz also conceives of a transitional phase between the intermediate and the objectal period: "This is the situation at 3 months when the pre-object is established. This stage is followed by an approximately eight-week transitional period of a step by step development: the transition from the pre-objectal stage to that of true object relations" (Spitz, 1954, p. 522).

[39] Spitz (1946b) points out that he never observed anaclitic depression before the age of 6 months, which he considers the chronological minimum on the basis of the development of the object concept.

A. THE OBJECTAL PERIOD IN TERMS OF EGO FORMATION

On this level we are less concerned with differentiation of psychic structures than with ego formation. Henceforth, the id and the ego are clearly differentiated in both their aims and their functions, while there is not yet any clear evidence of the existence of a superego. Thus, psychoanalysts write about the objectal period in terms of ego formation and emphasize the new functional maturity of the ego at this stage of development. This maturity becomes particularly clear when we analyze the five main functions of the ego in early childhood (cf. this chapter, footnote 18).

1. Perception has developed to a point where the love object is now visually distinguished from all other objects as indicated by the disappearance of the automatic smile and the eventual appearance of anxiety at the sight of a stranger.

"In our opinion, the disappearance of the indiscriminate smiling pattern marks the beginning of differentiation between 'friend' and 'stranger.' With this step the reaction to the 'human being in general' has progressed to a reaction to the emotionally welcomed individual. ... This disappearance of the indiscriminate smiling response after the sixth month is a sign of definite progress in environmental discrimination and it is also an indication of further emotional maturation [Spitz and Wolf, 1946, p. 90]."

"*In the third quarter* [of the first year of life] *the human object* and also the inanimate object are recognized by virtue of their objectal attributes and *perception has become truly objective. With this the period of the preobjects has ended, and object libidinal relations have become possible. ... Between the seventh and eighth months the libidinal object has become firmly established and the eight-months anxiety is the sign of the infant's discrimination of its love object from all other human beings* [Spitz, 1950e, p. 70]."

2. Motor activity is now sufficiently under ego control to make an intentional activity possible which can reach the goal it pursues.

"All this changes after the eighth month: at this point the child reaches straight for the one object which it desires among the many. As a pure function, grasping at this stage has lost its significance. In other terms, grasping has changed from a nonspecific to a purposive function [Spitz, 1951a, p. 146]."

3. The memory traces are stable and numerous enough to make a new intellectual activity possible, namely judgment.

"In the case of smiling, the sign-Gestalt is confronted by the memory traces of the human partners and accepted because it is homologous to them. In the eight-months anxiety, the perception of the stranger's face *qua* face is confronted with the memory traces of the mother's face. It proves to be different and is rejected. Through this functioning of his memory traces, the child evidences that it has formed a true object relationship with the mother as his libidinal object. At the same time he gives evidence of the acquisition of a new ego function: the function of judgment [Spitz, 1954, p. 519]."

4. The pleasure principle which dominated the infant's life almost exclusively gradually subsides letting the reality principle intervene more and more frequently and more and more efficiently. This becomes clearly evident from conformity to orders and prohibitions and (which means the same) from passing from fear of loss of the love object to fear of losing the love of the object.

"The relationship of the child to the world around him changes in character when the reality principle, at least in part, replaces the pleasure principle. ... This step becomes possible only if and when the urgency of demands can be reduced, when, as we said, future gratification can be substituted for immediate gratification. As a consequence, experience with those whom the child loves is no longer exclusively in terms of indulgence or deprivation. The child's attachment to them can outlast deprivation and they gain characteristics of their own that the child tries to understand [Hartmann, Kris, and Loewenstein, 1946, p. 30]."

Hartmann, Kris, and Loewenstein place this step toward the end of the first year, but Kris (1950) emphasizes that there is never an absolute demarcation between the two archaic dangers: the fear of loss of the love object which represents the anaclitic

needs, and the fear of losing the love of the object which represents a more integrated relationship regarding a permanent and
personalized love object. On this level one should undoubtedly
speak of secondary phases, substages or even in terms of ratio.[40]

5. The synthetic function of the ego leads, on this level, to a
first integration of the two basic drives: libido and aggression.
Here lies the extremely complex problem of the "good" and the
"bad" object. We shall not enter upon this problem because it
belongs to the development of aggression in the child and because
we have arbitrarily chosen not to deal with that development.
We emphasize here only the phenomenon of *drive fusion* because
it is highly representative for the synthetic function of the ego
during the objectal period.

"Around the sixth month a synthesis takes place. Meanwhile
the ego has taken on an increasingly important part. Its integrative function combines with countlessly repeated experiences with
the person of the mother and fuses the good and the bad object
with the perceptually single person of the mother. With this syn-
thesizing act the two drives become directed toward a single perceptual object. Through collaboration of perception, action and
the integrative function of the ego the fusion of the two drives is
achieved. The formation of the true libidinal object takes
place at this point. This is the beginning of true objectal relations [Spitz, 1954, p. 523]."

This new functional maturity of the ego is, by the way, a very
relative one; any recent acquisition makes the subject vulnerable
and multiplies the possibilities for regression.[41]

---

[40] "The fear of object loss never quite disappears; the fear of loss of love has
added a new dimension to a child's life and with it a new vulnerability. Quite
possibly, then, in studying child development further and in greater detail,
we might find it convenient to introduce not only 'sub-phases' but also to describe the simultaneous distribution of both types of object relation in one
child, e.g., in terms of a ratio" (Kris, 1950, p. 33).

[41] "... it appears relevant that newly acquired ego functions show a high
degree of reversibility in the child and that special devices are used by him in
his effort to counteract regression" (Hartmann, 1952, p. 26).

B. THE OBJECTAL PERIOD FROM THE DYNAMIC AND ECONOMIC VIEWPOINTS

1. The quantitative aspect

The intermediate period is marked by a first differentiation between self and environment, but it is only a first step in differentiation. On the objectal level, the infant clearly distinguishes himself from his environment. He recognizes his mother and other people of his immediate world as well as many familiar things. He understands a number of communications which (through imitation and/or identification) he becomes capable of using on his own. This simple understanding of such signs and the passage from passivity to activity are valuable objectal criteria.

"As the child learns to distinguish between himself and the mother, he develops understanding for her communications.[42] Little is known about the detailed processes by which this understanding is established; reactions to the actual handling of the child by the mother, to touch and bodily pressure, certainly play a part; gradually, the understanding of the child for the mother's facial expression grows. It seems probable that experiences concerning emotive processes and expressive movements in the infant itself form the basis or are a necessary condition for the infant's understanding of the mother's expression (Freud, 1905; Schilder, 1935 [1950]). But the cognitive side of the process, the understanding of signs of communication, is part of the libidinal tie existing between the two [Hartmann, Kris, and Loewenstein, 1946, p. 22]."

It is this deep interrelation between objectal development and semantics which Spitz (1957) attempts to analyze in *No and Yes*. He notes in this context: "On the age level of nine to twelve months at which primitive gesture identification[43] develops, the child also acquires the first understanding of commands and prohibitions" (p. 43).

For Escalona the eighth-month anxiety gives evidence of a more

---

[42] Italics added (T.G.D.). This development belongs in the objectal period, since it follows recognition of the mother.
[43] The term "gesture identification" is borrowed from Berta Bornstein.

complex differentiation between self and environment than most authors assume. She actually accepts the current interpretation of this indication but adds another meaning to it.

"As a matter of fact, it has seemed to me that so-called eight months' anxiety is a consequence of that step forward in the comprehension of the world about which enables the baby to perceive that the mother is an independent entity who can decide to be absent or present at will. If you will take these words in a somewhat metaphorical sense, it may be viewed as the final abandonment of a mode of experience corresponding to the notion of infantile omnipotence, and a very early step toward a mode of experience in which adults, and especially parents, are perceived as omnipotent [Escalona, 1953, p. 52]."

The sources consulted agree more in their analyses of the differentiation between self and environment than on the unperceivable dynamic processes underlying the differentiation, i.e., the distribution of cathexis.

Anna Freud explains the passage from the narcissistic to the objectal period on the basis of drive changes (i.e., on the basis of what she considers to be the quantitative aspect of cathexis development).[44] She distinguishes between certain steps in psychic energy distribution which are a direct function of the gradual decrease in the urgency of the drives.

[44] "The present writer's views on the same subject lean toward a quantitative rather than qualitative explanation. When studying a group of infants in situation of extreme need after separation from their mothers . . . , I developed the idea that the step from the first to the second stage of object relationship—from the milieu interne to the psychological object (Hoffer), from the need-satisfying object to object constancy (Hartmann), from part-objects to whole objects (Melanie Klein)—is determined by a decrease in the urgency of the drives themselves" (A. Freud, 1952, p. 44).

I am personally inclined to consider these changes as representing the *qualitative* aspect of cathexis development. Even if one assumes that certain needs can *by themselves* decrease in intensity (in which case the six-month-old would be less hungry than the newborn, which seems to be true for the adult whose visceral contractions usually do not attain the degree of intensity of those of the infant [cf. Pratt, 1946]) the ego development seems to remain the preponderant factor even in consideration of Anna Freud's statement. It requires an ego which grows capable of more and more effective controls in the face of the continued urgency of certain needs (e.g., the need to defecate).

"The needs have to lessen in strength, or have to be brought under ego control, before nonsatisfying (for instance, absent) objects can retain their cathexis. This statement is borne out by the behavior of young children under the influence of separation from their mothers. In the earliest months of life it seems possible to exchange the object, provided the form of need satisfaction given to the infant remains unaltered. Later (approximately after five months) the personal attachment to the object increases in importance; it becomes possible then to vary the satisfactions, provided the object remains the same. At that stage (approximately five to twenty-five months) separation from the object causes extreme distress, but the infant is so exclusively dominated by his needs that he cannot maintain his attachment to a nonsatisfying object for more than a given period (varying from several hours to several days). After this interval, which is most upsetting for the child, need satisfaction is accepted from and attachment (cathexis) is transferred to a substitute. As the ego matures and the pleasure principle yields to the reality principle, children gradually develop the ability to retain libidinal cathexis to absent love objects during separations of increasing lengths [A. Freud, 1952, p. 44f.]."

The possibility that the object retains the libidinal cathexis thus seems very relative even on the objectal level,[45] and highly dependent upon the continued presence of the object. Even at the age of two, a withdrawal of cathexis is still possible if not inevitable during an absence of the mother for more than a few days (Bowlby et al., 1952).

Spitz too occasionally uses the more or less traumatic impact of the separation from the mother as a criterion for the development of object relations, but he places himself, in these instances, within a clearly clinical framework[46] (Spitz, 1945a, 1946a, 1946b, 1950b, 1951c, Spitz and Wolf, 1949). When Spitz speaks of the loss of the love object in the framework of normality, he refers

[45] Anna Freud speaks of object love and of love object as soon as cathexis of something other than the gratifying experience or the self occurs. She places the possibility of object cathexis usually around the fifth or sixth month.

[46] A recent study (Schaffer and Callender, 1959) seems to prove that the effects of separation from the mother are very different for infants of 28 weeks or less and those of 29 weeks or more.

rather to the mother's short absences which occur necessarily in the course of the day. He attributes to them the following consequences on the objectal level.

"The loss of the object is therefore a diminution of the Ego at this age[47] and is as severe a narcissistic trauma as a loss of a large part of the body. The reaction to it is just as severe. Anxiety is the affect evoked by the threatening imminence of such a loss. This affect is produced in a constant flux during the daily contacts of the mother with the child. The child is assuaged when the mother is near it, when it sees her or hears her; it becomes anxious when she leaves it. The repeated anxiety attacks are short-lived; perhaps hallucinations replace the mother during her absence [Spitz, 1950a, p. 141]."

2. *The qualitative aspect*

In discussing the kind of cathexis which is characteristic of the objectal period some authors write about neutralization of libidinal and aggressive energies. It must be admitted that the quantitative and qualitative aspects of the cathexis cannot be separated easily.

"*It is in the third quarter that narcissistic energy becomes free; this is the reason why the period between the eighth and the fifteenth month is a particularly vulnerable one.* Environmental conditions which in one way or another retard the shifting of narcissistic cathexes into neutralized libido (Hartmann, 1950b) will make the formation of object relations impossible [Spitz, 1950e, p. 70f.]."

"At the end of the first year, in the early phases of ego development, the child has formed lasting object relations; his attachment can outlast deprivation, and libidinal energy directed toward the love object has been partly transformed into aim-inhibited libidinal energy, transient into permanent cathexis [Hartmann, Kris, and Loewenstein, 1946, p. 27]."

"The transition from the stage in which fear of losing the object dominates the child's life to the stage in which the fear of losing love predominates does not only make it essential that both li-

---

[47] I.e., the third quarter of the first year.

bidinal and aggressive energies should be neutralized; also their expression is 'socialized' [Hartmann, Kris, and Loewenstein, 1949, p. 32]."

The entire problem of drive interactions re-enters here. We can only touch upon it (cf. Hartmann, 1950b, 1952; Spitz, 1953).

Anna Freud seems to distinguish two modalities of objectal attachment: the first attachment to the mother pertains mainly to gratification; the second one seeks, above all, the love of the object.

"It is not difficult to pursue the line of development which leads from these crude beginnings of object attachment to the later forms of love. The infant's first love for the mother is directed towards material satisfaction (stomach love, cupboard love, egoistic love; 'to be fed'). In a next stage, object love is still egoistic but directed towards non-material satisfactions, i.e., to receive love, affection, approval from the mother; 'to be loved' [A. Freud, 1946, p. 125]."

However, most authors speak of a true object relation only when the wish for approval becomes stronger than the concern about material gratifications; yet, obviously, one kind of attachment never completely supplants another. It is a question of degree.

From a less theoretical point of view, namely from that of the analysis of the characteristic emotions of the objectal period, the qualitative aspect of the cathexis comes into sharper focus. Thus, we see that the *negative* affects are, from now on, possible not only in relation to people, but also in relation to things; the child may react with unpleasure to the loss of a toy.

"By the end of the fourth month, a well-developed baby will show displeasure if you stop playing with him, thus depriving him of your person, although at this same period, he will not scream if you take his rattle away. It is only two months later, in the sixth month, that he will cry at having his playthings removed [Spitz, 1947, p. 70]."

This reaction is indicative of objectal development, if one accepts the hypothesis (to which we shall return soon) that the relation to things is a direct function of the libidinal tie to people: "The establishment of pre-objectal relations makes the beginning of relationships with 'things' possible" (Spitz, 1954, p. 514; see also Hartmann, 1952).

Besides this unpleasure reaction toward things we notice a whole series of negative affects ranging from disappointment and fear to rage and anxiety. The most reliable criterion of object relations is, of course, the often-mentioned eighth-month anxiety which Spitz has described as follows.

"When one actively approaches an infant to whom one is not known, it will show a very characteristic behavior ranging from mere 'timid' lowering of the eyes to crying with or without tears. This behavior runs the whole gamut which we have observed and which corresponds to the way in which the child has established its object relations. The infant may hide under its covers, throw itself flat on its bed and hide its head under the sheets, raise its shirt over its face or hide its eyes behind its hand [Spitz, 1954, p. 516]."

Turning now to the positive affects we notice that:

"... by the tenth or the twelfth month, quite a wide gamut of emotion has developed from the originally meager reactions. On the positive side of the balance, he is able to show pleasure, love for one specific person, sympathy and friendliness toward other persons, enjoyment of his toys and a positive sense of property toward some special object [Spitz, 1947, p. 70]."

In this realm of emotional growth, probably one of the most characteristic signs of progress remains the passage from passivity to activity (expressed in imitation and identification). This forward movement shows itself very clearly in expressions of affection. At this level the child becomes not only capable of opening his arms toward someone, but of kissing and fondling an adult and even of repeating these gestures with a doll or a teddy bear. These manifestations have an undeniable objectal character.

"Imitation of and identification with the gesture are one of the child's major contributions to the formation of object relations. The first identifications with parental gestures appear in the third and fourth quarter of the first year and are echo-like reproductions of the adult's gesture. They arise in the course of the unfolding object relations, mostly as games, between the adult and the infant, as an immediate response, mirroring a gesture initiated by the adult. In the next phase the child takes the initiative; imitations of behavior observed in the libidinal object are placed by the child into the service of his spontaneous actions and games, even in the absence of the adult [Spitz, 1957, p. 42]."

C. THE OBJECTAL PERIOD IN TERMS OF OBJECT FORMATION

The objectal period is marked by the definitive formation of the libidinal object. It is time to define this object and outline its essential traits. Unfortunately the absence of a clear-cut terminology, which Glover and Hartmann deplored, makes it impossible to offer a general definition representative of contemporary psychoanalytic thought as a whole. Even at this point of our outline we must continue to talk about the libidinal object within each individual author's framework.

Hartmann, Kris, and Loewenstein cite permanence and objectivity as principal characteristics of the libidinal object. It is in this sense that we understand the term "object constancy" which appears again and again in their papers. Hoffer summarizes this state of "object constancy" as follows:

"This has to be considered the last and mature stage in the development of object relationships. It has a special bearing on the fate of the aggressive and hostile drives. In the state of 'object constancy,' the love object will not be rejected or exchanged for another if it cannot provide immediate and total satisfaction. It has ceased to be closely linked with the bodily needs, whose place in fact it has in part taken. In the state of 'object constancy' the absent object is still longed for and not rejected (hated) as unsatisfactory [Hoffer, 1955, p. 90]."

Most sources (Bowlby, Hoffer, Escalona, Wolf, Hartmann, Kris, Loewenstein, etc.) place this state of object constancy around the end of the first year.

Anna Freud, as stated before, conceives of object love from the moment when something other than the satisfying situation or the self is cathected. Hence she places the appearance of a love object around 5-6 months. Does this mean that the object attains object constancy as of that moment? Even for Anna Freud the object of that period possesses little stability and objectivity since, at the beginning of that attachment, the need for material gratification still rules almost exclusively. "After object cathexis has been established, the former attitudes which belong to the phase of need satisfaction continue to underlie it" (A. Freud, in Kris, 1954, p. 59). On the other hand, from this time onward the child's personal attachment to his mother increases incessantly and leads to the second part of the objectal period. Here, object constancy resists the fluctuations of satisfaction and the object ceases to be interchangeable. Having reached this stage the child seeks love rather than food. Yet even at this time and up to the age of about two years, object constancy does not resist the particular frustration evoked in the child by the object's more or less extended absence. The kind of object constancy which is implied in the continued cathexis of the absent object does not really appear before the beginning of the third year of life.

As far as we know, Anna Freud never clearly defined the constitutive elements of the object of objectal development. From her point of view, the *subject* of object relations and the feeling tone of the libidinal tie seem more important than the object. Spitz, on the other hand, has attempted to define the libidinal object as narrowly as possible. He places its appearance in the third quarter of the first year of life. The characteristics of the cathected object are, at that time, perceived objectively; at this age the child recognizes the mother on the basis of merely visual stimuli and external changes in the object no longer hinder its recognition; the object ceases to be interchangeable; it actually becomes a love object. "Trite as it may seem, love is not possible as long as objects are interchangeable" (Spitz, 1950e, p. 70). Due to the orders and prohibitions which the love object must issue, it frequently becomes a source of frustration. Yet, it remains cathected and preserves the state of object constancy which is the essential element in its newly gained status of libidinal object.

This does not mean at all that the object of the objectal period cannot lose this status. To the contrary: it is constantly in danger because to lose its status, its essential qualities need only be modified. Now, those qualities of the love object which normally meet the needs of the subject, which protect and gratify him, remain the essential qualities of the former. If those qualities cease to be associated with the love object (e.g., if the mother ceases to gratify the child's needs, as during her absence, or if, while present, she becomes the source of so many frustrations that the satisfaction-frustration balance is tipped), libidinal cathexis is withdrawn from the object. The concentration of the drive energy which was originally directed toward it is transformed into diffuse drive energy. In such a case the subject exchanges his original love object for another one which may, by the way, be himself or his ego (Hartmann, 1950b) or part of his body (Spitz and Wolf, 1949). But this does not occur in the ordinary course of events. Changes due to default of the love object always border on pathology and invariably have certain traumatic implications (Bowlby et al., 1956).

One must not conclude that, normally, the libidinal object is constituted by the same person from the objectal period onward. The maturing of the individual requires that the most cathected love object vary with the different phases of psychosexual development. The adult who has not given up his first love objects is sick. Object constancy means merely that the child has become capable of forming true object relationships with one or several human beings. Is it necessary to add that many adults have not reached this stage?

In conclusion, we repeat that the only really valid definition of the libidinal object remains its description in terms of the genetic stages which made the formation of the love object possible.

"... the libidinal object cannot be described by means of spatial and temporal coordinates except for the short or long period during which the subject does not transform it. How then can it be characterized and described? The libidinal object is described on the basis of its history, its genesis [Spitz, 1954, p. 488]."

CHAPTER IV

CONSTRUCTION OF THE
OBJECTAL SCALE

Chapter II specified the criteria for the construction of the Piaget series. The same criteria have dominated the construction of the objectal scale but two problems arose. In analyzing the different periods of object relations we realized that there are few clear landmarks for each period, and that these are not easily defined in operational terms.

There are, however, about ten items which at first seem fairly easy to scale as they are all found in one form or another in some of the tests for infants, be they the Cattell, Gesell, Brunet-Lézine, Hetzer-Bühler, or Griffiths. At this point of our work we were confronted with the following alternatives: we could either construct an original scale based solely on criteria drawn from psychoanalytic studies, or find a previously developed tool with items sufficiently representative of object relations to be used as is.

We have good reason for describing the objectal scale in greater detail than the Piaget series. The Piaget test items represent only a systematization of precise experimental observations. The entire Piaget series can be found in observations 1 through 66 of *The Construction of Reality in the Child* (Piaget, 1937). The objectal scale, on the contrary, had to be developed from more or less detailed observations and hints of various authors. Its rationale is necessarily less obvious and its scoring system more complex.

We considered the latter possibility first. After a brief investigation we realized that none of the existing tests could be administered as is and fully meet the requirements of our study. In order to be representative of object relations, several items (those coming nearest to psychoanalytic indicators) had to be altered.

But to alter the items of a standardized test even slightly means to decrease, if not to destroy, its validity. We thought it interesting, nevertheless, to have as a third working tool a test of recognized scientific value which could serve as control for our own study. We even hoped such a procedure might bring us closer to the solution of such complex and fascinating problems as: What relation exists between the development of fine motor co-ordination and the formation of the object concept? Is there a relation between a subject's mental age and his objectal level? Does language development go parallel with object concept formation or rather with object relation development? and so forth.

As suggested by the Reverend Father Dominique H. Salman, professor at the Institute of Psychology of the University of Montreal and at the Saulchoir, we selected as our third working tool *The Griffiths Mental Development Scale.* According to a method to be described later, we combined it with the objectal scale without prejudice to the test items. Thus the test remains valid and, in addition, supplies the necessary information for determining the subject's objectal level. Of course, the objectal scale can be understood only with constant reference to Griffiths (1954).

This insertion of the objectal scale in an existing test had many advantages. It saved us a pilot study, which would undoubtedly have been required by the vagueness of certain psychoanalytic observations, and it enabled us to place the objectal indicators in more reliable chronological order than would have been possible on the basis of the few suggestions found in our sources. We considered the similarity of the psychoanalytic indicators and certain test items and then could place the former on the same age level as the latter. This enabled us to adopt, with slight modifications,

Griffiths' instructions for the administration of the test items. For example:

"Any test may be taken twice, but no test more than twice.... Begin to test a child at a point equivalent to six items or two months below his actual age, e.g., a three-month's baby from the beginning of the test, a six-month's baby from about item 10, and so on. Then continue up and down the scale until the child has passed at least six items in succession in each subscale,[1] and also until he has failed six items in succession in each subscale [Griffiths, 1954, pp. 137-138]."

These instructions helped us to avoid the administration of the entire objectal scale to each subject (otherwise we might have had to ask a three-month-old to differentiate between an angry and a surprised face!). We shortened the experimental sessions, which is of paramount importance when working with babies. The insertion of the objectal scale also enabled us to work out a scoring method for the analytic criteria alongside Griffiths' scores. Thus a subject can be rated for his objectal development through a single reading of test results. Finally, the Griffiths Scale supplied us repeatedly with a valuable cross-check whenever a protocol was particularly difficult to interpret. We shall return to these issues in the chapters on method and on results and their discussion. They are mentioned here only to enable the reader to follow the very complex construction of the objectal scale.

We succeeded in isolating seven criteria which we consider representative of the development of object relations and which can be administered and scored objectively. We could not have reached the goal of our investigation without reducing the objectal indicators to (or better, translating them into) organized

[1] The Griffiths Scale consists of five individual scales each of which measures different aspects of behavior (Griffiths, 1954, Appendix II):
Scale A. Locomotor
    " B. Personal-Social
    " C. Hearing and Speech
    " D. Eye and Hand
    " E. Performance

tests. We hasten to add that all through this work we have tried to preserve the "sign- or signal-function" (exactly as stated by Hartmann, 1950a, p. 9) of these indicators; we speak of them as test items only by analogy.

THE FIRST OBJECTAL CRITERION: THE SPECIFIC REACTION TO FEEDING

Psychoanalytic theory asserts that the absolute undifferentiation of the beginning of the narcissistic phase gives way relatively soon to a first differentiation of certain global situations. From the first week on the infant responds to the feeding situation in a specific manner. This is evidence of the initial differentiation.

"Toward the eighth day the infant responds to signals. These are first signals of internal sensation. To be exact, these are sensations of balance. For instance, when a child is picked up from its cradle after the eighth day and placed in the feeding position, namely *horizontally,* it will turn its head toward the person who placed it in this position, be this person a man or a woman. If, on the contrary, one lifts the same child from its cradle to a *vertical* position it will not turn its head toward the person in question [Spitz, 1954, pp. 490-491]."

The significance of this first specific reaction in terms of objectal development is undeniable for it allows the conclusion that (1) certain signals are perceived; (2) a global experience is libidinally cathected, since the infant uses its perception of those signals to turn *toward* the stimulus. This primitive response of the infant has been known for a long time; it even appears in form of a test item in the Hetzer-Bühler Test. We are therefore content to use item 10 (age level: 2 months) as the first objectal criterion of that test[2] and to combine it with item B2, one of the

[2] Bühler's item 10 reads as follows: "S is brought into the feeding position, either on the lap of the experimenter in the case of breast-fed infants or turned sideways in bed with a cloth under his chin in the case of bottle-fed babies.

"The child reacts specifically by opening the mouth, turning the head sideways, perhaps by quieting down or by expressing impatience. Though not

very first items of Griffiths' Personal-Social Scale.[3] We do so in accordance with the chronological place suggested by psychoanalytic sources.

Criterion 1: *S is put in the feeding position which he is used to, whether it be in his mother's arms, in E's arms, or lying on his side in bed with a cloth under his chin.*
B2++: S reacts specifically by opening his mouth, turning his head sideways, making sucking-like movements. Though not always all of these reactions can be observed, a single one will not suffice for a positive score.
B2+ or B2—: no specific reaction.

The administration of the objectal test is obviously very easy: the mother or the experimenter takes the baby in her arms as soon as he becomes restless (B2) and brings him into the feeding position to which he is accustomed (Bühler's item 10).[4] In the case of subjects who are bottle-fed while held in someone's arms (a possibility not foreseen by Bühler) the subject is preferably held by the person who usually feeds him. Psychoanalysts emphasize that actually the response to feeding is at first a kinesthetic one (Spitz, 1954, 1955c; Brody, 1956). In this area some infants seem to be capable of noticing minimal differences from the first weeks on (Bergman and Escalona, 1949). The learning of the response may therefore be a function of such a specific person. In some institutions the rules require that the infants be fed while held in someone's arms during the first 2-3 months. Under these circumstances the subject is necessarily fed by several persons and

---

always all specific reactions can be observed, one will hardly suffice to show a definite response" (Bühler and Hetzer, 1935, p. 101).
[3] Griffiths' item B2 reads as follows: *"Quieted when picked up (first month)*. This is easily tested for during examination, for, should the child whimper at all, the mother may be asked to take him up and the child usually quietens down at once. If this opportunity does not arise, the mother should be asked about this item. Most happy normally developing babies cry very little and are readily quieted when taken up, unless very hungry" (Griffiths, 1954, p. 156).
[4] If the subject manifests no discomfort during the entire session, this test must be administered nevertheless.

there need be no objections if the experimenter rather than an aide holds the baby.

Passing of item B2, i.e., the subject who quiets down momentarily in his mother's arms (B2+), does not suffice for a positive score for the first objectal criterion. A passing score requires, besides the quieting, a further sign of the recognition of the feeding situation. This is the meaning of the double score of B2. Furthermore, the subject who fails B2 fails also on the objectal criterion, since he remains incapable of perceiving signals even if they are very clear.

In terms of periods, failure of the first objectal criterion, i.e., absence of the specific feeding response, places the subject in the first part of the narcissistic period; passing places him in the second part (for the relationship between scores, criteria, and periods see Table 3 at the end of the chapter).

THE SECOND OBJECTAL CRITERION: THE AUTOMATIC OR DIFFERENTIATED SMILE

Several psychoanalysts draw attention to a whole series of phenomena occurring around three months and which are extremely significant from an objectal viewpoint. Among them smiling plays an important part. We used the data of Spitz and Wolf (1946) for the construction of our second criterion because these authors have most minutely analyzed (from the theoretical as well as from the experimental angle) the deep significance of smiling in a psychoanalytic context. We relied also upon some more recent discoveries by Ahrens (1955).

Three of Griffiths' items underlie our second objectal criterion.[5]

---

[5] "B4. *Smiling (second month).* The average baby smiles at about six weeks old. The examiner should observe this himself, and a smile can usually be elicited, if the child is capable of it, by talking to the child or getting the mother to do so.

"B5. *Visually recognises mother (second month).* There is no doubt about this item when it is present. A glance at Plates 2 and 3 (Chapter II) will show an intelligent child recognising the mother, first with a lovely smile and afterwards with an intent expression attending to what she is saying. After the examiner

This complicates the administration and scoring, since the administration of the unchanged test items could have invalidated the evaluation of the objectal criterion. The reader is asked to be patient—the criterion is difficult to describe but the reality which it attempts to capture is of no lesser complexity (cf. Dennis, 1935, 1938, 1941; Szekely, 1954; Ahrens, 1955).[6]

Criterion 2: *E places himself alone, facing S, in S's immediate visual field, and smiles broadly while shaking his head several times (B8). E withdraws from S's visual field and the mother takes E's place. She smiles at S as E did previously (B5). The mother continues to smile but now speaks to S in her accustomed manner (B4).*

B8+: S responds by cooing at E.

B8++: S smiles at E.

B5+: S smiles at his silent mother.

B4+: S smiles at his talking mother.[7]

All other responses are scored minus (—).

---

has been holding the baby's attention, he should step aside and ask the mother to bend over the child. He will at once observe the change of expression if the child has reached this level of maturity.

"B8. *Returns examiner's glance with smiling or cooing (end of third month).* This item explains itself. By this age (about three months) the baby is capable of very definite social response to friendly persons. A smile, or a definite cooing sound, in response to the examiner's overtures is sufficient to pass this item. Smiling at mother or other familiar person (B4) is not a pass in this item" (Griffiths, 1954, pp. 156-157).

[6] Since 1960, time of completion of this experimentation, a tremendous amount of research has been done on smiling in infancy (Rheingold, 1961; Laroche and Tcheng, 1963; Wolff, 1963; Gewirtz, in press; and Miron-Brossard, 1965) wherein the theoretical and experimental contributions of Ambrose (1960, 1961, 1963a, 1963b) have been invaluable. The second objectal criterion would certainly need to be reformulated in the light of this recent accumulation of precise data.

[7] Griffiths interprets the fact that the baby smiles at his mother, who bends over him shortly after the examiner has held the baby's attention, as visual recognition of the mother. In the light of Spitz's and Ahrens' findings, we know that this is not the case. In order to remain faithful to the test instructions we have to give a plus (+) score to this item as soon as the baby smiles at the silent mother.

Meaning of scores

(B8— or B8+, B5—, B4—): No smiling.

(B8— or B8+, B5—, B4+): Automatic smiling at the adult heard and seen.

(B8++, B5+, B4+): Automatic smiling upon merely seeing the adult.

(B8— or B8+, B5+):[8] The smile is discriminating.

The score (B8— or B8+, B5—, B4—) indicates total absence of smiling whichever human face is perceived and whether a human voice is heard or not. The score places the subject below the level of the intermediary period.

An automatic smiling response requiring the combination of a visual and an auditory stimulus results in the following score: (B8— or B8+, B5—, B4+). This is, in a way, the first step of automatic smiling; it indicates that the subject is at the very beginning of the intermediate period. Theoretically, this score could be given a different interpretation. One could hypothesize that: a subject who smiles neither at the silent mother (B5—) nor at the silent experimenter (B8— or B8+) but at the talking mother (B4+) has reached the level of differentiated smiling; he recognizes the mother but not yet *visually;* the additional specific stimulus of the mother's voice is required for recognition. Or one

---

[8] When necessary, B20 may serve as control item, since B20+ has the same objectal meaning as (B8— or B8+, B5+). Here we find the eighth-month anxiety translated into operational terms. Item B20 reads: *"Knows strangers from familiar friends (eighth month).* The baby has now passed beyond the stage of being usually friendly to any stranger who takes notice of him. He now knows the various members of his own family and a few other friends, neighbours, etc., and is beginning to be less easy with strangers. This stage of development expresses itself by shyness (retreat) or resistance or even crying if a strange person is too attentive. The experienced examiner soon knows when a child has reached this stage in his social awareness by the child's first few reactions to himself. Insecurity is liable to be very operative at this stage and the child should be left on the mother's knee as much as possible, or the mother should be seated near him. The mother should be asked about the child's attitude to strangers, to confirm this stage of development. The child passes the item if he shows by his manner, especially at the beginning of the test, that the examiner is somebody new or strange" (Griffiths, 1954, p. 160).

could hypothesize that: this subject's vision does not yet enable him to recognize a familiar person but his smile is differentiated regarding sounds; thus he smiles specifically at *a given* human voice. However, in the four cases thus scored (B8— or B8+, B5—, B4+), these hypotheses were empirically untenable. According to the total record (Piaget series and Griffith scales) none of the subjects had yet reached such a capacity for differentiation.[9]

The automatic smile of the second step is evoked by the mere sight of the smiling human face, but the subject smiles instantaneously[10] at the experimenter and at the mother. There is, so far, no differentiation between the stranger and the mother or mother substitute. Thus one obtains the score (B8++, B5+, B4+). This is the typical response of the intermediate period.

There is a differentiated smile when the infant smiles at the silent mother but not at the experimenter (or at him only after a distinct pause). This "affective behavior" (Spitz, 1959, p. 84) proves the arrival at the objectal period and is expressed by the score (B8— or B8+, B5+). In the context of psychoanalytic theory one could conceive of a fifth score (B8++, B5—, B4—) indicating that the subject smiles at the mere sight of the experimenter but neither at the silent nor at the talking mother. We could therefore have a differentiated smile manifesting itself by the reversal of the smiling response (Spitz and Wolf, 1946, pp. 100ff.). In such a case the child reacts negatively to a familiar person who is the source of certain frustrations, but smiles at a stranger who interests him and who is not negatively cathected.

[9] A recent study on the development of smiling as a function of auditory stimuli reveals that smiling is not evoked *automatically* by the human voice (Lallier, 1961).

[10] ". . . in the first six months the infant smiles *indiscriminately* at *every* adult offering the appropriate stimulation, whereas in the second half it *may* smile at one person or another, if so inclined, but will not smile indiscriminately at anybody" (Spitz and Wolf, 1946, p. 73).

Once the child has reached the discriminative level he does not immediately smile at the experimenter—he habitually regards him for a few seconds before he decides to smile—whereas the smile at the mother is instantaneous and is easily recognized.

This would be a very exceptional case and, actually, this score did not come up in the course of our experiments.

THE THIRD OBJECTAL CRITERION: THE ABILITY TO WAIT

Psychoanalysts agree that the ability to wait is a sign of ego formation (specifically viewed as a first frustration tolerance) as well as a criterion for a self-environment differentiation and, generally, as an essential point in the development of object relations.

"Waiting is a condition in which libido is directed toward the outer world and constitutes the opposite of incorporation, or identification. It leaves the mother as a part of the outer world and prepares the object love step by step and thus functions as the forerunner of the development of object love [Benedek, 1938, p. 207]."

"We all agree that, in his development toward reality, the child has to learn to postpone gratification; the recognition, by the child, of constant and independent objects in the outside world already presupposes a certain degree of this capacity [Hartmann, 1950b, p. 78]."

"... the formation of a permanent object relation is, as has been shown elsewhere, dependent on the capacity of the individual to bear frustration; no permanent object relation, or no true constitution of a love object could be achieved without this capacity [Hartmann, Kris, and Loewenstein, 1949, p. 21]."

However, psychoanalysts (with the exception of Therese Benedek) are hardly explicit concerning what constitutes this ability to wait. They place it between three and five months and usually relate it to the feeding situation without supplying the necessary elements for the isolation of operational criteria.

A first construction of the third objectal criterion accounted only for Therese Benedek's relatively precise findings (1938); however, very early in our experiment, scoring difficulties forced us to analyze Griffiths' three items concerning quieting—B2 (cf.

this chapter, footnote 3), C2, B12—in greater detail.[11] This leads us to the separation of this criterion into two parts.[12]

Criterion 3: *S ceases to cry for at least 30 seconds.*

B7++: When seeing and hearing his mother who walks around and reassures him verbally.

B12++: When hearing the voice of his mother whom he cannot see and who reassures him while gradually coming closer.

Meaning of scores

(B7— or B7+): No ability to wait.

(B7++, B12— or B12+): Ability to wait for a seen and heard adult.

(B12++): Ability to wait at the mere sound of the voice.

[11] "*C2. Quieted by voice (first month).* At this early stage the child should quiet down, if restless, to the sound of an adult's voice, usually the mother's, and give evidence of hearing it and being reassured by the sound, the adult holding him or bending over the cot. (This is quite different from B12 in the Personal-Social-scale. There the older child accepts the comfort and reassurance of knowing from her voice and speech that mother is near at hand, although she is not holding him, and the child stops crying. At that later stage it involves a degree of self-control.)

"*B12. Stops crying when talked to (fifth month).* This item involves a five-months stage of maturity. Most younger babies require to be taken up when in distress before they will stop crying, but at this stage the child should be capable of being reassured by the mother's approaching voice and will stop crying on hearing her. Opportunity to observe this may occur during the test. If not, the mother must be carefully questioned about this. If the baby is not capable of this, the mother will say at once ruefully: 'Oh no! I always have to pick him up.' (*Note:* A child of this age is not likely to stop crying if he is very hungry.)" (Griffiths, 1954, pp. 171, 158).

[12] Actually, for 8 out of 90 subjects, we could not account for the subdivided third objectal criterion. For these subjects we decided arbitrarily to score B7++ those who passed one or several criteria beyond criterion 2 and to score B7 only those who did not get beyond it. On the basis of this scoring system 4 subjects were scored B7+ and 4 subjects obtained a score of B7++.

Item B7 reads: "*Follows moving persons with eyes (third month).* Moving a little way (about two yards) from the child, after holding his attention in some other test, the examiner should walk slowly about the room, still talking to the child. The test is passed if the child follows him with the eyes for a few seconds. The test may be tried a second time during the test period if the child does not succeed the first time. The child should be on the mother's lap in a comfortable sitting position" (Griffiths, 1954, p. 157).

Because of this item's chronological position and its similarity with the first step of the objectal criterion, we chose this item as a basis for the first part of "the ability to wait," although the Griffith item does not concern quieting.

If, during the entire session, S shows no discomfort and nothing makes him cry or become restless, E asks the mother: "When your baby is hungry and cries, how does he react (1) when he sees you? (2) when he hears you without seeing you?" Such replies as: "he quiets down," "he immediately stops crying," "he waits a while and then starts again," etc., to the first question are to be scored B7++, to the second question, B12++. Such replies as: "nothing will stop him," "he quiets down only when I pick him up," etc., indicate that a true ability to wait has not yet been attained.

The double score accounts for the time factor. It indicates not only that the subject quiets down on hearing and seeing a mothering person (B7++) or at the mere sound of her voice (B12 ++) but also that this period of quiet lasted for at least 30 seconds. Actually, an infant who can stop crying for such a short time is usually capable of waiting quietly for several minutes.

THE FOURTH OBJECTAL CRITERION: THE NEGATIVE EMOTION UPON THE LOSS OF A HUMAN BEING AND THE LOSS OF AN INANIMATE OBJECT

The hypothesis that there exists an essential genetic link between the cathexis of people and that of inanimate objects or "things" has been discussed especially by Spitz (1947, 1949, 1950d, 1954) and becomes more and more explicit in contemporary psychoanalytic writing (Kris, 1951b; Hartmann, 1952; Ritvo and Provence, 1953). We saw in Chapter III that the distinction between libidinal objects (which are usually people) and things is far from being constant in all individuals. The papers of Winnicott (1953), Stevenson (1954), Kestenberg (1956), and others indicate the complexity of this particular problem.

Be that as it may, generally, psychoanalytic theory presupposes a quantitative as well as qualitative link between the cathecting of people and of things. This link is explained by the fact that during early childhood the development of several ego functions (including the use of inanimate objects) depends directly upon the nature of the object relation (Kris, 1950, pp. 34ff.). This link is primarily of a genetic nature: "The establishment of pre-objectal relations makes the beginning of relationships with 'things' possible." It plays a part in perception, for instance, recognition of human faces precedes recognition of the bottle: "Two months after recognizing human faces as such the infant is able to recognize the bottle, this 'thing' which is offered to him several times per day, which he handles daily for extended periods, which he associates with food" (Spitz, 1954, p. 514). This link enters in the genesis of emotions. Thus pleasurable and unpleasurable affects arise in relationships with people before they appear in relationships with things:

"... after the third month the infant manifests his displeasure when he is abandoned by his human partner. But just as the child does not smile at that age at anything shown to him except a human face he does not show any displeasure either in response to being deprived of a toy. Only when his human partner leaves him will the infant begin to cry.

"At 5 months pleasure and displeasure responses become more specific and extend over a larger number of stimuli. Now the child will show his displeasure when a toy is taken away from him [Spitz, 1954, p. 515]."

One can add, from a clinical viewpoint, that any disturbance in the relation with people necessarily entails a disturbance in the relation with things. "So that we cannot encounter a disturbance of one sector of the objectal relations without its involving a disturbance of the relations to all other objects, be they even as insignificant as a toy" (Spitz, 1949, p. 109; cf. Ritvo and Provence, 1953).

The specificity of the unpleasurable affects seemed to us, among the different aspects of the psychoanalytic hypothesis, the criterion easiest to circumscribe for experimentation. Three Griffiths items (B10, B11 and B22)[13] were particularly suitable for this purpose. We used them to construct the fourth objectal criterion.

[13] "B10. *Resists adult who tries playfully to take ring or toy (end of fourth*

Criterion 4: (a) *After having played with S in her usual manner the mother stops her activity abruptly and withdraws from S's visual field.*

B11++: S reacts positively (smiling, babbling, laughing, etc.) to the mother's play and negatively (crying, fussing, scowling, etc.) to the interruption.

B11+: S reacts positively to the mother's play but shows no negative affect in response to the interruption.

B11—: S does not respond with pleasure to the mother's play.

(b) *While S is manipulating some object, E holds out his hand and says (asking for that object): "Give me the cup (ring, etc.)." When S holds on to the object, E takes it away deliberately.*

B22+: S reacts negatively to the loss of the toy.

B22—: S does not respond with displeasure to the loss of the toy.[14]

Meaning of scores

(B11— or B11+, B22—): No negative affect.

(B11++, B22—): Negative affect only in response to the loss of a human being.

---

month). After giving the child the ring in connection with testing for the ability to grasp an object (item D 9), the examiner makes sure that the child is holding it firmly and then gently tries to take it from him, asking playfully, 'May I have it?' or 'Give that to me,' etc. If the baby tries to hold on to the ring, he scores plus. A less mature child would relinquish it at once.

"B11. *Frolics when played with (fifth month).* Mother should be asked to play with the baby in her accustomed way, and the examiner should note the child's response. This should involve physical movement as well as laughter or smiling, and general signs of enjoyment at being played with.

"B22. *Displeased if toy is taken away (ninth month).* The object of this item is to see if the child has reached a stage such that he can express himself negatively in his own interest. He can, for example, make a fuss if a toy is taken from him. When the child is happily manipulating objects and holding on, for example, to the cup, the examiner holds out his hand and says: 'Give me the cup,' etc. When the child still hangs on, he gently but deliberately takes the cup away. The child passes this test if he shows displeasure, anger or annoyance. It should be immediately handed back to him and the child reassured. We do not like giving this item, as it is somewhat unkind or is liable to spoil the rapport in a sensitive child. There is usually, however, little danger of this if the attractive object is promptly restored to the child. It is sufficient to see that he is about to make a fuss, and the incident should not be allowed to develop to the point of tears" (Griffiths, 1954, pp. 158, 160).

[14] If from the subject's age and development it can be predicted that item

(B11— or B11+, B22+): Negative affect only in response to the loss of a toy.

(B11++, B22+): Negative affect in response to the loss of both human beings and inanimate objects.

Normally, negative affect in response to the loss of the human partner appears at about 3 months and places the subject in the intermediate period. Before reaching this period, the subject obtains the first score (B11— or B11+, B22—), whereas upon reaching this period he obtains the score (B11++, B22—).

In the objectal period, not only the human being but also the toy is cathected. The child continues to react negatively to the disappearance of the former and now protests also against the removal of the latter. This is expressed by the score (B11++, B22+).

We draw the reader's attention to the fact, to be discussed later, that within psychoanalytic theory the score (B11— or B11+, B22+) constitutes an anomaly since it indicates that a subject cathects inanimate objects but not human beings. Such a protocol obviously demands special analysis.

THE FIFTH OBJECTAL CRITERION: THE SIGNS OF AFFECTION

Psychoanalysts agree that identification plays an essential part in object relations; they diverge when it comes to distinguishing between such complex processes as incorporation and introjection, primary and secondary identification, and imitation. We are not concerned here with a discussion of these theoretical questions, but merely with circumscribing experimentally at least one aspect of identification which may reveal itself during the first two years of life. A twofold hypothesis (or rather two facets of a

---

B22 will not be administered, criterion 4b must be tested through B10. In this item manual resistance followed by negative affect after withdrawal of the toy is scored B10++ and permits the conclusion that the second part of criterion 4 has been reached.

single hypothesis) underlies the fifth criterion: one relating to the progress from passivity to activity, the other to imitation by means of partial identification.

Basing herself on one of Freud's theoretical formulations, Mack Brunswick (1940, p. 298) sees in any activity of the infant an indication of identification with the mother: "What we learn is that each bit of activity is based to some extent on an identification with the active mother. . . ."[15]

The meaning of this transition from passivity to activity in terms of object relations is particularly clear when libidinous manifestations regarding the love object are involved. The infant who can kiss, caress, embrace his mother has become capable of actively satisfying a drive which so far was mainly dependent on passive gratifications. A new step of "objectalization" has obviously been attained, as the baby no longer tries to be loved merely passively, but actively seeks love.[16] We do not claim that the infant thereby shows not only his desire for love but also that he *loves,* since a mere imitation may be involved; however, even if true affection is not yet manifest (i.e., the subject's behavior does not actually go beyond the level of imitation by gestures), the fifth criterion retains the objectal value. From the viewpoint of object relations, this very identification is significant, and during the infant's first year gestural imitation is only one aspect of this identification.

---

[15] This assertion definitely requires some restrictions. The majority of psychoanalytic writers do not interpret *any* activity as the result of an identification with the adult: "Abstraction is never the result of an identification: it is an autonomous achievement of the synthetic activity of the ego" (Spitz, 1957, p. 57).

[16] Some authors explain the absence of active search for satisfaction at the beginning of life by the incomplete motor development in addition to the immaturity of object relations: "This is so, not only because the object relationship is not developed, but also because of the absence of maturation of motility at that age. Thus, the aims, the gratification of drives, can only occur in the passive forms of being loved, being fed, being stimulated. The essential change probably occurs with the child's ability to stand up, to walk, to integrate, and also to impose changes on the objects" (Loewenstein, in Kris, 1954, p. 48).

"The prestages of identification become manifest in the child's early gesture identification, a concept introduced by Berta Bornstein. They appear after the sixth month of life, partly in the form of straight-forward imitation and partly in more advanced forms. Among the latter are those in which the child appears to conform with the libidinal object's attitudes [Spitz, 1957, pp. 40-41]."[17]

From a clinical point of view, the deficiencies in the imitative ability reveal, almost always, gaps in the identification processes and, in the final analysis, deviations of the object relation.[18]

Despite these theoretical complications, the fifth criterion is very straightforward and presents no problems either in its formulation, its chronological position, or its scoring. It consists of Griffiths' item B27 as is.[19]

---

[17] Spitz specified in earlier papers the time at which this particular form of identification appears: "The first attempts at identification become visible in the fourth quarter of the first year. They can be demonstrated experimentally in what Berta Bornstein has called 'identification with the gesture'" (Spitz, 1950e, p. 70; cf. Spitz, 1954, pp. 526-527).

[18] On the basis of the hypothesis that imitation is a part process of identification, Ritvo and Provence suggest, concerning autistic and symbiotic children: "For clues to the diagnosis, one may pay particular attention to the presence or absence of such games as 'pat-a-cake,' 'bye-bye,' 'kissing,' 'so big,' etc. which depend at least in part, upon the psychic representation of the human object and the presence in the child of an image of the bodily self" (Ritvo and Provence, 1953, p. 161; cf. Ritvo and Solnit, 1958).

Discussing COR (Corrective Object Relations) psychotherapy, Alpert (1959, p. 173) presents the following steps through which a schizoid subject went in his relations with other children: ". . . from incorporative—being the other child; to literal imitation—being like the other (identification by gesture); to doing like the other—representing a higher level of differentiation between the self and the other."

[19] "B27. *Gives affection (eleventh month).* The baby, to pass this test, gives affection to the mother or nurse or other member of the family. Earlier the child will have been content to 'accept' the expression of affection from others rather passively, now he returns the embrace or kiss. Many babies, however, at this stage cannot give a true kiss; they put their face to the mother, or their parted lips, or their arms round her, etc. Any of these manifestations that appear to be expressions of affection may be accepted.

"This is a valuable item in diagnosis of backward and sometimes maladjusted children, for they accept affection passively, without evincing any desire to return it, much longer than do normal babies, who, before the end of the first

Criterion 5: *After caressing the subject the mother asks for a sign in return: "Give me a kiss, give Mamma a big hug . . . ."*

B27+: The subject responds actively, e.g., he kisses or hugs the mother.

B27—: The subject does not respond at all to the mother's advances or responds only passively, e.g., he smiles, babbles, holds out his hands.

Passing of this item (B27+) indicates that the subject has reached the level of the fifth criterion and is in the objectal period. Failure indicates that this level has not yet been reached.

THE SIXTH OBJECTAL CRITERION: THE COMPLIANCE WITH REQUESTS AND PROHIBITIONS

We recognized the stability of the love object as characteristic of the last period of object relations. This stability enables the libidinal object to retain its status despite the frustrations it occasionally imposes on the subject. Compliance with requests and prohibitions gives evidence of the existence of this "objectal stability" and testifies to the following transformations:

(a) Another step in ego formation as the child becomes perceptually capable of understanding certain signs of communication. Without understanding what is asked of him and what is forbidden he could never comply with requests and prohibitions.[20] We are dealing here with a cognitive element which is surely connected with the development of intelligence in general and which can undoubtedly be explained otherwise than in an objectal framework;[21] but such a comprehension requires a sufficient distance between the subject who perceives the signs of communication and the person who emits them. We have seen that this differentiation between self and outer world is an essential element of the object relation.

---

year, are definitely giving evidence of affection towards others" (Griffiths, 1954, pp. 161-162).

[20] There is, however, no actual reciprocity: the subject may well understand what is asked of him and what is forbidden and yet refuse to comply.

[21] Cf. McCarthy (1954) and Lewis (1951).

(b) A further effectiveness of the reality principle. Certainly the ability to wait already reveals some frustration tolerance, but merely a physical or physiological one. The frustration on the present level is, however, of a psychological nature and its tolerance indicate a further grasp of reality.

(c) A further modification of cathexis. The child renounces an immediate pleasure rather than to risk losing the mother's or mother substitute's approval. Such postponement requires neutralization of libidinal and/or aggressive energies or, in Hartmann's terms, socialization. This compliance with demands and prohibitions is certainly also based on an identification with the commanding adult (Spitz, 1958) and to some extent implies the first elements of a rudimentary superego.

Be that as it may, the meaning of this sixth criterion in terms of object development is both complex and obvious. The construction of the criterion presents little difficulty. Its first part consists of Griffiths' item B30 located at 12 months.[22] Its second part consists of item 5 of the second quarter of the second year of the Hetzer-Bühler scale.[23] The chronological placement of this item is between 15 months and 17 months, 29 days with a base age of 15 months. According to Bühler, an interval of a few months thus exists between compliance with requests and compliance with prohibitions,[24] but most psychoanalytic writers do not bother in-

[22] "B30. *Obeys simple requests: 'Give me cup,' etc. (twelfth month).* To pass this test the child's social development must be such that he will on kindly request give up a toy or other object he is manipulating. If he will not give the object up to the examiner, the mother may be requested to ask the child for it. If he gives up the toy to an adult, he passes the test" (Griffiths, 1954, p. 162).

[23] This item reads as follows: "E gives the child some toys and plays with him for five or ten minutes. A toy is now placed in reaching distance of S and manipulated quite noticeably by E, whenever S looks at it. S is prevented from touching it and the admonition: 'Don't touch that! You can't have that!' is repeated as long as S continues to reach for the forbidden toy.

"S understands the commands, does not actually grasp the toy, but withdraws his hands as soon as E tells him to keep away from the toy or shows in any other ways that the command has been understood" (Bühler and Hetzer, 1935, p. 136).

[24] The Hetzer-Bühler scale contains another item which is actually representative of the compliance with requests. It is located at the first quarter of the second year. It has a base age of one year and ranges from 12 months to 14 months, 29 days.

dicating this distinction. We tried to take this into account by subdividing the sixth criterion with the expectation of obtaining, thereby, more agreement with the experimental findings and better differentiation even from an objectal point of view. Psychoanalytic theory supports the assumption that compliance with requests requires less drive control than does compliance with prohibitions and that, therefore, the former should precede the latter.

Criterion 6: _E (or if necessary the mother) says to S who is manipulating some object: "Give it to me" or "give me the cup (bell, etc.)."_
B30+: S relinquishes the object upon request.
B30—: S holds on to the object.
E places the object which S did or did not relinquish to him at a distance where S can easily grasp it. E manipulates the object very obviously whenever S looks at it. At the same time, E forbids S to take it by saying: "Don't touch it! No, you can't have it." E repeats his injunction as long as S attempts to grasp it.
B30++: Compliance with request and prohibition.
B30+: Compliance with request, but S does not accept the subsequent injunction and takes the object again.
B30—+: No compliance with request, but S accepts the injunction; he withdraws his hand and does not take the object.[25]

B30++ indicates complete passing of the criterion and places the subject near the end of object relation development. Mere passing of item B30 shows that the subject has reached the first part of the objectal criterion; failure indicates lack of compliance with requests and prohibitions and that the subject has not yet attained objectal stability. B30—+ indicates that the prohibition alone is effective.

THE SEVENTH OBJECTAL CRITERION: SUBTLE DISCRIMINATION OF SIGNS OF COMMUNICATION

Experimental psychologists have long been interested in the child's interpretation and reproduction of adult facial expres-

[25] The item must be administered to all subjects whether one year or 20 months old. Hence this item must in some cases be administered outside the regular procedure of the Griffiths scale on which B30 appears at 12 months.

sions and gestures. For some years, this problem has also attracted the attention of psychoanalysts. Ahrens' (1955) earlier-mentioned monograph probably represents the most specific scientific contribution to this subject. This seventh criterion was inspired by him. Yet this criterion remains in line with the objectal theory. However, the indications found in the psychoanalytic literature concerning this question were too sparse for transformation (without further elaboration) into operational criteria. We believe we did not distort the psychoanalytic concept by borrowing, in its entirety, an experiment from the methodology of comparative psychology, which concerns itself precisely with the finer discrimination of signs of communication.

We emphasized earlier the meaning of the progressive understanding of facial and gestural expressions of the mother in terms of object relations (Hartmann, Kris, and Loewenstein, 1946; Escalona, 1953; Spitz, 1957, 1958). But we are only beginning to understand the genetic processes which underlie this acquisition. We know today that one must wait over a year (whatever Charlotte Bühler[26] may have thought) before the child succeeds in grasping (from visual stimuli alone) the affect which is associated to a given expression when this affect is in any way complex. Spitz assumes that even at about 12-15 months the child differentiates only two affects:

"For the beginning of the second year of life I am inclined to assume that the child distinguishes in the adult partner two af-

---

[26] Item 7 on the 6-month level of the Hetzer-Bühler scale reads: *"Reflecting friendly and angry facial expression.* E bends over the child until his face is about 25 cm. from that of the child, smiles and talks in a friendly tone of voice for 30 seconds. He suddenly changes his tone of voice, frowns and talks angrily for 30 seconds. S reacts to this change by frowning and showing signs of negative expressive movements. These may again change back to normal after a few moments. Smiling and positive expressive movements are often noticeable in response to the friendly attitude of E" (Bühler and Hetzer, 1935, p. 114).

Bühler presupposes, in the 6-month-old, the capacity to reflect the affective tonality of these two different facial expressions. Ahrens has demonstrated that if the child reacts negatively to angry facial expressions at this age, he does so because of a feeling of strangeness attached to frowns, and not due to any understanding of the negative affect expressed by the adult.

fects only. I will call them the affect 'for' and the affect 'against.' In our usual terms, the child feels either that the love object loves him or that the love object hates him [Spitz, 1957, pp. 50-51]."

Ahrens' experiments indicate, in a different context, at what point a subject discriminates between perceptually very similar expressions with very different affective meanings, such as surprised and threatening looks. We constructed our seventh criterion from such experiments in combination with Griffiths' item B31.[27]

Criterion 7: *The mother (or, if necessary, E) places herself into S's visual field, frowns with horizontal lines on the forehead, lightly claps her hands, and repeats several times: "Oh . . . oh . . ." in an astonished and joyful voice. After having withdrawn from S's visual field, the mother returns. now frowns with vertical lines, shakes her index finger threateningly, and repeats several times: "tut . . . tut . . . tut. . . ."*

B31++: More marked negative reaction (expression of fear or sadness, lowering of eyes, slight withdrawal, etc.) to threatening than to surprised face.

B31—+: More marked negative reaction to threatening than to surprised face but without gestural imitation of hand-clapping (B31).[28]

B31+ or B31—: No more marked negative reaction to the threatening than to the surprised face.

On the one hand, in these two facial expressions, we have the wrinkling of the forehead which, through its strangeness alone, usually evokes a negative reaction in 6-month-old infants. On the other hand, each of the two expressions has totally different affective meaning: that of approving surprise in one case, and that of disapproving threat in the other. Obviously the child who is

---

[27] "B31. *Pat-a-cake (twelfth month).* This is a simple hand-clapping test. The examiner (or the mother) claps hands when the child is successful at some other test. The child imitates the gesture. The child is more likely to respond to the mother's clapping than to the examiner's, but either scores plus" (Griffiths, 1954, p. 162).

[28] The item must be administered to all subjects whether one year or 20 months old. Hence this item must in some cases be administered outside the regular procedure of the Griffiths scale on which it appears at 12 months.

capable of differentiating between these two facial expressions will himself react affectively in different ways.

We prefer the mother rather than the experimenter to administer the criterion because, according to psychoanalysis, the emotional meaning of the mother's facial expressions is perceived first. In order to facilitate the test we added visual signs (handclapping and threatening forefinger) and auditory signs (surprised voice and disapproving voice) to Ahrens' original experiment. We ascertained in a pilot study that the child understands the global situation: the majority of even 2-year-olds whom we tested in this respect did not distinguish between these two facial expressions when they were presented without any other sign. This is easily understood: the child must generally react to a mother who is surprised *by something* or to a mother who threatens because of a deed (past or future offense); he need not understand a facial expression which, in a sense, appears in a vacuum. Since in the context of object relations we are interested in the understanding of signs of communication in general (and not, as Ahrens is, in minimum visual stimuli capable of eliciting differential behavior), this does not in any way reduce the value of the criterion.

The scoring offers hardly any complications. Ahrens' slightly modified experiment is combined with Griffiths' item B31. The criteria for differentiation are those of Ahrens. A more marked negative reaction (i.e., quicker and/or more intense) to the threatening than to the surprised face is thus required in order that one may infer a differentiation (Ahrens, 1955, pp. 601-602).

The score B31++ indicates that not only the Griffiths item was passed but that the seventh criterion has also been achieved. B31—+ indicates failure of the test but passing of the objectal criterion. The other scores place the subject below this last criterion.

TABLE 3

Objectal Scale

Periods	Test Items	Griffiths Protocol	Score	Scale
Narcissistic	a) no specific reaction	B2—, B2+		0
	b) specific reaction to feeding	B2++	⌄	1
	2. automatic smile	± (B8— or B8+, B5—, B4+) + (B8++, B5 and B4+)	⌄	2 3
Intermediate	3. negative affect at play interruption	B11++	⌄	4
	4. ability to wait	± (B7++, B12— or B12+) + (B12++)	⌄	5 ⑥
	5. differentiated smile	(B8— or B8+, B5+		7
Objectal (a)	6. negative affect at loss of toy	B22+		8
	7. signs of affection	B27+		9
Objectal (b)	8. compliance with requests	B30+		10
	9. compliance with prohibitions	B30++, B30—+		11
	10. subtle discrimination of signs of communication	B31++, B31—+		12

In the above table, the subject is in the intermediate phase, at point 6 on the scale.

CHAPTER V

METHODOLOGY AND
PROCEDURE

In the introduction, we outlined this study in general terms and stated as its purpose the establishment of a parallel between objective development and objectal relation.[1] Our general hypothesis can be stated as follows: "Some relationship exists between the development of the object concept in terms of Piaget's theory and the development of the object relation in terms of contemporary psychoanalytic theory." In other words, our initial working hypothesis postulated a genetic parallel according to which a given *stage* of object concept formation corresponds to a given *phase* of object relation development. We have attempted to demonstrate experimentally the existence of this genetic parallel within the span of the first two years of life.

Two working tools were constructed to this end: the Piaget series and the objectal scale. The Piaget series consists of 5 items representing the stages of object concept formation and a 9-point scale. Any subject can be placed on some point of this scale. The objectal scale consists of 7 criteria representing the periods of object relation development and a 13-point scale. Any subject can be placed on some point of this scale as well.

[1] Cf. Chapter III, footnote 3.

The objectal scale was superimposed upon the Griffiths Mental Development Scale, a test for babies providing a global mental age and a specific mental age on each of 5 subtests, namely the previously mentioned scales A, B, C, D and E. This scale was standardized on the infant population of Kensington (a London suburb) born mainly between 1947 and 1951 (Griffiths, 1954, p. 47). Thus this test was not immediately applicable to our French-Canadian infant population and its results could not be used as is. However, we wish to emphasize that in the area of baby tests, standardization need not be as rigorous as in tests for children of speaking age and adults. A perusal of Bowlby's (1951) work on the effects of lack of mothering on infants shows how little concerned well-known researchers in this field are about the use of nonstandardized working tools, be they those of Gesell, Cattell or Hetzer and Bühler.[2]

Besides, our problem was of a very specialized nature. We did not investigate mental age, but the relationship of the latter, according to the Griffiths, to, let us say, object concept formation. It was of little concern to us whether or not the mental age represented the subjects' true intellectual achievement. All we needed was a general measure enabling us to make statements of the following kind: on the average, the higher a score a subject obtains on Griffiths' subscale C (Hearing and Speech) the more advanced is he in terms of the Piaget series; or, the lower an over-all score a subject obtains on the Griffiths scale, the less advanced is he in terms of object relations. The lack of standardization of our third working tool, thus, was for us of minor importance.

SUBJECTS

Our population consisted of 90 subjects, 46 boys and 44 girls. The subjects were equally divided into 3 environmental catego-

---

[2] Pinneau (1955b) seems well justified in his criticism concerning this very point. It is difficult to understand why Spitz constantly used the tests by Hetzer and Wolf instead of their revised form, i.e., the Hetzer-Bühler. Cf. also Ackerman (1942).

ries and into 6 age groups. Category A consisted of 30 children living with their real parents, category B of 30 children living in a foster home awaiting legal adoption by their present foster parents, and category C of 30 institutionalized infants.

We set up these three categories under the assumption that the object relation would show up differently in each one of them. Theoretically, it should be good in category A (home) and extremely poor in category C (institution). We were looking for an intermediary environment in which the object relation might prove to be better than in an institution but not as good as in a home environment. Therefore, we selected third category subjects who lived in adoptive homes but who were not as yet legally adopted. We felt that the object relation would be disturbed by anxiety because the adoptive mother is usually deeply attached to the child of her own choice, but her affective contacts with the child are more often than not colored by anxiety, especially as long as the adoption has not become legalized.[3] We need not explain here to what degree tension in the mother may influence the baby's object relation. This is a well-known psychoanalytic finding.

Actually, we based our selection of these three populations on the simple assumption that a parallel between object concept development and object relation would show up more clearly if either of these presented extreme variations. Our population fell into the following six age groups: 3 months, 6 months, 9 months, 12 months, 16 months, 20 months. The permissible deviation was ± 3 days for the first three and ± 5 days for the last three age groups. This means that the maximum age difference between subjects in any given age group was 6 days for the 3-, 6- and 9-

---

[3] Empirically, the existence of this anxiety left no room for doubt. Despite the introduction through the adoption and child welfare agency, an adoptive mother left the female experimenter standing at the door because she believed the latter to be the real mother who was attempting to get her child back. Frequently the father left his job to be present during the test, and both adoptive parents asked for constant reassurance that this was not a mysterious measure which might delay the legal adoption.

month-old groups and 10 days for the 12-, 16- and 20-month-old groups.

We selected these intervals in order to stay within developmental norms. The developmental rhythm is actually much faster at the beginning of the first year of life than after one year, when a kind of plateau has been reached. The choice of specific age levels was based both on psychoanalytic statements concerning the time of appearance of the various objectal criteria and on Piaget's assertions as to the timing of the various stages of object concept formation. However, we indicated earlier that Piaget left a wide margin in his chronology for the various stages. Hence our age groups correspond only partially to the levels suggested by Piaget. For example, Piaget places the first cycle of object concept formation within the first 18 months. We selected 20 months as ceiling age because our pilot study indicated that the systematic use of representations (whether tested by screens or superimpositions) appears only rarely before this age.

On the other hand, we remind the reader that Spitz (who, after all, is the psychoanalyst who specifies a chronological order most clearly) speaks frequently of objectal development in terms of quarters. Our first-year age groups are thus reasonably close to the proposed norms. However, the first great step of objectal development is usually considered to end at about 12 months, since the libidinal object has normally been formed at this time. According to most psychoanalysts this first cycle of objectal development is thus completed at about one year; according to general psychology certain objectal criteria appear more slowly (cf. the second part of the sixth objectal criterion). Not even from the point of view of object relation need we consider the last two age levels superfluous. Table 4 shows the distribution of our 90 subjects in terms of age, sex and environmental categories.

PROCEDURE

The author and two other psychologists administered to the 90 subjects and generally in the following order: (1) the second ob-

TABLE 4

Distribution of Population by Age, Sex and Category (N=90)

Age group	Sex	Category			Total
		Home	Adoptive	Institution	
3 months	f	3	3	3	9
	m	2	2	2	6
6 months	f	3	2	3	8
	m	2	3	2	7
9 months	f	2	2	1	5
	m	3	3	4	10
12 months	f	2	3	4	9
	m	3	2	1	6
16 months	f	2	1	3	6
	m	3	4	2	9
20 months	f	3	2	2	7
	m	2	3	3	8

jectal criterion (the automatic or differentiated smile)[4]; (2) the five items of the Piaget series; (3) the Griffiths Mental Development Scale and the remaining six objectal criteria.

We did not always follow this order as the testing of infants has quite different requirements from the testing of adults. To follow the baby's lead[5] is more important than to follow a rigid sequence in the administration of the items of a test. Efficiency requires that one proceed (without consulting the manual) from a locomotor item to one of imitative audition. The subject must be caught whenever he may be up to giving his optimum performance—possibly a fleeting moment. Among factors to be avoided are that the baby be hungry, sleepy or in any way uncomfortable as these would invalidate the test.

The length of the experimental session is also an important fac-

[4] The second objectal criterion was deliberately selected as the first item to be administered. In order to know whether or not the subject distinguishes between familiar and unfamiliar people one must avoid leaving the baby sufficient time to become acquainted with the experimenter.

[5] "Everything will be done in due order, in the child's order and his own good time; only thus can he give his maximum attention and effort" (Griffiths, 1954, p. 129).

tor. On the average a 3-month-old baby must not be tested for more than 30 minutes, and a one-year-old for longer than 50 minutes. This does not mean that the infant is subjected to the actual testing for 30 to 50 minutes. Normally this period covers the administration of test items demanding special attention and concentration from the subject, as well as observation and recording of all spontaneously occurring behavioral items by the experimenter.

We followed, throughout our experimentation, Griffiths' general directions (1954, pp. 126ff.) and tried to proceed as systematically as possible.[6] While the administration of the Piaget series presents few problems (the material is limited, and there are only 5 items which overlap, giving the procedure a certain continuity), this cannot be said of the administration of the Griffiths scale and the interspersed objectal scale. Griffiths indicates how difficult she considers the administration of her instrument by limiting its use to technicians who have attended her courses. We ourselves started our experimental series only after several weeks of training and administered an average of 4 pilot tests for each age level. During the beginning of our experimental series we worked in pairs of two female experimenters; one of us worked with the baby while the other recorded the results. To ensure a homogeneous procedure, the author participated during the first sessions as one of the experimenters in either the active or the passive role.

We soon realized that it would be absurd to administer all the items of the Piaget series regardless of the subject's age. A 3-month-old cannot be expected to search for a toy which is hidden under three superimposed screens (item 5). At that age he can-

---

[6] Only one who has worked with infants knows what flexibility this requires: "This is a skilled technique and implies special training. It also involves in some sense a veiled conflict for the psychologist. In one sense the whole situation is in the hands of the examiner to manipulate: in another sense the child is himself master of the situation and, indeed, at times master of ceremonies! Yet the scientific score of exact observation and recording of results must remain unimpaired, while there is at the same time fluidity of procedure, involving a constant adjustment to circumstances on the part of the examiner, while the child apparently leads him where he will" (Griffiths, 1954, pp. 126-127).

not even maintain the posture necessary for attempting this test. We decided arbitrarily to administer the Piaget series until at least two consecutive items were failed, indicating that the subject had missed either a whole stage or the end of one and the beginning of the following stage. Considering the wide age span covered by each stage, failure on two consecutive items seemed to sufficiently guarantee that no later item might be passed by the subject. Moreover, this was an experimental precaution since, theoretically, Piaget's stages are irreversible and do not allow for the passing of an item which follows one that was failed.

At the termination of our experiments we had collected the following data on each of the 90 subjects (see Table 4): (1) the subject's name as represented by a code number; (2) the subject's sex; (3) the subject's environmental category (home environment, adoptive home, institution); (4) chronological age in weeks as indicated by Griffiths; (5) passed and failed items of the Piaget series; (6) object concept development level in terms of stages and the point reached on the Piaget scale; (7) a specific mental age on scales A, B, C, D and E; (8) global mental age; (9) passed and failed criteria on the objectal scale; (10) object relation development level in terms of periods and the point reached on the objectal scale; (11) the subject's psychological profile based on the Griffiths scale results and expressed by quotients; (12) those few biographical data required by Griffiths (birth weight, birth order, father's occupation, etc.); (13) period of institutionalization for subjects of category C. It remains to report the analysis of these data. As a first step, we shall attempt to distil the significance of the raw data and simply summarize the general conclusions emerging from a superficial analysis. As a second step, we shall present the quantification of the same data and the results of our statistical analyses.

CHAPTER VI

ANALYSIS OF THE DATA

PART ONE: ANALYSIS OF RAW DATA

The analysis of the protocols and the compiling of the data were not without problems. Since the observations concerned qualitative data and the research design was new, we inevitably encountered some ambiguous and unforeseen cases.

We instructed our research assistants to inform us of any test which seemed difficult to score, and to take as many notes as possible concerning the behavior of each subject. The investigator herself placed the subjects—both from the objective and from the objectal viewpoints—in accordance with the score indicated by the two scales.

We thus realized that, in the borderline cases, a mere enumeration of the data without due attention to the total protocols would have easily falsified the results and, eventually, the true significance of the study. At this point in the investigation, therefore, the author acted as genetic psychologist rather than as statistician. She was convinced that this was the only valid scientific method, because it alone was in Piaget's spirit and yet in line with the subtleties of psychoanalytic theory, since "an acute observation ... surpasses all statistics" (Piaget, 1948, p. 72).

150

I. INDEPENDENT ANALYSIS OF THE RESULTS OF THE TWO SCALES

Analysis of the data from the Piaget series

A. *Sequence of the stages.* Our data revealed at first sight that the conclusions which Piaget had reached on the basis of the observation of his three children were fully supported by a larger sample. The sequence of the six stages of the construction of the object concept proved to be the same as that predicted by Piaget. Not one of our ninety subjects passed a stage which was considered to follow one which he had failed. Within each stage, we found the same consistency. Not a single subject passed an item which was considered typical for the end of a stage and failed one considered characteristic for the beginning of that stage.

B. *Distribution of the subjects by stages.* With one exception, our subjects were distributed over the stages approximately as one would expect on the basis of the number of subjects and our six age groups (see Figure 1). The cluster of subjects within the first step (I and II) can easily be explained: it corresponds to the three-month level and merely means that, in addition to 14 of our 15 three-month-olds, 7 older subjects demonstrated no active search for the vanished object. It is more surprising that a single subject is at stage Vb. This subject was from an institution, 20 months old, and his protocol showed no other abnormalities, considering the category to which he belonged. Thus, the large majority of subjects around this step succeeded in mastering the sequence of visible displacements without mastering the simplest of invisible displacements: we have 20 subjects at Va. On the other hand, the majority of subjects who have mastered one invisible displacement, can also master two: we have 7 subjects at VIa. The mastery of a single invisible displacement (Vb) appears to be the exception.

How is this to be explained? As discussed earlier, Piaget (1937, pp. 70ff.) sees the mastery of a single invisible displacement as the outcome of a concrete learning process into which representa-

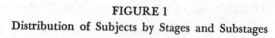

FIGURE 1

Distribution of Subjects by Stages and Substages

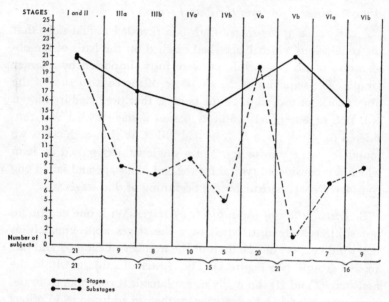

tion hardly enters and no awareness of the relationship of positions exists as yet. He clearly distinguishes this behavior from the subsequent mastery of at least two invisible displacements. He places the latter behavior at the sixth stage when there is definite and systematic intervention of representation. But could deduction not already participate in the mastery of even a single invisible displacement? The last stage would thus already have been reached; but a delay between the mastery of a single invisible and simple displacement (Vb), two invisible and simple displacements (VIa) and, finally, several invisible and complex displacements (exchange of screens and of their locations, VIb) would have been caused by the law of shifting—in this case a horizontal shift like the one which is characteristic of the residual reaction of the fourth stage. Deduction could intervene as of Vb, but only if the problem to be solved is not too complex. This new capacity would, therefore, not be utilized when the task is too difficult, as in the case of successive invisible displacements. Actually, systematic or, better, habitual use of deduction is ensured only when the subject masters a complex sequence of invisible displacements.

To us this explanation seems more plausible than that of a concrete learning process without deduction when the subject masters the first invisible displacement. In the latter case, it would be difficult to understand the cluster of subjects at Va. Moreover, if deduction intervenes as of Vb, the seeming gap[1] between Va and Vb would be easier to understand. It is reminiscent of the transition from the total absence of active search (I and II) to a first search for the vanished object (IIIa) at the beginning of the development of the object concept.

Certainly, our experiment with its age limits does not enable us to conclude that stage Vb constitutes a fictitious step within a stage. We know that this behavior exists. Piaget observed it in two of his children and we recorded it in one of our 90 subjects. However, we wonder whether this behavior has the necessary (relative) stability which would permit its being considered as characteristic for the completion of a stage, or whether it would be better to consider it as a sign of the very beginning of a final stage, that of the appearance of deduction? Probably only a longitudinal study could refute or support such an interpretation.

C. *Distribution of subjects by stages and chronological age.* Obviously, chronological age is an important factor in our research, as it is in every aspect of genetic psychology. "Time is growth," wrote Gesell. According to Piaget, the integration and co-ordination of individual heterogeneous and mutually independent sensorimotor schemas requires several months. (Integration and co-ordination were seen to constitute the substructure of the formation of the object.) If intelligence is an ultimate goal, it takes some time to get there.

Thus we knew a priori that the distribution of the sub-

---

[1] This gap is obviously not a real one, but due to our method of observation.

jects among the various stages would be, to a large extent, a function of their chronological age. Hence, one of the reasons for dividing our population into six age levels was to collect more data concerning this particular issue. However, we cannot and never intended to derive definitive chronological norms from our sample. We are well aware that no such conclusions can be drawn because of the specific heterogeneity of our sample, which is far from being representative of the population as a whole, and because of the small number of subjects (15) in each age group.

Our data may, nevertheless, permit us to draw some conclusions concerning age ranges. These conclusions may not have statistical value, but they carry more weight than those drawn by Piaget on the basis of his three children.

Obviously, the exact weight of the CA factor can be evaluated only when other variables such as mental age and environment are controlled. We shall attempt this in the second part of this chapter. Meanwhile, we shall analyze briefly the distribution of the 90 subjects by stage and CA as presented in Figure 2.

The spread in Figure 2 is much larger than expected: at a CA of 20 months, two subjects from institutions (87 and 90) are still at the very beginning of the fourth stage, i.e., they search for the

FIGURE 2

Distribution of Subjects by Stages and Chronological
Age Levels (15 subjects per age level)

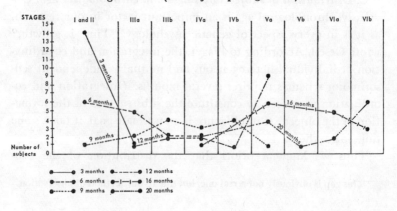

vanished object only after initiating the grasping movement, and they remain incapable of taking the visible displacements into account. This is a most limited active search, and it is difficult to imagine such a primitive construction of reality in children almost two years old.

However, we find a subject from an adoptive home with a CA of 9 months (39) who has already reached the fifth stage: he searches for the vanished object where it is and takes all its visible displacements into account, while another child of the same age, but from an institution (43), fails even the first test of the Piaget series and is placed below the level of any search for the vanished object.

These extreme cases suggest trends which must be studied in the light of the total protocols (environment, objectal phase, mental age, etc.). This analysis follows later on. Yet, some trends show up in a mere survey of the data. The distribution of the subjects by stage, chronological age, and environment (Figure 3) clearly shows, at all age levels, a much wider range for children from adoptive homes and institutions than for those from home environment.

Piaget suggests the following age ranges which he keeps deliberately flexible:

Stages I and II: between 0 and 4 months
Stages IIIa and IIIb: between 4-5 and 9 months
Stages IVa and IVb: between 8 and 10 months
Stages Va and Vb: between 12 and 18 months
Stages VIa and VIb: between 16 and 20 months

Despite the heterogeneity of our population, the chronological age and the attainment of stages permit us to make the following statements in terms of limits. Among our 90 subjects:

1. Not a single subject of three months was capable of reconstructing the whole from a visible fraction (IIIb) and almost all subjects of this age group (i.e., 14 out of 15) demonstrated no active search, i.e., were in the first two stages.

2. Not a single six-month-old exceeded the stage of active search

FIGURE 3

Distribution of Subjects of the Three Categories
by Stages and Chronological Age

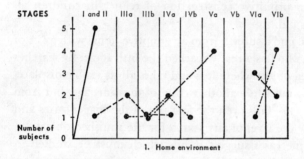

1. Home environment

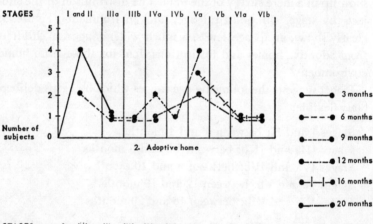

2. Adoptive home

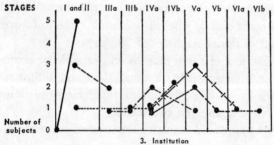

3. Institution

following upon the act of prehension (IVa). Thus, these subjects were incapable of active search except as an immediate extension of the act of accommodation.

3. Although the majority (9 out of 15) of the twelve-month-olds proved able to master the sequence of visible displacements (Va), not one of them demonstrated a search for the vanished object, if the latter was subjected to the slightest invisible displacement (Vb).

4. From 16 months on, all stages become accessible. However, two thirds of the subjects (21 out of 30) between 16 and 20 months had not yet reached the final step of the last stage (VIb) and could not make systematic use of deduction.

Analysis of data from the objectal scale

A. *Absence of a rigid sequence of the criteria in the objectal scale.* The sequence of the stages in the development of the object concept was supported by our experiment. This sequence forms a basic assumption of Piaget's theory. Nothing of the sort exists in psychoanalytic theory. Although the objectal relation is hypothesized to develop normally from a narcissistic, through an intermediate, to the objectal period, the order of appearance of the behavior which indicates whether a subject belongs to one or the other phase is rather flexible. An analyst would hardly be astonished to find a subject who can distinguish between a stranger and a familiar person but has a very limited ability to wait: the child who is able to stop crying only when he sees and hears the adult. There is just as little rigidity within any given period and nothing in psychoanalytic theory rules out the possibility of reversals, e.g., a subject who has already acquired the differentiated smile, shows no negative affect at the loss of the toy. No doubt, in these cases, we are getting away from the ideal object development, but in the realm of affectivity, it is finding the ideal which is surprising.

Yet, theoretically, some criteria cannot be inverted without casting some doubt upon certain psychoanalytic hypotheses. There are three series within which the irreversibility of the tests is presupposed by objectal theory.

The first series consists of: the specific reaction to feeding (1),[2] the automatic smile (2), the differentiated smile (5), the signs of affection (7).

The second series consists of: the negative affect at play interruption (3), the negative affect at the loss of the toy (6).

The third series consists of three tests, two of which are usually combined and, therefore, can be inverted in relation to each other but not to the third: the compliance with requests (8) and/or with prohibitions (9), the subtle discrimination of signs of communication (10).

The objectal meaning of these criteria has been sufficiently discussed above so that a detailed justification for their irreversibility is not required here. A few reminders will suffice.

First series. The automatic smile is a specific reaction analogous to the reaction to feeding, but it is a reaction to an object which is, to some extent, more "objectalized" than the global situation of feeding. Thus, theoretically, passing of the first test item must precede passing of the second one.

From a certain age on, however, it becomes difficult to elicit the specific reaction to feeding within the narrow framework of the test item as we have described it. The four-month-old may suddenly make sounds of pleasure instead of making sucking-like movements when he is placed into the feeding position. The specific reaction to feeding is a transitory behavior which will disappear when a certain level of maturity has been achieved (Gesell and Amatruda, 1948). The automatic smile indicates that that reaction has already existed and been outgrown, if it does not appear at present. Beginning with four months, if the undifferentiated smile is observed, one must automatically give credit for the specific reaction to feeding.

The differentiated smile cannot appear before the automatic smile. Today we know that the infant who does not smile spontaneously at the experimenter has already passed through a period of undifferentiation in which he smiled at strangers as well as at a Halloween mask. Thus, passing of the fifth test presupposes that the second test was passed earlier; differentiated smile excludes simultaneous automatic smile.

Active show of affection marks the beginning of the objectal period; it signifies identification with the libidinal object. This object can attain its status as libidinal object only under the condition that it is differentiated from all other objects in the environment. Signs of affection must, therefore, be subsequent to this differentiation. Thus, theoretically, the seventh test cannot be passed without previous passing of the fifth.

Second series. The hypothesized genetic relationship between the cathexis of persons and the cathexis of inanimate objects could show up in the progressive specificity of displeasure affects. Because the child has cathected a human being positively and, therefore, reacts negatively to his loss, he becomes capable of positive cathexis of "things" and hence of showing a negative affect at the loss of the toy. This hypothesis, which is still rarely encountered in contemporary psychoanalytic literature, obviously requires that the sixth and third test not be interchangeable.

Third series. More and more developed perceptual objectivity corresponds to a progressive structuralization of the ego. In this light, the understanding of requests and prohibitions seems to belong to the same level, and we have seen that psychoanalysts make no distinction between the two. The discrimination of the adult's facial expressions demands a much greater perceptual objectivity and, in the final analysis, an "objectalization." How can a child who can differentiate between affects as complex as surprise and disapproval be unable to understand such clear communicative signs as those of requests and prohibitions? Theoretically, then, the tenth test cannot be passed without passing the two immediately preceding tests.

These are the hypotheses derived from psychoanalytic theory. What are our findings?

Findings. Separate analyses of the three series give very different results.

First series. Tests 1, 2, and 5 proved to be irreversible. This followed irrevocably from the scoring system. Forty-five subjects passed the seventh test, one of them (20) failed test 5. This subject, therefore, actively showed affection although he had not yet arrived at discrimination between strangers and familiar persons. What does this mean? One out of 45 is doubtless a very small number. But this exception cannot be attributed to chance. There is no chance in clinical findings. Hence, we must try to understand these anomalies. Actually, more detailed analysis of this atypical protocol was most enlightening.

Subject 20 comes from a home environment, is 25 weeks and 6 days old (age group: 6 months) and scored a mental age (MA) of 31 weeks and 6 days on the Griffiths test. This girl's objectal development corresponds to her chronological age (CA), except for signs of affection which, statistically, do not appear until 11 months. Her psychological profile in terms of quotients is the following (Figure 4):

FIGURE 4

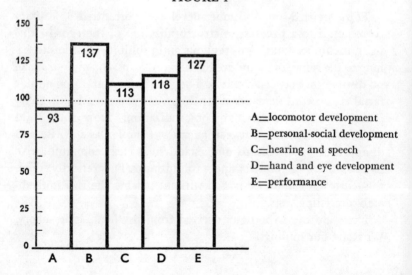

A=locomotor development
B=personal-social development
C=hearing and speech
D=hand and eye development
E=performance

As can be seen from Figure 4, performance and personal-social development are clearly superior according to the scale, whereas locomotor development shows up as below average. We believe that this profile may explain the anomaly of the objectal protocol. This might be a socially overstimulated girl, not in the sense of socialization, but in the narrow sense of training, who was very early taught tricks, e.g., to help to hold her cup (she passed item B23, placed by Griffiths at the 9-month level). The child has a learning capacity which enables her to be trained, but this drill does not really change the objectal relation which lies on a much deeper level. Actually, compared to the other children from home environment and of the same age group (even including those of lower MA), subject 20 is late in her objectal development except for test 7. This precocious training may well indicate a lack of affect in the mother.

These findings teach us that test 7 requires a careful analysis and that the mere imitation of a caress—in the presence of a model—may have a very relative objectal meaning, since this behavior may appear before there is the possibility of an object choice. Piaget's (1945) minute observations of the numerous stages of gestural imitation would, no doubt, enable us to outline Berta Bornstein's vague concept of "gesture identification."

Conclusion. Our over-all data enable us to conclude that the irreversibility of the tests within the first series was, in general, experimentally confirmed.

Second series. Forty-six subjects passed the sixth test. However, 14 of them failed the third. These 14 thus reacted negatively to the loss of the toy, whereas they had not shown any displeasure when the adult left them. Within this second series, the (hypothetically) exceptional cases can be seen to represent almost one third of the subjects.

How are these results to be interpreted? Three explanations come immediately to mind: (1) We misunderstood the psychoanalytic hypothesis, and the third test consists of a transitory behavior which, in this sense, is analogous to the specific reaction to feeding: it is outgrown when the child passes the sixth test, and the negative affect at the loss of the toy implies absence of negative affect at play interruption. If so, the protocols of the remaining 29 subjects who passed both the sixth and the third test have to be explained. (2) The psychoanalytic hypothesis of a genetic link between the cathexis of persons and that of things is inaccurate or, rather, was not supported by our experiments. (3) The objectal criterion as set up by us, on the basis of Spitz's and Wolf's indications, does not tap the psychoanalytic hypothesis concerning the specificity of negative affects.

The first interpretation can easily be checked. If it is correct, the distribution of successes and failures on the two tests must vary with chronological age. Thus, from 6 months onward, the large majority of subjects who show an absolutely normal objectal development with respect to the other items must not show any negative affect at play interruption. Yet, this is not the case.

The second interpretation is more difficult to verify. The psychoanalytic hypothesis cannot be supported or rejected on the basis of our data alone. The lack of a genetic link between the cathexis of people and that of things cannot be established on the sole basis of a lack of experimental proof of the presence of negative affects at different points in objectal development. If the presence of negative affects indicates the existence of a prior cathexis of persons or inanimate objects, the converse is not true; the absence of negative affects does not necessarily imply the absence of a prior positive cathexis. We shall see that psychoanalytic findings allow for a quite different explanation of the absence of negative affect in tests 3 and 6.

Even the derived hypothesis of the progressive specificity of affects of displeasure is far from being refuted by our results. Possibly our fourth criterion itself (and here we come back to our third interpretation) camouflages that progressive specificity. If this is so, the existence of this particular development of negative affects can be proven experimentally only by longitudinal studies.

Even in a study such as ours, further reading of the protocols may throw some light on these problems. In 6 of the 14 diverging protocols the absence of the negative reaction to play interruption was the only failure. The over-all objectal development of these subjects is, therefore, remarkably consistent. Their lack of negative affect in the third test cannot be interpreted in terms of an absence of person cathexis, since all these subjects completed the criterion of differentiated smiling. In four other protocols, the absence of negative affect at play interruption and at the loss of the toy are the only two failures. Thus, if one considers only the last item passed, three of these protocols place the subjects in the second part of the objectal period, that is, among the most advanced subjects.

Thus it seems to us that the supposed objectal importance of the presence of negative affect at play interruption and/or loss of the toy has been overemphasized. The absence of that affect may occasionally even be interpreted positively. In certain cases (which, we insist, represent a minority) the absence of negative affect may indeed be conceived rather as a sign of ego strength than as an indication of spotty objectal development.

In such a perspective, in the case of the subject who failed only tests 3 and 6, he did not cry when the adult left because he had already attained a certain tolerance level and had sufficient personal resources to turn immediately toward other things in the environment. Similarly, he did not cry when he was deprived of the toy because he was able to tolerate that material loss or because he believed the adult was playing a game.[3]

As for the subject who failed only test 3, he did not cry when the adult left him because he was secure enough to tolerate the frustration of being left alone; he knew the adult would soon re-

[3] The absence of affects of displeasure can be interpreted in many other ways. In this respect, we find the hypothesis of a relative genetic independence between negative and positive emotions of particular interest (Bridges, 1932, 1933). The systematic exploration of this hypothesis would undoubtedly offer numerous clinical extensions. We refer, in particular, to the very different distribution of affects of pleasure and displeasure in certain neuroses.

turn. This same basic trust (Erikson, 1950) enabled him to express his displeasure when his toy was taken away. He could be aggressive without fearing to lose the love of the object.

We have here a small example of the difficulties inherent in setting up experimental controls for the testing of psychoanalytic concepts. The same manifest behavior can and must be interpreted differently for different individuals, and according to developmental level for the same individual (Hartmann, 1958a).

Third series. Only two of our subjects passed the last criterion. Their protocols corroborated the irreversibility of the compliance with both requests and prohibitions with respect to the differentiation of signs of communication.

B. *Distribution of subjects by periods.* Our experimental findings clearly enabled us to determine the level reached by each subject in his development of the object concept. We did not expect the same concerning objectal development but had no concept of the problems which would confront us. For 44 of our subjects, i.e., almost 50 per cent of the sample, the objectal level reached could be determined without difficulty. Their protocols consist of a continuous series of plusses. Hence, the last item passed sufficed for placing the subjects in the appropriate objectal period. The following example provides an illustration.

Tests:	1	2±	2	4±	3	4	5±	5	6	7	8	9	10
Subject 22:	+	+	+	+	+								
Subject 76:	+	+	+	+	+	+	+	+	+	+	+	+	+

Subject 22 is in the intermediate period; subject 76 in the second part of the objectal period.

Interpretation of the objectal protocols. Here we must insert a long explanatory note concerning the bizarre numbering system which we have adopted for the coding of the individual protocols of the objectal series. This code is the result of our groping. As mentioned above, the third objectal criterion, i.e., *the ability to wait,* was subdivided only after the beginning of experimentation.

In order to keep the chronological sequence of the tests it seemed necessary to insert the third test, i.e., *negative affect at play interruption*, between the first (4±) and the second (4+) part of that ability to wait. The two parts of *differentiated smile* (5± and 5+) could be distinguished only after termination of the experimentation. As a matter of fact, the analysis of the individual protocols made us realize that the fifth test (*differentiated smile*) and the Griffiths item B20 (*knows strangers from familiar friends*) presented a scoring problem in some cases. We mentioned that psychoanalysts believe that the differentiated smile reveals a distinction between familiar and unfamiliar persons and that they therefore attribute to it an objectal meaning. The protocols in question, all of which were from subjects from institutions, showed, on the one hand, an automatic smile (2+) and, on the other hand, a very clear expression of anxiety in relation to the experimenter; item B20 had therefore been passed. Hence the subject was able to distinguish between familiar and unfamiliar persons, yet he smiled indiscriminately at anyone. The protocols were accompanied by comments such as the following:

"The baby smiles at me immediately in the day room but not once in the testing room where he soon begins to cry. He is inconsolable as long as he sees me. On my lap, he quiets down for a short while. The remainder of the test is administered in the day room where he becomes happily active again [subject 59, boy from institution, age level 12 months]."

All protocols contained a common element: an expression of anxiety (the infant cries or becomes solemn) which did not appear when the experimenter was noticed for the first time, but only when the infant was no longer in the room where he spent most of his time.

We interpreted the concomitant appearance of the automatic smile and the delayed expression of anxiety as evidence of a first step in the differentiation between familiar and unfamiliar persons, a differentiation which remained embryonic and relative and which could not be evoked by merely visual stimuli, i.e., smiling-human-face. In these instances the experimenter would be perceived as a stranger only in an unknown or little familiar environment and/or when he made unusual gestures. The change in environment itself certainly does not explain the anxiety reaction, since the latter does not appear when the subject is brought into the testing room by the nurse or the nun, or even if the experimenter is not within the subject's immediate field of vision.[4] There seem to be very different degrees of recognition of familiar persons.[5]

In order to account, if possible, for the progressive differentiation between familiar and unfamiliar persons we gave a score of 5± to all subjects who passed item B20 but could not make that differentiation from visual cues alone. We believe that we are dealing here with a normal step in objectal relations but which appears obviously much earlier in children who live with their parents, probably around 4-5 months.

In view of these adjustments, the reader is asked to refer to the following coding system:

1 Specific reaction to feeding.
2± Automatic smiling at the heard and seen adult.
2 Automatic smiling upon merely seeing the adult.
3 Negative affect at play interruption.
4± Ability to wait for a seen and heard adult.
4 Ability to wait at the mere sound of the voice.
5± Limited differentiated smile.

[4] We have here a confirmation of Spitz's observations. He stated that the eighth-month anxiety disappears as soon as the stranger turns his back to the child: "When therefore the approaching stranger has provoked anxiety in the child by his approaching face, but withdraws the distinctive signal of the face for an appreciable time, the child will be confronted by something which is no longer either its object, the mother, or the proof of the mother's absence, the stranger's face" (Spitz, 1950d, p. 141).

[5] These different degrees of recognition seem to explain in part the non-recognition of the mother which is so frequent in children between 15 and 18 months. At first, they remain indifferent when the mother returns after a six- to seven-day absence (most often due to hospitalization for the birth of another child). Psychoanalysts explain this behavior very differently, but we agree with them only partially on this issue.

5 Differentiated smile without limitations.
6 Negative affect at loss of toy.
7 Signs of affection.
8 Compliance with requests.
9 Compliance with prohibitions.
10 Subtle discrimination of signs of communication.

Obviously, few protocols were as homogeneous as the two mentioned above. Actually, 46 protocols show irregularities which range from the mere failure of item 3 with passing of item 6, to the following kind of incongruity:

1	2±	2	4±	3	4	5±	5	6	7	8	9	10
+	+	+	—	—	—	—	—			+		

Protocol 42 must be read as follows: this subject has achieved the automatic smile at the sight of even a silent adult. He shows no capacity for waiting and no negative affect when the adult leaves him. Despite his chronological age (subject is 9 months old), he cannot differentiate between familiar and unfamiliar persons. Yet, we notice a clear negative affect at the moment of losing the toy.

Where should one place such a subject? If one went merely by the last test item passed, he would be placed in the same period and at the same point on the objectal scale as subject 32 who is of the same age and obtained the following protocol:

1	2±	2	4±	3	4	5±	5	6	7	8	9	10
+	+	+	+	+	+	+	+		+		+	

Subject 32 has the ability to wait even without seeing the adult, provided he can hear the adult's voice. He distinguishes unrestrictedly between familiar and unfamiliar persons and expresses his displeasure when the adult leaves him or takes the toy away.

Can subjects 42 and 32 really be given identical ratings? Such a classification seemed to us unjustifiable from the psychoanalytic point of view. At this point in the analysis of the data we were thus faced with the following dilemma.

For more than half of our subjects, the irregular sequence of passed and failed tests made their placement at any specific *point* on the objectal scale impossible, whereas the classification in terms of objectal *periods* offered little assurance of objectivity. Classification in terms of objectal periods might have been possible on the basis of the detailed qualitative analysis of the 46 irregular protocols. However, after the collection of all the data, it did not promise to be of great discriminatory power. We had, after all, only three periods which, even with their subdivisions, gave us no more than five possible classifications. Furthermore, since our first age level began with three months, it was predictable that not a single subject was in the first part of the narcissistic period and only one in its second part. There remained only three categories for the classification of 89 subjects: intermediate period and periods objectal *a* and objectal *b*. But, even from our small sample and within the narrow framework of the first twenty months, we obtained 46 different kinds of protocols. This shows that even within the first phase of life the objectal relation can show up in a multitude of ways. It also shows, contrary to the notion of stages, that the concept of periods is too complex and fluid to serve as a valid experimental criterion.

Under these circumstances we had to take recourse to a different rating system and a more highly differentiated form of quantification of our data. The latter will be described in the second part of this chapter. We regretted having to abandon the idea of correlating stages and periods. The hope of making this parallel explicit was the basis of this investigation. Hence, before setting in motion the formidable machinery of statistics, we attempted a last analysis of our raw data in terms of the concept of periods. We present that analysis for what it may be worth. We know very well that certain conclusions from it could have only a very relative significance. Yet we believe that the trends, suggestions, hypotheses which can be derived from it are not without importance for future research.

II. ANALYSIS OF THE TWO JOINED SERIES ON THE BASIS OF THE HOMOGENEOUS PROTOCOLS ALONE

The term homogeneous protocols refers to those protocols which consist of an uninterrupted sequence of passed items. The term heterogeneous protocols refers to those in which at least one failed test precedes one which the subject passed. The above-mentioned 46 heterogeneous protocols could not be rated in terms of periods or last item passed. For the remaining 44 protocols, which were homogeneous, our initial rating procedure was applicable. Although this was a very small sample, we felt that the analysis of the stage-period distribution of these subjects was worth the effort, and that it might enable us to qualify Piaget's global statement: "Corresponding to the affective level of 'object choice'[6] there is construction of substantial objects and organization of external space" (Piaget, 1945, p. 185). Or, allow us to throw serious doubt upon the psychoanalytic hypothesis of the primary model of thought: *mounting drive tension—absence of drive object—hallucinatory image of it* (Rapaport, 1951, p. 690).

The following pages will present the distribution by Piagetian

[6] Piaget's frequently used term, "object choice," is not easy to define. Can one speak of object choice with the appearance of differentiated reactions to people in general? "I come now to a last problem with respect to the affectivity which corresponds to the sensorimotor level; it is the problem of reactions to people and especially the problem of 'object choice' in the Freudian sense of the term" (Piaget, 1954, p. 54). Or does "object choice" appear only when the infant has differentiated reactions "toward people whom he loves, in the first place his mother ..." (*ibid.*, p. 58), an "object choice" which Piaget places, for good reasons, toward the end of the first year? Piaget's constant references to Freud hardly simplify the matter, since psychoanalysis distinguishes various kinds of object choice (Stanton, 1959). However, Freud spoke (usually) of object choice after the child had outgrown primary narcissism and the cathexis no longer centered on the activity itself. We believe that the "object choice" to which Piaget refers must be understood in the same way. In this case, the choice would intervene as soon as there is a reaction to someone else, and the mother would represent, somewhat paradigmatically, the reaction to others (Freud's assumption that, at the time of the reaction to others, the mother is recognized as such would be erroneous). These formulations of Piaget are difficult to understand because they come from lecture notes, and we therefore hesitate to use this work systematically.

stages of the 44 subjects with homogeneous protocols according to the period in which they belong and the last objectal criterion which they have passed (Figure 5).

FIGURE 5
Distribution of the 44 Subjects with Homogeneous Protocols by Stage, Period, and Last Criterion Passed

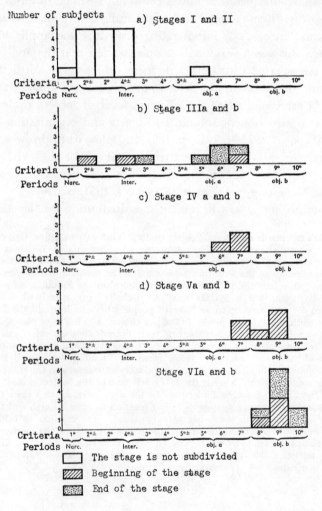

What does this distribution suggest? A mere glance at the various graphs immediately reveals a clear-cut trend: the majority of subjects who are in the first stages of the search for the vanished object are also at the beginning of objectal development; the majority of the subjects who are in the last stages of the search for the vanished object are also in the last stages of objectal development.

The relationship is most blurred for the subjects in the intermediate stages of the search for the vanished object. One can try to increase this correspondence somewhat by (1) not subdividing the stages into a phase of development and a phase of completion and (2) using the general concept of period without rigidly adhering to the last test passed. Under these conditions the following general correspondence is obtained:

Piaget stages	*Periods of object relation*
I and II	intermediate
III and IV	objectal (a)
V and VI	objectal (b)

The majority of the subjects (15 out of 17) who do not search for the vanished object at all can be seen to belong to the beginning of the intermediate period. This means that a child who, from a conceptual point of view, is still incapable of constructing an inanimate[7] object which is permanent, substantial, identical to itself and external to the ego, can, nevertheless, react affectively to the smiling human face by means of the automatic smile.

Of 11 subjects who are in the transitional stages (III and IV) of object formation, 3 are still at this intermediate emotional level, whereas 8 subjects have reached the first step of the objec-

---

[7] The reader must not assume that the construction of the object concept is the same in the case of the human being as for inanimate objects. Neither should he jump to the conclusion that to any given stage in the search of the vanished object there is a corresponding specific degree of concreteness, permanence, externality, etc., of the love object.

Within the context of Piaget's theory, the person and the inanimate object do not necessarily reach object status *at the same time:* "persons are obviously the most easily substantiated of all the child's sensorial pictures" (Piaget, 1937, p. 46f.).

tal period. This means that a child who is not yet able to attribute permanence to a vanished object which has undergone even the slightest visible displacement, can nevertheless distinguish a familiar person from the rest of his environment. Even one subject who has hardly reached the beginning of an object concept (III) demonstrates the ability for such objectal development.

Of the 16 subjects who have reached the last two stages of the search for the vanished object (V and VI), 14 have reached the second step of the objectal period. This means that both the infant who believes in the permanence of the inanimate object provided that he can watch all its displacements, and the infant who systematically uses deduction, can endow the love object with that "objectal stability" which characterizes the end of the first cycle of the objectal relation. We are aware that we are generalizing from a specific sample. However, everything leads us to believe that even if we were to increase the number of our subjects considerably, the general, although very vague correlation stated above would not be changed.[8] Thus, the most important conclusion to be drawn from this brief analysis of the 44 homogeneous protocols and of their objective and objectal distributions seems to be that it is impossible to establish a rigid parallel between the beginning or the end of a given stage and some objectal criterion, or even between any given single stage and some objectal period.

There remains, indeed, considerable variance in the stage-period correlation. There are, however, certain limits which must not be minimized, as not one subject from stages I and II reached the period "objectal *b*"; nor did a single subject from period "objectal *b*" remain below stage V. The above variance is another indication of the great diversity in psychological development from the first years of life on.

---

[8] Another calculation reveals that this correlation is increased when, instead of making use of only the 44 homogeneous protocols, the 46 heterogeneous protocols are added and are assigned quite concretely to an objectal period on the basis of the last objectal criterion passed.

Distribution of homogeneous and heterogeneous protocols by environmental categories

Before concluding the analysis of the homogeneous protocols we wanted to see whether a relationship existed between homogeneity (or heterogeneity) of the protocols and a subject's category. We obtained the following results (Figure 6).

A comparison of the two environments, which we hypothesized to be at opposite poles from an objectal viewpoint, shows an almost perfect inverse relationship between homogeneous and heterogeneous protocols. Although these proportions are not statistically significant, they reveal a tendency which one may attempt to explain.

The more advanced a subject is on the objectal scale, the higher is the possibility of an intermingling of successes and failures, i.e., of heterogeneity. Hence the relationship between homogeneous and heterogeneous protocols might be explained by means of the relative number of subjects who are little advanced and very far advanced on the objectal scale. If this were the case, the inverse relationship of homogeneous to heterogeneous protocols from children from home environments and those from institutions would be related to a lesser objectal development of the children from home environments as compared to children from institutions. As expected, this is not the case (Figure 7).

Of 18 subjects with homogeneous protocols and from home environments, 16 are in periods "objectal *a*" and "objectal *b*"; of 11 subjects with homogeneous protocols and from institutions, 11 are within the intermediate period. The subjects from adoptive homes again fall between the two extremes; 7 are in the intermediate period and 8 in the objectal periods *a* and *b*. This distribution makes the inverse relationship between homogeneous and heterogeneous protocols as a function of the environment even more significant.

As counterpart to Figure 5, it seemed interesting to compare the distribution again in terms of the environment of the 46 subjects with heterogeneous protocols, but according to the absolute num-

FIGURE 6
Distribution of Subjects with Homogeneous Protocols and with Heterogeneous Protocols According to Categories

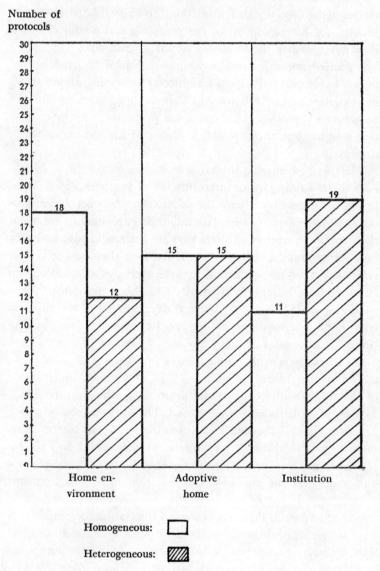

Homogeneous: ▢

Heterogeneous: ▨

ber of passed and failed items. Obviously, this presentation must disregard the position of the items on the objectal scale as these are heterogeneous protocols. We believe however that the relative percentages of failed and passed tests indicate the degree of heterogeneity of these protocols.

Category	Tests passed	Tests failed	Per cent
Home environment	90	18	20
Adoptive home	129	25	19.5
Institution	138	45	32.6

The differences in percentage are certainly not very marked. Yet the two extreme environments always reflect the same trend the meaning of which we must now attempt to understand more precisely. It is evident that, despite the high number of protocols belonging to the last period of objectal development, children from home environment failed relatively few tests. On the other hand, children from institutions are less advanced on the objectal scale and have more failures interspersed. Is a qualitative analysis of such sparse data permissible? As stated before, our three categories are not directly comparable, since the only con-

FIGURE 7

Distribution by Category of Subjects with Homogeneous Protocols According to Last Criterion Passed (and Period)

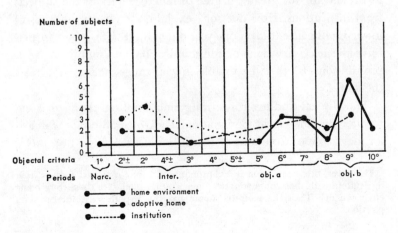

trolled variables are sex, number of subjects, and age. We offer the following interpretations merely as hunches in the hope that further research may confirm or reject them as explanations.

The profound differences in the mother-child relationship between home environment, adoptive home, and institution ensured, in advance, very different objectal developments in our three groups of subjects. But we could not foresee how these differences would manifest themselves in the objectal scale or even whether our working tool would discriminate between them.

In view of the close connection between mental development and the structural development of the ego (the latter represents an essential aspect of object relations) the decreasing intellectual efficiency (Gratton, 1954) and the initial below average intelligence of our subjects from institutions in general may be assumed inevitably to influence the objectal performance of that group. The poor intellectual potential and the absence of sensorimotor stimulation could perhaps by themselves explain why even the subjects from institutions with ideal development (i.e., with homogeneous protocols) very clearly manifested objectal retardation in comparison with children from home environment and from adoptive homes.[9] Yet this intelligence factor probably cannot account for the relatively large number of heterogeneous protocols and for the greater degree of heterogeneity of the subjects from institutions. How does one explain, merely on the basis of lower intelligence, that a one-year-old subject (58), who can perceive the necessary signs of communication for compliance with prohibitions, is otherwise unable to wait unless he sees and hears the adult?

The clinical findings concerning emotional development seem to offer the only valid explanation. Lack of mothering, which is an inevitable concomitant of institutional life, causes not only a

[9] However, this retardation is less pronounced if one compares infants from institutions with those from adoptive homes rather than with those from home environments. Thus the adoptive home has the hypothesized intermediary position.

retardation in objectal development, but profound deviations. It is normal that the objectal development of most of our subjects from institutions is abnormal as reflected by the heterogeneity of the protocols. The distribution of passed and failed objectal tests would give us, then, an experimental index of the nature of a given subject's object relationships.

In other words, we hope that if, genetically, the position of a subject on the objectal scale will some day enable us to speak of objectal progress or retardation with some accuracy, then, clinically, the degree of a protocol's homogeneity or heterogeneity will perhaps make possible a more precise diagnosis of normal or pathological objectal development.

PART TWO: ANALYSIS OF QUANTIFIED DATA

So far we found the period to which a child belonged and the last test he passed insufficient indices for the determination of his objectal level. This discovery forced us to look for a different method for the objectal classification of each of our subjects. After several unsuccessful attempts, we adopted the following method at the suggestion of Jacques Saint-Pierre, Director of the Statistics Center of the University of Montreal and of Professor Zinger of the same center. We entered the 46 protocol patterns which we had obtained from the objectal scale[10] on individual cards and gave these in random order to our two experimenters (and assistants). We asked them to arrange the 46 cards in one continuous series representing the objectal development as revealed by the sequence of passed and failed tests. The author served as third judge. The Spearman correlation coefficient for the classification of judges whom we shall call A, B and C was the following: A and B = .9947; A and C = .9859; B and C = .9875. The Kendall coefficient of concordance was W = .9928.

[10] Among the 44 homogeneous and the 46 heterogeneous protocols there were only 46 different ones, since a number of the 90 subjects obtained exactly the same protocols.

Obviously these coefficients are very significant. They would enable us, within the frame of our experimental design, to determine objectively the level of objectal development of a subject from his performance on the objectal scale. At this point in our research we expected to use, as is, the mean ranks assigned to the 46 sample protocols by the three judges and then to compare this single series with our other data.

However, we realized that, actually, our data were not directly comparable, and that the ranks assigned on the basis of the objectal scale could not be correlated directly with the ranks obtained on the Piaget series. The latter is truly one-dimensional, which means that we do not distort the data by assigning to the eighth rank the subject who has reached stage VIb and to the third rank the subject who has reached stage IVa (see Table 2, in Chapter II). Piaget's theory assumes the continuity of the stages, since the very degree of decentralization of the perceptual pictures distinguishes a given stage from the preceding stage and from the subsequent one. This decentralization is a gradual process. Each stage has an additive element relative to the preceding stage and a restrictive element relative to the following stage; these elements are directly comparable from one stage to the other. An analysis of the objectal scale does not show up anything equivalent. We had 46 kinds of protocols which were arrived at empirically and could be ranked from 1 to 46 with relative ease, but nothing guarantees that this seriation corresponds to reality.

As a matter of fact, from the objectal point of view, our sample is far from being representative of the general population: it is arbitrarily broken down into specific age groups and drawn from three particular environments. It could easily be conceived that our 46 protocol patterns might be part of a larger number of such patterns and that this would change their classification. Only an exhaustive longitudinal study would make it possible to scale the objectal development on a continuum the existence of which can be assumed in this area just as in the realm of intelligence.

In order to improve the comparability of our data, we have

attempted to list all protocol patterns which could, hypothetically, be extracted from our objectal scale. A certain number of combinations have been shown theoretically and empirically to be impossible. However, in view of the complexity of some psychoanalytic assumptions, we were extremely careful concerning the theoretical limitations and were mainly guided by our experimental findings. These indicated the possibility of a larger number of combinations.

We came up with 168 protocol patterns ranging from total absence of any item passed to passing of all criteria on the objectal scale. Interspersed among these 168 protocol patterns and in no way distinguishable from them were the 46 patterns which we had found empirically. We then asked the judges to scale these 168 protocol patterns on the basis of the following instructions.

"Hypothetically 168 different protocols can be derived from the objectal scale. They consist of a sequence of plusses and minuses ranging from complete failure, i.e., a protocol consisting only of minuses, to passing of all criteria, i.e., the following protocol:

1	2±	2	4±	3	4	5±	5	6	7	8	9	10
+	+	+	+	+	+	+	+	+	+	+	+	+

"You will find the coding system explained on a separate sheet.[11] You are to assign ranks to these protocols from 1 to 168 in terms of objectal development.

"This ranking should be based on two main criteria: (A) order of signs: the closer a minus sign is to the beginning of the scale, the less advanced is the subject and (B) number of minus signs: the more minuses precede the last plus sign, the less advanced is the subject.

"Since both criteria interplay and since the scale is not reversible as we had hoped, a number of protocols will present special problems. You are to judge where, in terms of psychoanalytic theory, a given subject is to be placed in relation to the other subjects.

"To facilitate the ranking, you may first distribute the cards in

[11] See this chapter, pp. 166-167.

thirteen piles according to the last objectal criterion passed; the protocol without any minus sign should serve as the end point for each pile. Then play around with the cards of each pile and, if necessary, move some borderline cases to an adjoining pile.

"Remember that you are to rank the protocols in terms of an increasing development of object relations. Thus a given subject may develop less harmoniously than another one and yet be more advanced from a strict objectal viewpoint. Example:

	1	2±	2	4±	3	4	5±	5	6	7	8	9	10
A:	+	+	+	+	+	+	+						
B:	+	+	+	−	−	−	+	+	−	−	+		

"Subject A is undoubtedly developing better than B, but from a strictly objectal viewpoint is less advanced than B. Thus an overall IQ of 130 with great discrepancies between the verbal and performance subscores is higher than an IQ of 100 with a minimal difference between subscores.

"Certainly, a higher index may lose all its weight due to the preceding minuses which change its meaning. Example:

1	2±	2	4±	3	4	5±	5	6	7	8	9	10
+	+	+	−	−	−	−	−	−	+			

"The active show of affection without discrimination between familiar and unfamiliar persons occurs before the choice of the love object.

"After ranking all the protocols list them on the attached cross-ruled sheets as follows:

1+
2++
3+++, etc."

As can be seen, our instructions were very precise and with good reason. During the first ranking (when the instructions were more ambiguous) we had found that agreement was greater between judges A and B than between judges A and C and B and C. This reflected itself in the correlation coefficients. We looked for the reasons by further analyzing the three seriations. The analysis of judge C's rankings lead us to the following conclusion: this judge had frequently taken a clinical rather than a strictly genetic approach and thus evaluated a number of subjects in terms of the normality or abnormality of their protocols. Certainly, the genetic aspect had been taken into consideration also, but the analysis of this third ranking showed that judge C had (more or less consciously) utilized the two criteria, and that it was their interplay which lowered the correlation between C's rank ordering and that of the other two judges who had adhered rather closely to the genetic criterion. The validity of an evaluation of objectal level on the basis of clinical criteria can be defended of course, but in that case the data under comparison must be seen in the same light. We deliberately embraced a genetic outlook at the beginning of our research. The concepts of development, growth, evolution, etc. have guided us, while we systematically discarded the concepts of equilibrium, disequilibrium, regression, etc. We gave the judges very explicit instructions in the hope of maintaining this genetic perspective, knowing how easily one slides toward clinical evaluations when one deals with the realm of emotions. In short, we asked the judges to make a blind analysis of a number of difficult protocols with the qualification that these were to be evaluated in terms of progress or retardation rather than in terms of normal or pathological development. Obviously, clinical data cannot but enter into a genetic context, but we wanted to avoid their being the determining factor in the final ranking of our subjects. The mean ranks of the 46 empirically obtained protocols which had been interspersed among the 122 hypothetical protocols then formed our definitive objectal scale which we shall call ABC ranks.

The correlation matrix obtained from our principal data appears in Table 5. The following variables were studied: ranking on the Piaget series (Piaget ranks), global mental age and specific mental ages on subscales A, B, C, D and E obtained on the Griffiths, ABC ranks, chronological age, environment, and sex. These correlation coefficients lead to a number of conclusions which we shall now discuss in detail beginning with the simplest ones. What follows is essentially a literal presentation of these final quantified findings.

TABLE 5

Variables	1	2	3	4	5	6	7	8	9	10	11
1 Piaget ranks											
2 Global mental age	.916										
3 Griffiths A*	.869	.968									
4 Griffiths B	.912	.982	.936								
5 Griffiths C	.882	.968	.909	.955							
6 Griffiths D	.912	.983	.937	.965	.939						
7 Griffiths E	.902	.973	.919	.984	.929	.966					
8 ABC ranks	.816	.860	.830	.877	.833	.842	.825				
9 Chronological age	.857	.946	.943	.912	.881	.931	.927	.794			
10 Environment	.178	.220	.147	.229	.297	.211	.210	.333	.—002		
11 Sex	.080	.059	.060	.036	.055	.070	.065	.063	.078	.027	

* See this chapter, Figure 4.

Sex and environment

As was to be foreseen, there exists no correlation between sex and Piaget rank or between sex and any other variable. On the basis of simple correlation coefficients, the influence of the environment does not show up either. We remind the reader of the structure of our sample and of our original hypotheses. We have never attempted to determine the influence of the environment as such. In order to do so, we would have had to match the subjects of the three categories and to control such variables as intellectual endowment, the time spent in institutions for the subjects from adoptive homes, the occasional presence or absolute absence of the mothers of the subjects from institutions, etc. We did none of this. Our population was selected so that at each age level only five subjects came from each of our three environmental categories. However, the influence of the environment remains undeniable. It showed up already in the analysis of the raw data (heterogeneity of the protocols, age distribution of the subjects, etc.). It reflects itself also in the mean IQ (which decreases as the age of the subjects from institutions increases), in the psychological profiles (a typical profile seems to crystallize for the children from adoptive homes and for those from institutions), and even in the experimental techniques themselves. This influence shows up clearly, even in the formation of the object concept, if one makes a more detailed statistical analysis.[12]

A. *Study of the variability of the measure of development of the object concept (Piaget ranks, multiple regression model)* (Snedecor, 1950; Fisher, 1952). As can be seen from Table 6, environment taken by itself is hardly a significant variable, since it accounts for only 3 per cent of the variability of the Piaget ranks. However, the picture looks quite different if one takes into account only the basic variables (mental and chronological age and ABC ranks) and evaluates the role of the environment by means of a multiple regression model. When the weight of the different factors is thus correctly distributed, one notes that at an explanation level of 84.8 per cent (Table 7) the environment obtains a student t of 1.81. We must conclude that, even if the environment explains the variability of the measure of the development of the object concept much less than mental age does, the former nevertheless remains an important explanatory factor in its own right just like the chronological or the ABC ranks which obtain similar student t's.

Chronological age. The coefficient of correlation between chronological age and Piaget ranks is .857, which is not at all surprising.

Chronological age by itself can be seen to account for 73 per cent of the variability of the measure of the development of the object concept. It thus plays an extremely important role. When subjected to the multiple regression model and analyzed in combination with the other basic variables, the variable CA obtains a Student t of -1.59,[13] which is slightly lower than that of en-

---

[12] We emphasize again that this analysis was made possible only by the close collaboration of Jacques Saint-Pierre and frequent use of the electronic computer. Guy Lavoie, Professor of Statistics at the Institute of Psychology, helped us with the reading of the data, and we are deeply grateful.

[13] This negative t value does not represent an inverse relationship (there

TABLE 6
Percentage of Variability of the Piaget Ranks Explained by Each Individual Variable

Variable	Per cent
Sex	0.64
Environment	3.27
Chronological age	73.4
Griffiths A	75.5
Griffiths B	83.2
Griffiths C	77.8
Griffiths D	83.2
Griffiths E	81.4
Global mental age	83.9
ABC ranks	66.6

The per cent of variance is the square of the correlation coefficients of the Piaget ranks and the variable in question.

TABLE 7
The Piaget Ranks as a Function of the Basic Variables
Per cent of Explained Variability: 84.8 Per cent

Variable	Regression coefficient	Variance of regression coefficient	Student t
Environment	.36	.039	1.81
CA	−.030	.00035	−1.59
MA	.12	.00046	5.75
ABC ranks	.0074	.000018	1.74

vironment and ABC ranks and clearly lower than that of mental age (Table 7).

Mental age. We obtained from the Griffiths a global mental age and five specific mental ages. The correlation coefficient of the global mental age with the Piaget ranks is .916, one of the highest of the entire correlation matrix. The correlation coefficients of the specific scales are of the same order and vary from .869 (Grif-

was a very high positive correlation between Piaget ranks and CA). It is only a compensation mechanism inherent in the multiple regression model used.

fiths A: locomotor development) to .912 (B: personal social development, and D: hand and eye development). Global mental age alone thus accounts for 83.9 per cent of the variability of the Piaget ranks, which is more than any of the other variables do. Considered individually, each specific mental age accounts for at least 75.5 per cent of the variability of that measure. This is rather high. Table 6 shows further that personal-social development and hand and eye development have almost as much weight as global mental age.

If the specific mental ages are placed hierarchically within the global mental age, the latter accounts on an explanatory level of 84.8 per cent for more of the variability of the measure of Piaget than does any other basic variable. Its *t* value is at least three times higher than that of any other basic variable (see Table 7).

ABC ranks. The correlation between ABC ranks and Piaget ranks was .816. Therefore, there exists a statistically demonstrable relationship between the development of the object concept as measured by the Piaget series and the development of the objectal relation as measured by our ABC ranks. Moreover, objectal development seems to be related to all aspects of development, as indicated by the relatively high correlation coefficients obtained. We shall revert to this problem. If, for the time being, we attempt merely to understand the actual meaning of the correlation coefficient for the two parallels under investigation, we find that the ABC ranks in themselves account only for 66.6 per cent of the variability of the Piaget ranks; this is somewhat less than chronological age (Table 6). On the other hand, if combined with the other basic variables, the influence of the ABC ranks (still as explanatory factor for the variability of the measure of the development of the object concept) appears slightly greater than that of chronological age, but less than that of environment and much smaller than that of mental age (Table 7).

B. *Study of the variability of the measure of the development of object relations (ABC ranks).* To complete this work we must now analyze the other half of our initial parallel—the objectal development as expressed by the ABC ranks. We must go through the same statistical steps using the ABC ranks as our independent variable.

Sex and environment. The absence of a correlation between sex and any other variable including the ABC ranks has already been mentioned. This poses no problem. The low correlation of .333 between environment and ABC ranks (Table 5) is more surprising. One may remember that one of our subproblems dealt precisely with the influence of the environment on objectal relations (Chapter V). As Tables 8 and 9 show, a more sophisticated statistical analysis changes the picture. Environment by itself accounts for only 11 per cent of the variability of the ABC ranks (Table 8), but combined with the other basic variables and analyzed by means of the multiple regression model at a level of explanation of 77.2 per cent, environment obtains a student *t* value of —3.03 and is the most explanatory basic variable for this variability (Table 9).

TABLE 8

Per cent of Variability of the Measure of Objectal Development (ABC Ranks) Explained by Each Individual Variable

Variable	Per cent
Sex	.4
Environment	11.1
CA	63.0
Griffiths A	68.9
Griffiths B	76.9
Griffiths C	69.4
Griffiths D	70.9
Griffiths E	68.1
MA	74.0
Piaget ranks	66.6

Chronological age. The correlation between chronological age and ABC ranks is .794 (Table 5). Chronological age by itself accounts for 63 per cent of the variability of the ABC ranks, which

TABLE 9

The ABC Ranks as a Function of the Basic Variables

Per cent of Explained Variance: 77.2 Per cent

Variable	Regression coefficient	Variance of regression coefficient	Student t
Environment	−14.50	22.93	−3.03
CA	.5946	.2215	1.26
MA	.8041	.3898	1.29
Piaget ranks	4.607	7.041	1.74

is rather high. In a combined analysis, at a level of explanation of 77.2 per cent, the chronological age obtains a t value which remains significant and is directly comparable to that of mental age and that of the Piaget ranks, but definitely lower than that of the environment (Table 9).

Mental age. The coefficient of correlation between mental age and ABC ranks is .860 (Table 5). Mental age by itself accounts for 74 per cent of the variability of the ABC ranks. It therefore plays approximately the same role as chronological age in relation to the variability of Piaget ranks. In combination with the other basic variables, again at a level of explanation of 77.2 per cent, it remains an explanatory factor of the same importance as chronological age and Piaget ranks, but its contribution is only half as important as that of the environment.

Piaget ranks. The relationship between ABC ranks and Piaget ranks has already been shown. Since, according to Table 8, the percentage of variability of the ABC ranks consists of the square of the coefficients of correlation, the Piaget ranks necessarily account for 66.6 per cent of the variability of the objectal measure. This is exactly the same percentage as that of the ABC ranks in relation to the variability of the objective measure. The real influence of the objective development is brought forth only in a combined analysis with the other basic variables. Then one notices that at a level of explanation of 77.2 per cent its contribution is clearly inferior to that of the environment but slightly higher than that of mental age and chronological age (Table 9).

Subscales A, B, C, D and E

At the beginning of this research we asked ourselves the following questions. Is there a relation between a subject's mental age and his objectal level? What is the relation between the development of dexterity and the construction of the object concept? Is language development parallel with the construction of the object concept or with the development of object relations? We are now in a position to answer the first of these questions, but in order to answer the others we must first attempt to evaluate the influence of the measure of Griffiths' scales A, B, C, D and E concerning the measures of objective and objectal development. This will be the next and final step in the analysis of our data.

A. *The Griffiths scales and the variability of the Piaget ranks.* Table 10 indicates that the Griffiths subscales, when analyzed in combination with all the variables at a level of explanation of 85.7 per cent, have very low student t values. Subscales A (locomotor development) and D (hand and eye development) seem to account for more of the variability of the measure of objective development than any of the other subscales. When only these two subscales are combined with the other basic variables and analyzed with the aim of discovering which of the two is more influential, one finds that, at a level of explanation of 84.3 per cent, subscale D has a much higher student t value (4.97) than subscale A (.48) (see Table 12[a]).

B. *The Griffiths scales and the variability of the ABC ranks.* Table 11 indicates that subscale B (personal-social development) when analyzed in combination with all the variables at a level of explanation of 81.2 per cent has a student t value almost as high as that of environment. When the subscales are compared with each other, subscale A (locomotor development) too seems to account for some variability. But when only the two subscales with

TABLE 10
Piaget Ranks as a Function of All Other Variables
Per cent of Explained Variability: 85.7 Per cent

Variable	Coefficient of regression	Variance of coefficient of regression	Student t
Sex	0.16	0.053	0.68
Environment	0.36	0.045	1.71
Chronological age	−0.028	0.00045	−1.32
Griffiths A	−0.025	0.0014	−0.66
Griffiths B	0.0087	0.0016	0.22
Griffiths C	−0.016	0.0012	−0.43
Griffiths D	0.022	0.0011	0.67
Griffiths E	0.007	0.0013	0.19
Mental age	0.13	0.022	0.85
ABC ranks	0.0072	0.000023	1.50

the highest *t* values are combined and analyzed with the other basic variables, one finds that at a level of explanation of 79.5 per cent subscale B becomes the most important variable to account for the variability of the ABC ranks (see Table 12[b]).

TABLE 11
ABC Ranks as a Function of All Other Variables
Per cent of Explained Variability: 81.2 Per cent

Variable	Coefficient of regression	Variance of coefficient of regression	Student t
Sex	2.318	29.22	0.43
Environment	−18.02	21.36	−3.90
Chronological age	1.026	0.2371	2.11
Griffiths A	1.098	0.7429	1.27
Griffiths B	3.104	0.7456	3.60
Griffiths C	0.3138	0.6673	0.38
Griffiths D	0.1436	0.6170	0.18
Griffiths E	0.4765	0.7026	0.57
Mental age	−4.596	11.86	−1.33
Piaget ranks	3.888	6.695	1.50

TABLE 12

(a) Piaget ranks as a function of Environment, CA, Griffiths A & D, and ABC ranks		(b) ABC ranks as a function of Environment, CA, Griffiths A & B and Piaget ranks	
Explained Variability: 84.3 per cent		Explained Variability: 79.5 per cent	
Variable	*Student t*	*Variable*	*Student t*
Environment	1.02	Environment	−2.97
Chronological age	− .47	Chronological age	.87
Griffiths A	.48	Griffiths A	.21
Griffiths D	4.97	Griffiths B	3.04
ABC ranks	2.15	Piaget ranks	.85

CHAPTER VII

CONCLUSIONS

> *". . . nothing more desirable could happen to psychoanalytic theory than a corroboration of Piaget's findings. Psychoanalysis would find itself for the first time confronted with a genetic theory of broad scope, using a method of observation which is in some ways akin (if not derived from) its own. The mutual stimulation of this confrontation could not but prove productive"* (Rapaport, 1960, p. 119).

The experiments have proven the existence of a close link between intellectual development analyzed under the specific aspect of the object concept and measured by the Piaget ranks, and affective development analyzed under the specific aspect of object relations and measured by the ABC ranks. This link is such that, as the subject gets older, he reaches increasingly advanced levels from the objective, and an increasingly higher rank from the objectal points of view. We are thus confronted with a parallel of a genetic order.

SOME CONCLUSIONS RESULTING FROM THE QUANTITATIVE ANALYSIS

The quantitative analysis of the first half of our parallel permits the following conclusions:

1. In the construction of the object concept, mental age represents a variable of primary importance. This is not surprising. Indeed, if the construction of the object concept is in fact a dimension of intelligence, and if the global mental age as measured by the Griffiths is a valid measure of intellectual performance of the infant, these two variables cannot but obtain a high coefficient of correlation. The profound significance of this correlation coefficient shows up in a more advanced statistical analysis, namely in the multiple regression model which allows us to conclude that mental age, more than any other factor, accounts for the variability of the measure of object concept development, and that its influence clearly exceeds that of the other basic variables, i.e., environment, ABC ranks, and chronological age. These results contradict the assertions of certain psychologists who see in Piaget's analyses nothing but vague philosophical speculations divorced from reality. The steps observed by Piaget (1937) in *The Construction of Reality in the Child* appear indeed to be indicative of a subject's mental level. We are convinced that by adding to the first series of the construction of the object concept tests concerning space, time, and causality, one would obtain an excellent working tool for testing the intellectual performance of infants. Yet we do not think of this testing in terms of intelligence quotients (as in most tests of this kind) but rather in terms of a constellation of stages. This seems much more in the spirit of a structural theory of intelligence.

2. The second most important factor to account for the variability of the measure of objective development is the environment. Its influence is, however, not comparable to that of mental age but rather to that of ABC ranks and chronological age, the other two basic variables. This seems surprising at first, since Piaget almost never speaks of the environment which he assumes to be normal when he studies the construction of reality. Piaget grants that this environment influences the development of sensorimotor intelligence, but he considers it rather as a problem belonging to differential psychology, and sees it very differently from

the way the psychoanalysts do. According to Piaget, if the mother's absence results in general retardation of infants in institutions, this is so because, especially during the first year of life, the mother is not only the foremost affective object but also the cognitive object *par excellence* (Piaget, 1954, pp. 66ff.).[1] Be that as it may, within the framework of our experiment, environment is an extremely complex variable; it involves not only profound variations in the mother-child relationship but also in mental age, learning possibility, and freedom of movement. These various elements must be taken into consideration in the evaluation of the influence of the environment upon the formation of the object concept.

3. The correlation between Piaget and ABC ranks is high. Provided that one accepts the working tools we constructed as valid, the coefficient of correlation reflects a close link between object concept formation and object relation. In a more sophisticated statistical analysis, this link is maintained: The variability of the measure of objective development is accounted for by the ABC ranks better than by chronological age, less well than by the environment, and considerably less well than by mental age. We see these results as a confirmation of the relative interdependence of intelligence and affectivity, the two complementary aspects of personality. We shall return to the discussion of the possible theoretical extensions of this interdependence.

4. Chronological age is the last basic variable accounting for the variability of the measure of objective development. Intellectual growth requires time; it takes several months to progress from sensorimotor to representative intelligence and no researcher in genetic psychology can dissociate chronological age from development in general. Moreover, since mental age is obviously closely related to chronological age, the latter must be an impor-

---

[1] In this context, we can imagine a fascinating and difficult research in which the relative presence of the mothering one would be kept constant while one varied the sensorimotor stimuli presented by some cognitive object with as much *Prägnanz* as possible but which would not be a human being.

tant factor in accounting for the variability of the measure of objective development. Yet its influence is definitely not as great as that of mental age. As shown in Figure 2 (Chapter VI), a certain lability exists in the construction of the object in regard to CA despite our age groupings, and we are tempted to say of chronological age what Piaget (1954) asserts for maturation: "Maturation alone causes nothing; it merely determines the range of possibilities for any given level" (p. 24).

5. The comparative analysis of the Griffiths subscales reveals that hand and eye development (subscale D) is one of the most important factors in accounting for the variability of the Piaget ranks. This result was to be foreseen in view of the fact that Piaget attributes considerable importance, from a strictly intellectual viewpoint, to the integration of the heterogeneous and independent schemas of vision and prehension (Piaget, 1948, pp. 90ff.), and in view of the very theory of object concept formation and of the structurization of the tests of the Piaget series. Eye-hand co-ordination must certainly not be assumed to determine the construction of the object concept: certain items of hand and eye development are passed or failed (e.g., D18: "looks for fallen object") according to the subject's construction of the object, and not the reverse.

The high coefficients of correlation between the measure of locomotor development (subscale A) and all other psychological variables, including objective development, are harder to understand. These results are evidence for the internal consistency of the Griffiths and for the existence of what Spitz calls "somato-psyche," but we cannot easily see locomotor development as very representative of psychological development in general and intellectual development in particular. Furthermore, a more sophisticated statistical analysis reduces the role of locomotor development (Table 12[a], Chapter VI).

The quantitative analysis of the second half of our parallel permits the following conclusions:

1. The ABC ranks do not show up as clearly related to the environment on the basis of a simple coefficient of correlation. However, the multiple regression model makes the relationship evident: environment becomes the preponderant factor to account for the variability of the ABC ranks. Provided that one accepts our working tools as valid, this indicates a close link between the environment and the development of object relations. We see in these results a confirmation of our subhypothesis according to which the category to which a subject belongs influences his objectal level. The analysis of the raw data had already supported this hypothesis, but not statistically (Figures 6 and 7, Chapter VI). Yet the reservations made concerning the influence of the environment upon object concept formation also hold true for the analysis of the link between environment and objectal development. Factors other than emotional certainly play a role. The environment still seems to affect emotional development more directly than mental development.[2] The mere contact with things can in itself be a source of knowledge and even of socialization (in the narrow sense of progressive decentralization), but by prohibiting exchange and learning of co-operation such contact leads only to limited decentralization, to a depersonalized relationship with others.

2. Object concept formation as measured by the Piaget ranks is the second most explanatory factor for the variability of the objectal measure. Its influence remains considerably below that of environment but slightly exceeds that of CA and even of MA. This may be a weak indication that Piaget's intelligence stages are more closely linked with emotional development than genetic scales conceived of as the sum of items of knowledge.

3. Mental age is the third most explanatory factor of the variability of the ABC ranks. If the Griffiths truly measures intellectual performance and the objectal scale measures emotional development, this link is a very natural one. This agrees with our

---

[2] Our models are never directly comparable, since they are at different levels of explanation.

aforementioned results and underlines again the existence of a close relationship between the development of intelligence, however measured, and the development of affectivity. It must be noted, however, that subscale B of the Griffiths clearly measures personal-social development and thus may accentuate the relationship between Griffiths MA and the ABC ranks. From this perspective, the Piaget ranks seem to be a much more affect-free measure of intellectual performance than the Griffiths, and their relationship to the ABC ranks is all the more conclusive.

4. Chronological age as an explanatory factor of the variability of the ABC ranks is directly comparable to mental age. This is not surprising, and what we said in analyzing the relationship of this variable to the Piaget ranks applies here as well. Moreover, considering the inevitable link between CA and objectal development, we deem the attitude of certain authors somewhat unrealistic (although historically very understandable) when they show little concern for this variable while claiming to use genetic psychoanalysis. Discussions with genetic psychologists will become possible only when psychoanalysts will attempt a narrower chronological delimitation of certain affective phenomena following the example of Spitz, Escalona, Fries, and others. Let no one reply that psychoanalysts need speak only in terms of years (pregenital phase, latency period, adolescence, etc.)—Within the first two years of life, three months equal years of later development (Spitz, 1959, p. 10).[3]

5. Among the Griffiths subscales, subscale B accounts for the variability of the ABC ranks more than the others. Any other result would have been surprising. The objectal scale was combined with Griffiths' subscale B and even shared three of its items. Must one conclude that the objectal scale could easily be reduced to a simple scale of social activities? We do not think so, since passing

---

[3] The importance of chronological age is highlighted by Bowlby (1960), Anna Freud (1960), and Spitz (1960). In this discussion, the differences of opinion are due mainly to the fact that some speak of children of one year or less, others of children of one and a half years or more.

or failure of an objectal criterion had to be interpreted in terms of the total protocol, and since its meaning could change from one subject to the next (cf. Chapter VI, first part). We believe that the objectal scale approaches projective techniques rather than psychometric tests, and we would hesitate to attempt a rigid standardization.

Finally, the comparison of the various models shows definitely that the attained level of explanation, depending on the part of the parallel under analysis, is evidently never exactly the same and proves to be slightly higher in the case of the measure of objective development (84.8 per cent compared to 77.2 per cent [see Tables 7 and 9]; and 84.3 per cent compared to 79.5 per cent [see Table 12]). This is hardly significant. These differences in the percentage of the explained variability may, however, be due to our measures. The ranking of our subjects in terms of objective development certainly did not present as many difficulties as the ranking of these subjects in terms of their objectal level; the measure of the Piaget stages seems to be more rigorous than the ABC ranks. This may also be tied to the very nature of the two aspects of development which we tried to study; emotional phenomena remain more elusive than cognitive phenomena.

These various results supply abundant material for thought. We could continue this analysis, but we prefer to leave it up to the reader to construct new hypotheses on the basis of our findings. We shall, instead, make a last attempt to explain the central problem of our research: the possible correlation between objective and objectal development.

SOME CONCLUSIONS RESULTING FROM THE QUALITATIVE ANALYSIS

The qualitative analysis of the findings enables us to answer some of the questions raised in the beginning. Does the construction of the object parallel the development of object relations? If so, is this a perfect parallel? Or, in Piaget's terms, does a given intellectual structure necessarily correspond to a given form of energy regulation? Can one predict a specific objectal level from a given objective stage?

We have seen that the fixed sequence of the Piaget stages does not recur for the phases of emotional development and that the absence of irreversibility of the objectal criteria makes a rigid correlation impossible. There is certainly never an inverse relationship but, within certain limits, there is a considerable amount of freedom between the two sides of our parallel allowing for numerous combinations and underlining the extreme diversity of psychological development during the first years of life. An over-all comparison of the Piaget stages and the psychoanalytic periods reveal, on the basis of our over-all data, the following general parallel:

Stages	Periods
I and II	intermediate
III and IV	objectal a
V and VI	objectal b

It must be emphasized that this parallel is derived only from subjects who, according to our hypothesis, had a harmonious objectal development. Nevertheless, as we have just seen, the close link between object concept formation and objectal development expressed by the ABC ranks remains the same even if subjects with certain emotional problems are added to this first group.

Our findings constitute a more explicit form of the parallel suggested by Piaget in 1954. They support it on some points and contradict it on others. A systematic comparison of our findings with the particular Piagetian hypotheses seems superfluous. It would require an interpretation of his lecture notes. Such an interpretation could easily do injustice to his ideas. In those notes Piaget analyzed emotional development essentially in terms of the evolution of drives, while we are concerned not only with the object of the drive but also with the much more flexible object of object relations. Our two parallels are not directly comparable.

Moreover, Piaget's criticisms of Freudian theory largely disappear if, instead of clinging to the extremely simplified concept of psychosexual development as per Freud's early theory, one considers object relations as described by contemporary psychoanalysis. The vast majority of psychoanalysts agree with Piaget that the development of affectivity involves a restructuring of the universe, a restructuring which is actually the result of a decentralization in which the perceptual and intellectual processes play a considerable part. Most genetic psychoanalysts would fully endorse Piaget's statement that:

"This displacement of affectivity from action itself onto someone else, which Freud discusses, and which will free the child of its narcissism in order to invest some other person with affectivity, is in reality much more than a displacement. It is much more than a transfer since previously there was neither anyone in the sense of an autonomous object, of an autonomous source of causality, of a body similar to one's own body, etc., nor an independent object.

"This displacement is much more than a displacement because it is accompanied by a total and general construction, a *restructuring* of the entire environment [Piaget, 1954, p. 65]."

The disagreement remains when the relationship between intelligence and affectivity is viewed in terms of antecedents or causes. But even in this respect, the great theorists of psychoanalysis have considerably reduced these differences between Freud's and Piaget's theories by following Hartmann and suggesting the existence of autonomous ego functions. Be that as it may, this problem cannot be resolved on the basis of our data alone.[4]

[4] Is this not as Piaget strongly asserts a pseudo problem? "There is no affective behavior and cognitive behavior. Behavior is always both. Thus, only an analysis, an abstraction for the study of their respective mechanisms separates these two aspects which in reality are always present *simultaneously*. Hence, if one acknowledges affectivity and cognition (perceptual or intelligent) as two aspects of behavior, it makes no sense to wonder which causes which or even which precedes which. One aspect does not cause another aspect or precede another aspect. They are complementary because neither process can function without the other" (Piaget, 1954, p. 67).

The author does not wish to leave the reader with the impression that her investigation leads to a blending of the basic psychoanalytic theories and certain findings of the Geneva school. There remain between them differences and even contradictions, one of which is of primordial importance and concerns the genesis of representation. We shall conclude with a discussion of this last question, since our findings may throw some light upon it.

THE GENESIS OF REPRESENTATION ACCORDING TO PIAGET AND TO PSYCHOANALYTIC THEORY

According to Piaget, representation does not exist at birth. It appears during the first eighteen months and becomes the habitual mode of thought at approximately two years. It is hard to say exactly what Piaget means by "representation." Concerning the sixth and final stage of sensorimotor intelligence, Piaget mentions true, real, and actual (*vraie, réelle, véritable*) representation, indicating thereby the existence of a different and earlier kind of representation (Piaget, 1948, pp. 341ff.). In *The Construction of Reality in the Child* he speaks of a representation which begins with the third step (stage IV) of the construction of the object and again leaves true representation for the end of the sixth stage (Piaget, 1937, p. 83f.). In later works, Piaget is even less explicit. Whereas according to his earlier writings representative intelligence followed immediately upon sensorimotor intelligence (Piaget, 1937, 1948), he now sees the typical behavior patterns of the sixth stage as proof for "the beginnings of representation, but beginnings which scarcely go beyond the rather rudimentary representation of chimpanzees" (Piaget, 1947, p. 106); he mentions "pre-representative" intelligence (*ibid.*, p. 116) and speaks of "dawning representation" (Piaget, 1956, p. 39) as succeeding sensorimotor intelligence. However, in *Play, Dreams and Imitation in Childhood* Piaget makes an important distinction which throws light on these divergences:

"We use the word 'representation' in two different senses. In its broad sense, representation is identical with thought, *i.e.*, with all intelligence which is based on a system of concepts or mental schemas and not merely on perceptions and actions. In its narrow sense, representation is restricted to the mental or memory image, *i.e.*, the symbolic evocation of absent realities [Piaget, 1945, p. 67]."

According to Piaget, representation in the wider sense (when he analyzes sensorimotor intelligence in general) is likely to appear at the same time as representation in the narrower sense (when he discusses the development of gestural imitation and speech); but in another passage he is careful to specify that if invention by mental combination and the specific deduction of the sixth stage require representation, the latter does not necessarily imply either invention or deduction, since it can be defined as "evocation of absent objects" (Piaget, 1937, p. 293).

If we limit ourselves to the construction of the object concept (which we shall attempt to do), can we conclude that representation exists from the beginning of the evocation of absent objects, i.e., of stage four, since at that level the infant, for the first time, searches for an object which is entirely covered by a screen? This is not the case, as Piaget distinguishes between simple and real evocation and considers only the latter to constitute true representation:

"Doubtless this representation of the object which we call the characteristic of the sixth stage is already budding in the preceding stages. As soon as the child at the fourth stage begins to search actively for the vanished object it can be claimed that there exists a sort of evocation of the absent object. But never until the present stage has this behavior led to real evocation, because it has merely utilized a system of signs linked with the action; searching for an object under a screen when the subject has seen it disappear there (stages IV and V) does not necessarily presuppose that the subject 'imagines' the object under the screen but simply that he has understood the relation of the two objects at the moment he perceived it (at the moment when the object was covered) and that he therefore interprets the screen as a sign of the actual presence of the object. It is one thing to assume the permanence of an object when one has just seen it and when some other object now in sight recalls its presence, and it is quite another thing to imagine the first object when there is nothing in sight to attest its hidden existence. True representation therefore begins only when no perceived sign commands belief in permanency, that is to say, from the moment when the vanished object is displaced according to an itinerary which the subject may deduce but not perceive [Piaget, 1937, p. 84f.]."

Thus true evocation or memory image or representation exists only when deduction intervenes, i.e., in the sixth stage, according to Piaget. According to some of our findings, deduction may be assumed to intervene as of the end of the fifth stage, but this hardly changes the following observations, since only one 20-month-old subject was at stage Vb. Among our 90 subjects (CA range 3 to 20 months) 16 reached the sixth stage. In these we can be sure of the existence of representation if we accept Piaget's theory. All of these subjects were at least 16 months old. This means that representation makes its appearance probably only around the beginning of the second year of life (not one of our one-year-old subjects went beyond the beginning of stage V) and that the symbolic ability in the form of internalized images becomes possible only from that age on.

Obviously these conclusions are valid only if one accepts Piaget's theory. It would seem difficult to doubt the accuracy of the observations from which Piaget derived his theory since they could be repeated with a population of 90 infants from very different environments, yet one can refuse to interpret the facts in the way Piaget does. He would be the first one to admit that the nonexistence of a psychological process can never be proven conclusively. However, if the nonexistence of such a process is a sufficient explanation for hitherto incomprehensible facts, the hypothesis must be accepted as long as no better explanation is available. For the time being, Piaget's theory about object formation seems to account fully for the various behavior patterns of the infant between three and twenty months when it searches for a vanished object.

We shall now briefly analyze contemporary psychoanalytic theory regarding the beginning of representation. For most psychoanalysts, the existence or nonexistence of mental images at the beginning of life is not a real problem or at least is a minor problem within the total context of Freudian theory.[5] Various authors differ on this point, but this entails no controversy. Theorists and practitioners of genetic psychoanalysis hardly seem to be sensitive to this question, which is easy to understand in view of the origin of the theory.[6] The psychoanalysts' deliberate vagueness concerning chronological points of reference hardly facilitates matters. A comparison of Piaget's and psychoanalytic theories concerning the genesis of representation results in a comparison of a series of minute observations, resulting in an explicit hypothesis with a dearth of observations and hypotheses which most often must be extrapolated from various texts. We have, on the one hand, a single author for whom the problem of the advent of representation is a fundamental one, treated at length in his major works (Piaget, 1937, 1945, 1948); on the other hand, we have numerous authors for whom this question is relatively unimportant and who therefore refer to it only occasionally. Under these circumstances we must constantly make inferences, and one runs the danger of falsifying the ideas of the psychoanalysts by making them say much more than they had ever wanted to say. Hence we shall limit ourselves to the most explicit texts and to the familiar authors.

In discussing the major sources of data incompatible with psychoanalytic theory Rapaport mentions Piaget's observations and

[5] I am grateful to Mr. André Lussier, Professor of Psychology at the University of Montreal and President of the Canadian Psychoanalytic Society, for his friendly criticisms of my initial interpretation of the hallucinatory object.

[6] However, some psychoanalysts are especially alert to this question. Their interest originated mainly in the controversy between Kleinians and orthodox Freudians (cf. Glover, 1945). We have deliberately disregarded Melanie Klein's theory, but it is clear that her postulates are absolutely irreconcilable with Piaget's theory.

theory and asserts that, if confirmed, these data could become a source of contradictions. He mentions only motivation as a point of contention (Rapaport, 1960, p. 119). In earlier works (Rapaport, 1954a) he had seen certain works of Piaget (1931, 1948) as a confirmation of psychoanalytic hypotheses concerning the origins of thought; he did not seem to find contradictions between these two theories in this respect.

Wolff compared classical Freudian theory with Piaget's hypothesis that representation (characteristic of stage VI) is both the result of learning and the most economic means of adaptation to reality. In the following statement, Wolff refers to the primary model of thought processes as conceived by psychoanalysis.

"When integrated into this classic conception of psychoanalysis, Piaget's findings would describe the mechanisms by which primary-process ideations are reorganized according to reality considerations, and by which secondary-process thought functions to some extent independent of the environment while maintaining an internal representation of it. Piaget's findings also emphasize the potentially adaptive role of early fantasies and caution us against making psychoanalytic reconstructions of early mental life which assume that the infant already hallucinates discrete objects, objective spatial and causal relationships, etc. [Wolff, 1960, p. 166]."

When the study of dreams, of perceptual illusions, and of hallucinations had revealed to Freud that, in certain instances of intense frustration, the tension increase due to the absence of the gratifying object led to hallucinations of that object and/or the gratifying experience itself, he constructed from these findings the basic model of mental functioning (Freud, 1911, 1915). This model was adapted and clarified by Rapaport[7] as follows:[8]

Drive→ $\left\{ \begin{array}{l} \text{absence of drive object:} \\ \text{delay of discharge} \end{array} \right\}$ → $\left\{ \begin{array}{l} \text{hallucinatory image of the} \\ \text{memory of gratification} \end{array} \right.$

---

[7] "I am not embarking on the task of creating a new model, but only of spelling out the psychoanalytic one, which to my knowledge has never been explicitly done" (Rapaport, 1954a, p. 222f.).

[8] From Rapaport, 1954a, p. 227. Even if some psychoanalysts reject certain

Due to the inevitable delay in drive gratification the memory traces of a gratifying experience are cathected to the point of perceptual hallucinatory intensity. These particular dynamics characterize the very beginnings of life.[9] Part of the behavioral repertory of the infant is explained by this conceptual model which is at the root of the adult's intellectual functioning since ideas spring from these hallucinatory images. What do these hallucinatory images consist of originally? Here, "hallucinatory" means essentially that the subject believes the hallucinated drive object to be real;[10] the exact meaning of the word "image" poses a problem. Rapaport, the most explicit author in this connection, writes:

"From the genetic point of view a more complete description of the hallucinatory image must be made, and from it important conclusions may be derived concerning the primary process. From developmental psychology we know that the original experience of the need-satisfying object is a diffuse undifferentiated experience in which visual, acoustic, tactile, thermal, cutaneous, kinesthetic, and other stimulations are fused. Discrete objects do not as yet exist, and thus the need-satisfying object itself is not differentiated from the context in which it appears nor even from the experiences immediately preceding or following it.

"It is this diffuse global image of the need-satisfying object which is pushed into consciousness when instinctual tension mounts. In the course of development this diffuse image differentiates into discrete objects and experiences, all of which are still related to instinctual drives in the same fashion as was the original undifferentiated image of the need-satisfying object [Rapaport, 1954b, p. 262]."

In this context the hallucinated object is far from being the permanent, substantial thing, external to the I, which Piaget means

---

modalities of this primitive conceptual model (e.g., Spitz), most of them accept this hypothesis without reservations (Stanton, 1959). Rapaport realizes, moreover, that he deals with what is essentially an assumption, but one which he considers plausible (Rapaport, 1951, 1954a).

[9] ". . . all that is assumed here is that the sequence *restlessness→absence of breast→hallucinatory image* occurs *in infancy*" (Rapaport, 1954a, p. 227).

[10] ". . . hallucinatory phenomena are perceptions without objects in the outside world" (Hartmann, Kris, and Loewenstein, 1946, p. 14).

when he speaks of an "object." The hallucinatory image differs
from the image of which Piaget writes: ". . . the image itself raises
a problem, for far from being an immediate continuation of perception as such, it does not seem to intervene in mental life before
the second year" (Piaget, 1945, p. 3). Yet this hallucinatory image
of the need-satisfying object does seem to be a primitive form of
representation since, in the absence of that need-satisfying object,
it evokes a vague, diffuse, undifferentiated object. This is not yet
true representation but rather analogous to representation in
stage IV, in which visceral hunger sensations play the role of perceptual indicators of a forthcoming feeding and lead the infant to
believe that the object is already present. Due to its reviving force,
and because it goes beyond simple sensation, the hallucinatory
image approaches the percept but is different from the latter in
being a vague awareness of past perceptual data rather than of
perceptual data which are present in the environment at the time.
Due to its diffuse, syncretic, undifferentiated character and its
condensation of visual, tactile, and kinesthetic stimuli, it approaches the eidetic image, but without the photographic precision which eidetic images sometimes have (see especially Russell,
1956 and Werner, 1957).

Even if the contradiction between Rapaport's specific primitive
model of cognition (many authors are less cautious than he) and
Piaget's hypothesis is not obvious, the two seem unavoidably con-
tradictory from a strict chronological viewpoint. The hallucinatory
image characterizes the beginning of existence (it will take a few
days or even weeks for memory to register the various stimuli connected with the total feeding situation) since it belongs to the primary process which marks the phase of nondifferentiation between id and ego (Rapaport, 1954b, pp. 268ff. and Hoffer, 1950a,
p. 19). This period of nondifferentiation normally does not outlast
the first three or four months. However, according to Piaget, representation, even in this primitive form,[11] does not appear until stage

[11] We are by no means sure that the hallucinatory image *is nothing but this
primitive form* of representation. Our interpretation, if we accept Piaget's

IV, i.e., at approximately 8 to 10 months.[12] Furthermore the contradiction continues and becomes even more obvious if one compares the moment at which Piaget places the appearance of the true mental image, or of representation in the narrow sense (1945, p. 67), with the time at which psychoanalysts assume its existence. We find that the infant is capable of evoking the image of the vanished object—relatively early according to some (A. Freud, Hoffer), and somewhat later according to others (Spitz, Benedek)—that this image (most frequently visual) represents a differentiated object (smiling-human-face, breast, the whole mother), and that this object may be evoked in the absence of perceptual cues.

Because they do not make the distinction between affective and objective permanence, psychoanalysts assume that as soon as the infant has formed an attachment to a given human being, and hence shows regret in his absence, the baby is able to visualize the one he loves and misses. As far as we know, no psychoanalytic author denies the existence of this capacity from 6 to 7 months on, and most of them seem to admit implicitly the existence of mental images when they describe the cathexis of the love object, the differentiation between familiar and unfamiliar persons, and oral fantasies.

"Negative hallucination refers to the temporary abolition of a stimulus, inside or outside the body, not to the abolition of the mental representation of such stimuli like in repression. Negative hallucination . . . connotes one of the earliest and most primitive of mental processes [Hoffer, 1950a, p. 19]."

"Following Freud's argument, the infant's visual recognition of the human face, the smiling response, marks the establishment of

---

theory, gives the psychoanalysts the benefit of the doubt and minimizes the contradiction with Piaget's data.

[12] In our study, out of 52 subjects who reached or passed stage IV, only 2 were less than 9 months old. Moreover, they were at the very beginning of that stage, when there is active search in the immediate extension of the act of accommodation. The beginning of representation of which Piaget speaks (1937, p. 84f.) seems to be characteristic of the end of the stage, so that the behavior of the two six-month-old subjects who reached stage IVa can be explained in the absence of any representation.

the reality ego, for it establishes that 'something which is present in the ego as an image can also be discovered in perception [that is, in reality]' (Freud, 1925) [Spitz, 1959, p. 19]."

"The recognition of the human face confirms that the infant has acquired the capacity to rediscover in reality the object which corresponds to what is present in his imagination [Spitz, 1959, pp. 19-20]."

"Libidinal cathexis shifts gradually from the experience of satisfaction to the image of the object without whom satisfaction would not have come about. With this step forward in development, the infant enters into the stage of object love [A. Freud, 1954, p. 13]."

"Recent studies of institutionalized children [Spitz, 1945b] show that infants who did not develop object relationships or had to give them up because of neglect, withdrew from the environment and lived the life of preverbal fantasies which are expressed in the monotonous repetition of some form of autoerotic manipulation [Benedek, 1952, p. 69]."

We believe that there is a real contradiction between these statements (to which we could add) and Piaget's theory. This difference becomes particularly important in its extensions, since the moment of the beginning of representation is at the root of a number of propositions which, when reduced to their most simple form, can be stated as follows:

Propositions by Piaget	*Psychoanalytic Propositions*
The infant is incapable of true representation before the second year (16-20 months).	The infant is capable of true representation from the intermediate period on (3 to 6-7 months).
Before this time the infant is incapable of symbolic play.	Elements of symbols are acquired as of that period (e.g., thumb symbolizing breast).
Before this time the infant is incapable of imitating an internal model.	The infant is capable of imitating an internal model (identification) before age 12 months.

Before this time the infant is incapable of imagination in the strict sense.	Before age 12 months the infant has a universe of fantasies at his disposal.

No dialectics seem to be able to reduce the discrepancies between these propositions,[13] but the facts may help us to choose one or the other set of hypotheses. The emotional behavior patterns analyzed in this study make us wonder whether they necessarily require the intervention of representation. If they do, the fact that a subject shows himself capable of a single one of these behavior patterns before having reached the sixth stage may throw some doubt on Piaget's interpretations; if, however, these behavior patterns can be explained without resorting to representation, Piaget's theory is supported, and some psychoanalytic propositions need reformulation.

In brief, the following emotional behavior patterns were observed between the ages of three and twenty months: (1) specific reaction to feeding, (2) automatic smile (2 stimuli required), (3) automatic smile at the mere sight of the adult, (4) ability to wait for a seen and heard adult, (5) negative affect at play interruption, (6) ability to wait at the mere sound of the adult's voice, (7) specific smile with certain limitations, (8) absolutely specific smile, (9) negative affect at loss of toy, (10) active show of affection, (11) compliance with requests, (12) compliance with prohibitions, (13) subtle discrimination of signs of communication. According to Piaget's theory, none of these behavior patterns requires representation, with the possible exception of active show of affection in the absence of any gesture of affection on the part of the mother.

The specific reaction to feeding is a simple sensorimotor recognition of postures. The automatic smile is a recognitory response to sensory pictures which are either only visual or both visual and

---

[13] This time we are accentuating the discrepancy instead of minimizing it. We believe that despite the simplification most psychoanalysts would agree with the propositions in the right column.

auditory. The ability to wait requires, besides frustration tolerance, perception of and accommodation to a certain number of
signals. The negative affect at play interruption or at the loss of
the toy presupposes only an affective permanency of people and
things and is closely related to anticipatory behavior. The specific smile itself may be no more than the recognition of sensory
pictures more complex than the simple picture of the smiling human face.[14] The active show of affection creates a problem
if it consists of a complex gesture which the infant cannot see in
relation to his own body (e.g., kissing), which he does spontaneously and not in direct imitation of a model before him. This is
an instance of "deferred imitation" which presupposes representation (Piaget, 1945, pp. 63ff.). But we have seen that our criterion requires only the direct imitation of an affectionate gesture,
and that the objectal meaning of this affective behavior remains ambiguous and calls for clarification. We do not have to
analyze the last three behavior patterns because the subjects who
reached this level were all at least at the beginning of the sixth
stage and thus, according to Piaget, already capable of representation. If the behavior patterns 11 and 12, which occur prior to
the internalization of social norms, may not require representation from this perspective, they must require it in terms of their
objectal meaning. According to psychoanalytic theory, these behavior patterns actually testify to the object constancy of the love
object, and this constancy is inconceivable without the capacity
for representation of the absent object.

Before turning to the facts, let us note that the attempt to verify
psychoanalytic data by means of Piagetian data and vice versa
requires extreme caution. One must remember that the objectivation of the human being, and thus at some time the representation of that person, precedes (even according to Piaget) the ob-

[14] The later-appearing eighth-month anxiety is probably already an evocation,
although not yet a real one. According to this hypothesis the stranger's face
plays a role comparable to that of the screen (object construction, stage IV)
and constitutes the perception which attests to the existence of the familiar
person.

jectivation of the inanimate object. It does so not only because the human being forms the emotional object *par excellence,* but also because, strictly from the point of view of intelligence, persons are at the crosspoint of numerous assimilatory and accommodatory schemata.

"The other person is of course an emotional object to the highest degree but at the same time it is the most interesting cognitive object, the most alive, the most unexpected, at this level the most instructive one, an object, I repeat, which is the source of perception, of actions of any kind, of imitation, of causality, of spatial structuring. Thus, the other person is an object which implies a multitude of exchanges in which cognitive as well as affective factors play a role, and if this object is of paramount importance in one of these respects, it is, I think, equally important in the other [Piaget, 1954, p. 66]."

A number of problems can be solved and the analysis of our data facilitated by allowing for a two- to three-month interval to account for the shift between the objectivation of persons and that of things, as Spitz did for the cathexis of persons and things. What can we learn from our data after making this last correction and focusing on the specific problem of representation? The distribution of our subjects by Piagetian stages and psychoanalytic periods was presented in Figure 5 (Chapter VI). We refer the reader to these histograms with the reminder that they are based only on data from one half of our population, but since "an acute observation ... surpasses all statistics" (Piaget, 1948, p. 72), the author ventures to believe that there is material for thought here.

HISTOGRAM 1 (STAGES I AND II)

The last objectal test passed by the subjects who do not yet search for any vanished object (stages I and II) and are therefore still far from the stage of representation, is the specific smile. However, this is an exceptional behavior (1 out of 17 subjects). We have seen that this behavior can be explained on the level of simple recognition of complex sensory pictures (a typical behavior of stages I and II). Hence this distribution presents no problem in terms of Piaget's theory. The behavior of the infant remains coherent without resorting to representation.

HISTOGRAMS 2 AND 3 (STAGES III AND IV)

The last objectal test passed by the subjects who, from the objective point of view, have become capable of transitional behavior (visual accommodation to rapid movements and reconstructions of an invisible whole from a visible fraction, stage III) or of even more advanced behavior (active search for the entirely vanished object with or without grasping attempt, stage IV) is the active show of affection. Since direct imitation suffices to pass this criterion, this kind of emotional expression does not require representation for its explanation. Thus, this distribution of our subjects presents no problem.

HISTOGRAM 4 (STAGE V)

The last objectal test passed by the subjects who have become capable of accounting for visible displacements in their search for the vanished object (stage Va) is the compliance with prohibitions. From the Freudian viewpoint, this behavior presupposes representation: it is evidence of object constancy. Here the psychoanalytic assumption seems perfectly sound and is in fact in complete agreement with our findings. There is probably, as mentioned before, a three-month interval between the representation of inanimate objects and of human beings. Therefore, the fact that our subjects are just before the representation of inanimate objects (stage V) does not prevent their having attained the level of representation (stage VI) of human beings. This is in full agreement with Piaget's theory and avoids a possible contradiction with the psychoanalytic hypotheses which place the beginning of object constancy at about the end of the first year of life. Our 12-month-old subjects cluster in stage Va.

HISTOGRAM 5 (STAGE VI)

The distribution of our remaining subjects presents no problem, whatever theory one espouses. Subtle discrimination of signs of communication is the last objectal criterion passed by the subjects who are, from then on, capable of deduction. Furthermore, it should be emphasized that the two subjects who passed this objectal criterion were not at the beginning but at the end of objective stage VI.

We have now reached the end of the analysis of our data concerning the specific problem of the genesis of representation. We certainly did not succeed in resolving the theoretical discrepancies between the two giants of psychology, Freud and Piaget, but we hope to have sharpened some of their hypotheses believing, with Etienne Gilson (1939, p. 7) "that a good disagreement ... is better than the semblance of agreement amidst confusion."

At the end of this study, we find it necessary to accept the plausibility of Piaget's hypotheses concerning both the specific problem of the genesis of representation and the general problem of the formation of the object concept. On the other hand, we believe that the psychoanalytic hypotheses relative to the specific question of the beginning of representation require reformulation. As to the more general assumptions which underlie the psychoanalytic theory of object relations, they were to a large extent supported by our experiments—with the possible exception of the assumed genetic link between the cathexis of persons and that of things which is extremely difficult to translate into operational terms.

We come to the practical conclusion that any study of affective phenomena must take cognitive processes into account, and that any study of intellectual phenomena must not disregard affective modalities. All evidence points to the inseparability of these two aspects of personality and to the intertwining of all aspects of development (be it locomotion or learning) which clearly shows up on our correlation matrix (Table 5, Chapter VI). Infantile psychopathology could only profit from an interpretation of neurotic and psychotic problems taking Piaget's findings into account. Many symptoms of symbiotic and autistic patients seem more accessible in the light of the different steps of the construction of the object concept, of the spatial field, of the temporal field or of causality (Décarie, 1953; Anthony, 1956b).

But we leave it up to others to develop research studies which may complete, support, or reject our hypotheses as we remember that:

"even the most beautiful of theories is never as beautiful as truth or fact. I do not believe that a single true and absolute theory exists either in physiology or even in physics or chemistry. Everything is only relative. At the end of all ends we shall have the absolute. To have destroyed a theory is therefore an excellent thing. It is a step forward. And one need not tremble lest a fact destroy a theory, even one's own. One must seek it. Underneath lies a discovery, a revolution so to speak, for science is revolutionary and does not advance by successive additions as many believe [from the manuscripts of Claude Bernard]."

REFERENCES

Ackerman, D. B. (1942), Critical Evaluation of the Viennese Tests as Applied to 200 New York Infants Six to Twelve Months Old. *Child Devel.,* 13:41-53.

Aebli, H. (1950), *The Development of Intelligence in the Child* (summary of the works of Jean Piaget published between 1936 and 1948). Minneapolis, Minn.: Institute of Child Welfare, University of Minnesota.

Ahrens, R. (1955), Beitrag zur Entwicklung des Physiognomie- und Mimikerkennens. *Zeitschr. exper. angewandte Psychol.,* 2:412-454, 599-633.

Ajuriaguerra, J. de (1955), Intervention. *Rev. fr. psychanal.,* 19: 295-299.

Alpert, A. (1959), Reversibility of Pathological Fixations Associated with Maternal Deprivation in Infancy. *The Psychoanalytic Study of the Child,* 14:169-185. New York: International Universities Press.

Ambrose, J. A. (1960), The Smiling and Related Responses in Early Human Infancy: An Experimental and Theoretical Study of Their Course and Significance. Unpublished doctoral dissertation, University of London.

——— (1961), The Development of the Smiling Response in Early Infancy. *Determinants of Infant Behaviour,* 1:179-201, ed. B. M. Foss. New York: Wiley.

——— (1963a), The Age of Onset of Ambivalence: Indications from the Study of Laughing. *J. Psychol. Psychiat. & Allied Disciplines,* 4:167-181.

———— (1963b), The Concept of a Critical Period for the Development of Social Responsiveness in Early Human Infancy. *Determinants of Infant Behaviour*, 2:201-225, ed. B. M. Foss. New York: Wiley.

Anthony, E. J. (1956a), The Significance of Jean Piaget for Child Psychiatry. *Brit. J. Med. Psychol.*, 24:20-34.

———— (1956b), Six applications de la théorie génétique de Piaget à la théorie et à la pratique psychodynamique. *Rev. suisse psychol. pure et appliquée*, 15:269-277.

———— (1957), The System Makers: Piaget and Freud. Symposium on the Contribution of Current Theories to an Understanding of Child Development. *Brit. J. Med. Psychol.*, 30:255-269.

———— (1958), An Experimental Approach to the Psychopathology of Childhood: Autism. *Brit. J. Med. Psychol.*, 31:211-225.

Apostel, L. (1959), Logique et apprentissage. *Études d'epistémologie génétique*, 8:1-138.

Balint, M. (1953), *Primary Love and Psycho-Analytic Technique.* New York: Liveright.

Benedek, T. (1938), Adaptation to Reality in Early Infancy. *Psychoanal. Quart.*, 7:200-215.

———— (1952), Personality Development. *Dynamic Psychiatry*, eds. F. Alexander and H. Ross. Chicago: University of Chicago Press, pp. 63-113.

Bergman, P. and Escalona, S. (1949), Unusual Sensitivities in Very Young Children. *The Psychoanalytic Study of the Child*, 3/4:333-352. New York: International Universities Press.

Bernassy, M. (1956), Evolution de la psychanalyse. *La psychanalyse d'aujourd'hui*, 2:761-784, ed. S. Nacht. Paris: Presses Universitaires.

Blum, G. S. (1953), *Psychoanalytic Theories of Personality.* Toronto: McGraw Hill.

Bouvet, M. (1956), La clinique psychanalytique. La relation d'objet. *La psychanalyse d'aujourd'hui*, 1:1-68, ed. S. Nacht. Paris: Presses Universitaires.

Bowlby, J. (1951), *Maternal Care and Mental Health.* Geneva: World Health Organization, Monograph 2.

———— (1958), The Nature of the Child's Tie to His Mother. *Int. J. Psychoanal.*, 39:350-373.

———— (1960), Grief and Mourning in Infancy and Early Childhood. *The Psychoanalytic Study of the Child*, 15:9-52. New York: International Universities Press.

————, Ainsworth, M., Boston, M., and Rosenbluth, D. (1956), The Effects of Mother-Child Separation, a Follow-up Study. *Brit. J. Med. Psychol.*, 29:211-247.

————, Robertson, S., and Rosenbluth, D. (1952), A Two-Year-Old Goes to the Hospital. *The Psychoanalytic Study of the Child*, 7:82-94. New York: International Universities Press.

Brandt, L. W. (1961), Some Notes on English Freudian Terminology. *J. Am. Psychoanal. Assn.*, 9:331-339.

Bridges, K. (1930), A Genetic Theory of the Emotions. *J. Genet. Psychol.*, 37:514-527.

———— (1932), Emotional Development in Early Infancy. *Child Devel.*, 3:324-341.

———— (1933), Emotional Development in the Young Child. Doctoral thesis, University of Montreal.

Brierley, M. (1951), *Trends in Psychoanalysis*. London: Hogarth Press.

Brody, S. (1956), *Patterns of Mothering*. New York: International Universities Press.

Brunet, O. and Lézine, I. (1951), *Le développement psychologique de la première enfance*. Paris: Presses Universitaires.

Bühler, C. (1930), *The First Year of Life*. New York: John Day.

———— (1954), The Reality Principle. Discussions of Theories and Observational Data. *Am. J. Psychother.*, 8:626-647.

———— and Hetzer, H. (1935), *Testing Children's Development from Birth to School Age*. New York: Farrar & Rinehart.

Carmichael, L., ed. (1954), *Manual of Child Psychology*. New York: Wiley.

Cattell, P. (1940), *The Measurement of Intelligence of Infants and Young Children*. New York: The Psychological Corporation.

Chambers, J. (1957), Maternal Deprivation as a Retarding Effect in the Development of Temporal Concept. Doctoral thesis, University of Montreal.

Davis, H. V., Sears, R. R., Miller, H. C., and Brodbeck, A. J. (1948), Effects of Cup, Bottle and Breast Feeding on Oral Activities of Newborn Infants. *Pediatrics,* 2:549-558.

Décarie, T. Gouin- (1953), Quelques symptômes d'enfants atypiques en regard des théories de Jean Piaget. *Contrib. étude sciences de l'homme,* 2:87-93.

———— (1960), La notion d'objet chez Jean Piaget et la relation objectale. Doctoral thesis, University of Montreal.

Dennis, W. (1935), An Experimental Test of Two Theories of Social Smiling in Infants. *J. Soc. Psychol.,* 6:214-233.
——— (1938), Infant Development under Conditions of Restricted Practice and of Minimum Social Stimulation. A Preliminary Report. *J. Genet. Psychol.,* 53:149-159.
——— (1941), Infant Development under Conditions of Restricted Practice and of Minimum Social Stimulation. *Genet. Psychol. Mon.,* 23:143-189.
Dolto-Marette, F. (1948), Les sensations coenesthésiques de bien-être et de malaise, origines des sentiments de culpabilité. *Psyché,* 18/19:468-482.
Drever, J. (1953), *A Dictionary of Psychology.* Melbourne: Penguin Books.
Eissler, R. S. et al., eds. (1949), *The Psychoanalytic Study of the Child,* 3/4:9-493. New York: International Universities Press.
English, H. B. and English, A. C. (1958), *A Comprehensive Dictionary of Psychological and Psychoanalytical Terms: A Guide to Usage.* New York: Longmans, Green.
Erikson, E. H. (1950), Growth and Crises of the Healthy Personality. Symposium on the Healthy Personality, Suppl. 2. *Transactions of the Fourth Conference on Problems of Infancy and Childhood.* New York: Josiah Macy Foundation.
Escalona, S. (1945), Feeding Disturbances in Very Young Children. *Am. J. Orthopsychiat.,* 15:76-80.
——— (1953), Emotional Development in the First Year of Life. *Transactions of the Sixth Conference on Problems of Infancy and Childhood.* New York: Josiah Macy Foundation.
——— and Heider, G. M. (1959), *Prediction and Outcome.* New York: Basic Books.
Fenichel, O. (1945), *The Psychoanalytic Theory of Neurosis.* New York: Norton.
——— (1954), Early Stages of Ego Development. *The Collected Papers of Otto Fenichel,* Second Series. New York: Norton.
Fisher, R. A. (1952), *Statistical Methods for Research Workers.* Edinburgh: Oliver Boyd.
Flavell, J. (1963), *The Developmental Psychology of Jean Piaget.* Princeton, N. J.: Van Nostrand.
Fodor, N. and Gaynor, F., eds. (1950), *Freud: Dictionary of Psychoanalysis.* New York: Philosophical Library.
Freud, A. (1946), The Psychoanalytic Study of Infantile Feeding Disturbances. *The Psychoanalytic Study of the Child,* 2:119-132. New York: International Universities Press.

———— (1947), Aggression in Relation to Emotional Development, Normal and Pathological. *The Psychoanalytic Study of the Child,* 3/4:37-42. New York: International Universities Press.

———— (1951a), The Contribution of Psychoanalysis to Genetic Psychology. *Am. J. Orthopsychiat.,* 21:476-497.

———— (1951b), Observations in Child Development. *The Psychoanalytic Study of the Child,* 6:18-30. New York: International Universities Press.

———— (1952), The Mutual Influence in the Development of Ego. *The Psychoanalytic Study of the Child,* 7:42-50. New York: International Universities Press.

———— (1953), Some Remarks on Infant Observation. *The Psychoanalytic Study of the Child,* 8:9-19. New York: International Universities Press.

———— (1954), Psychoanalysis and Education. *The Psychoanalytic Study of the Child,* 9:9-15. New York: International Universities Press.

———— (1958), Child Observation and Prediction of Development. *The Psychoanalytic Study of the Child,* 13:92-116. New York: International Universities Press.

———— (1960), Discussion of Dr. Bowlby's Paper. *The Psychoanalytic Study of the Child,* 15:53-62. New York: International Universities Press.

Freud, S. (1905), Three Essays on Sexuality. *Standard Edition,* 7:130-243. London: Hogarth Press, 1953.

———— (1911), Formulations Regarding the Two Principles in Mental Functioning. *Standard Edition,* 12:218-226. London: Hogarth Press, 1958.

———— (1914), On Narcissism, an Introduction. *Standard Edition,* 14:73-81. London: Hogarth Press, 1957.

———— (1915), Instincts and their Vicissitudes. *Standard Edition,* 14:117-140. London: Hogarth Press, 1957.

———— (1925), Negation. *Collected Papers,* 5:181-186. London: Hogarth Press, 1950.

Fries, M. E. (1946), The Child's Ego Development and the Training of Adults in his Environment. *The Psychoanalytic Study of the Child,* 2:85-112. New York: International Universities Press.

———— (1947), Diagnosing the Child's Adjustment through Age-Level Tests. *Psychoanal. Rev.,* 34:1-31.

Germain, C. (1954), Test individuel d'intelligence générale pour enfants de deux à douze ans. M.A. dissertation, University of Montreal.

Gesell, A. (1946), The Ontogenesis of Infant Behavior. *Manual of Child Psychology*. New York: Wiley, pp. 295-331.

—— et al. (1940), *The First Five Years of Life*. New York: Harpers.

—— and Amatruda, C. (1945), *The Embryology of Behavior*. New York: Harpers.

—— and —— (1948), *Developmental Diagnosis*. New York: Boeler.

—— and Ilg, F. (1943), *Infant and Child in the Culture of Today*. New York: Harpers.

Gewirtz, J. L. (in press), The Course of Infant Smiling in Four Child-Rearing Environments in Israel. *Determinants of Infant Behaviour, 3*, ed. B. M. Foss. New York: Wiley.

—— and Gewirtz, H. B. (in press), Stimulus Conditions, Infant Behaviors, and Social Learning in Four Israeli Child-Rearing Environments. *Determinants of Infant Behaviour, 3*, ed. B. M. Foss. New York: Wiley.

Gilson, E. (1939), *Réalisme thomiste et critique de la connaissance*. Paris: Vrin.

Glover, E. (1945), Examination of the Klein System of Child Psychology. *The Psychoanalytic Study of the Child,* 1:75-118. New York: International Universities Press.

—— (1950), Functional Aspects of the Mental Apparatus. *Int. J. Psychoanal.,* 31:125-131.

—— (1953), *Psychoanalysis and Child Psychiatry*. London: Imago.

—— (1956), *Selected Papers on Psychoanalysis,* Vol. I. New York: International Universities Press.

Gratton, P. (1954), Aspect psychologique du développement d'enfants de quatre à huit mois dans un milieu institutionnel. M.A. dissertation, University of Montreal.

Greenacre, P. (1952), *Trauma, Growth and Personality*. New York: Norton.

Greene, W. A. (1958), Early Object Relations, Somatic, Affective and Personal, An Inquiry into the Physiology of the Mother-Child Unit. *J. Nerv. Ment. Dis.,* 126:225-253.

Griffiths, R. (1954), *The Abilities of Babies*. London: University of London Press.

Harriman, S. (1952), *The New Dictionary of Psychology*. London: Vision.

Hartmann, H. (1950a), Comments on the Psychoanalytic Theory of the Ego. *The Psychoanalytic Study of the Child*, 5:74-96. New York: International Universities Press.

———— (1950b), Psychoanalysis and Developmental Psychology. *The Psychoanalytic Study of the Child*, 5:7-17. New York: International Universities Press.

———— (1952), The Mutual Influences in the Development of Ego and Id. *The Psychoanalytic Study of the Child*, 7:9-30.

———— (1955), Notes on the Theory of Sublimation. *The Psychoanalytic Study of the Child*, 10:9-29. New York: International Universities Press.

———— (1956), Notes on the Reality Principle. *The Psychoanalytic Study of the Child*, 11:31-53. New York: International Universities Press.

———— (1958a), Comments on the Scientific Aspects of Psychoanalysis. *The Psychoanalytic Study of the Child*, 13:127-147. New York: International Universities Press.

———— (1958b), *Ego Psychology and the Problem of Adaptation*. New York: International Universities Press.

———— and Kris, E. (1945), The Genetic Approach in Psychoanalysis. *The Psychoanalytic Study of the Child*, 1:11-30. New York: International Universities Press.

————, ————, and Loewenstein, R. M. (1946), Comments on the Formation of Psychic Structure. *The Psychoanalytic Study of the Child*, 2:11-38. New York: International Universities Press.

————, ————, and ———— (1949), Notes on the Theory of Aggression. *The Psychoanalytic Study of the Child*, 3/4:10-36. New York: International Universities Press.

Hendrick, I. (1942), Instinct and the Ego during Infancy. *Psychoanal. Quart.*, 11:33-58.

———— (1951), Early Development of the Ego: Identification in Infancy. *Psychoanal. Quart.*, 20:44-61.

Hilgard, R. E. (1952), Experimental Approach to Psychoanalysis. *Psychoanalysis as Science*. New York: Basic Books, pp. 3-45.

Hinsie, L. E. and Campbell, R. J. (1960), *Psychiatric Dictionary*, 3rd ed. New York: Oxford University Press.

—— and Shatzky, J. (1948), *Psychiatric Dictionary*. New York: Oxford University Press.

Hoffer, W. (1949), Mouth, Hand, and Ego-Integration. *The Psychoanalytic Study of the Child*, 3/4:49-56. New York: International Universities Press.

—— (1950a), Development of the Body Ego. *The Psychoanalytic Study of the Child*, 5:18-23. New York: International Universities Press.

—— (1950b), Oral Aggressiveness and Ego Development. *Int. J. Psychoanal.*, 31:156-160.

—— (1952), Mutual Influences in the Development of Ego and Id. Earliest Stages. *The Psychoanalytic Study of the Child*, 7:31-41. New York: International Universities Press.

—— (1955), Psychoanalysis, Practical and Research Aspects. *The Abraham Flexner Lectures*, Series 12. Baltimore: Vanderbilt University.

Inhelder, B. (1943), *Le diagnostic du raisonnement chez les débiles mentaux*. Neuchâtel: Delachaux & Niestlé.

—— (1956a), Die affective und kognotive Entwicklung des Kindes. *Rev. suisse psychol. pure et appliquée*, 15:251-268.

—— (1956b), Criteria of the Stages of Mental Development. *Discussions on Child Development*, 1:75-86, eds. J. M. Tanner and B. Inhelder. New York: International Universities Press.

Jacobson, E. (1953), The Affects and their Pleasure-Unpleasure Qualities in Relation to the Psychic Discharge Processes. *Drives, Affects, Behavior*, ed. R. M. Loewenstein. New York: International Universities Press.

—— (1954), The Self and the Object World. *The Psychoanalytic Study of the Child*, 9:75-127. New York: International Universities Press.

Jankelevitch, S. (1929), *Essais de psychanalyse*. Paris: Payot.

Jensen, K. (1932), Differential Reactions to Task and Temperature Stimuli in New-Born Infants. *Genet. Psychol. Mon.*, 12:373-479.

Jones, E. (1923), Cold, Disease and Birth. *Papers on Psychoanalysis*. London: Bailliere, Tindall & Cox, 1948.

Kestenberg, J. (1956), On the Development of Maternal Feelings in Early Childhood. *The Psychoanalytic Study of the Child*, 11:267-291. New York: International Universities Press.

Koupernick, C. (1951), Développement psycho-moteur du nourrisson. *Psychiat. soc. de l'enfant,* 2:17-25. Paris: Centre International de l'Enfance.

———— (1954), *Le développement psycho-moteur du premier âge.* Paris: Presses Universitaires.

Kris, E. (1950), Notes on the Development and on Some Current Problems of Psychoanalytic Child Psychology. *The Psychoanalytic Study of the Child,* 5:24-46. New York: International Universities Press.

———— (1951a), Psychoanalytic Child Psychology. *The Psychoanalytic Study of the Child,* 6:9-17. New York: International Universities Press.

————(1951b), Some Comments and Observations on Early Autoerotic Activities. *The Psychoanalytic Study of the Child,* 6:95-116. New York: International Universities Press.

————, Chairman (1954), Problems of Infantile Neurosis: A Discussion. *The Psychoanalytic Study of the Child,* 9:16-71. New York: International Universities Press.

Lacan, S. (1949), Le stade du miroir comme formateur de la fonction du je. *Rev. fr. psychanal.,* 4:449-455.

Lallier, L. (1961), Étude du sourire chez le nourrisson en fonction de stimuli auditifs. M.A. dissertation, University of Montreal.

Lampl-de Groot, J. (1947), On the Development of the Ego and Superego. *Int. J. Psychoanal.,* 28:7-11.

———— (1950), On Masturbation and Its Influence on General Development. *The Psychoanalytic Study of the Child,* 5:153-174. New York: International Universities Press.

Laroche, J. L. and Tcheng, F. (1963), *Le sourire du nourrisson.* La voix comme facteur déclenchant. Louvain: Publications Universitaires.

———— and ———— (in press), Phases du sommeil et sourires spontanés. Observation longitudinale d'un nouveau-né. *Acta psychol.* (Amsterdam).

Laurendeau, M. and Pinard, A. (1962), *Causal Thinking in the Child.* New York: International Universities Press.

Lebovici, S., Ajuriaguerra, J. de, and Diatkine, R. (1958), À propos de l'observation chez le jeune enfant. *Psychiatrie de l'enfant,* 1:436-474.

———— and Diatkine, R. (1954), Étude des fantasmes chez l'enfant. *Rev. fr. psychanal.,* 18:108-159.

———, ———, Favreau, J. A., Luquet, P., and Luquet-Porot, J. (1956), La psychanalyse des enfants. *Psychanalyse d'aujourd' hui,* ed. S. Nacht. Paris: Presses Universitaires, pp. 169-235.

Leitch, M. and Escalona, S. (1949), The Reaction of Infants to Stress, A Report on Clinical Findings. *The Psychoanalytic Study of the Child,* 3/4:121-140. New York: International Universities Press.

Lewis, M. M. (1951), *Infant Speech: A Study of the Beginnings of Language.* London: Routledge and Kegan Paul.

Loewenstein, R. M. (1950), Conflict and Autonomus Ego Development during the Phallic Phase. *The Psychoanalytic Study of the Child,* 5:47-52.

Mack Brunswick, R. (1940), The Preoedipal Phase of Libido Development. *The Psychoanalytic Study of the Child,* 9:293-319. New York: International Universities Press.

Mahler, M. S. and Gosliner, B. J. (1955), On Symbiotic Child Psychosis. *The Psychoanalytic Study of the Child,* 10:195-211. New York: International Universities Press.

Malrieu, R. (1952), *Les émotions et la personalité de l'enfant.* Paris: Vrin.

——— (1958), Étude génétique des émotions. *Psychol. française,* 1:76-84.

Marty, P. and Fain, M. (1955), Importance du rôle de la motricité dans la relation d'objet. *Rev. fr. psychanal.,* 19:205-322.

Maslow, A. H. and Szilagyi-Kessler, L. (1946), Security and Breast Feeding. *J. Abnorm. Soc. Psychol.,* 41:83-85.

McCarthy, D. (1954), Language Development in Children. *Manual of Child Psychology,* ed. L. Carmichael. New York: Wiley, pp. 476-481.

Miron-Brossard, L. (1965), Etude différentielle du renforcement du sourire chez le jeune nourrisson. M.A. dissertation, University of Montreal.

Mittlemann, B. (1954), Mobility in Infants, Children and Adults: Patterning and Psychodynamics. *The Psychoanalytic Study of the Child,* 9:142-177. New York: International Universities Press.

Nacht, S. (1951), Les nouvelles théories psychanalytiques sur le moi. *Rev. fr. psychanal.,* 15:142-177.

Odier, C. (1947a), *L'angoisse et la pensée magique.* Neuchâtel: Delachaux and Niestlé; (1956) *Anxiety and Magic Thinking.* New York: International Universities Press.

———— (1947b), *Les deux sources consciente et inconsciente de la vie morale*. Neuchâtel: Baconnière.

Osterrieth, P. A. (1955), Les stades du développement selon d'autres écoles de psychologie, le problème des stades en psychologie de l'enfant. *Troisième symposium de l'association psychologique française*. Paris: Presses Universitaires, 1956, pp. 43-49.

Piaget, J. (1924), *Judgement and Reasoning in the Child*. Patterson, N. J.: Littlefield, Adams, 1959.

———— (1926a), *The Child's Conception of the World*. Patterson, N. J.: Littlefield, Adams, 1960.

———— (1926b), *The Language and Thought of the Child*. London: Routledge & Kegan Paul.

———— (1931), Children's Philosophies. *A Handbook of Child Psychology*. Worcester: Clark Univ. Press, pp. 377-391.

———— (1937), *The Construction of Reality in the Child*. New York: Basic Books, 1954.

———— (1945), *Play, Dreams and Imitation in Childhood*. New York: Norton, 1962.

———— (1947), *Psychology of Intelligence*. Patterson, N. J.: Littlefield, Adams, 1960.

———— (1948), *The Origins of Intelligence in Children*. New York: International Universities Press, 1952.

———— (1949), *Introduction à l'épistémologie génétique*, Vol. I. Paris: Presses Universitaires.

———— (1954), *Les relations entre l'affectivité et l'intelligence dans le développement mental de l'enfant*. Paris: Centre de Documentation Universitaire.

———— (1956), Les stades du développement intellectuel de l'enfant et de l'adolescent, le problème des stades en psychologie de l'enfant. *Troisième symposium de l'association psychologique scientifique de langue française*. Paris: Presses Universitaires, pp. 33-42.

———— (1957), Logique et équilibre dans les comportements du sujet. *Études d'épistémologie génétique*, 2:27-117. Paris: Presses Universitaires.

———— (1959), Apprentissage et connaissance. *Études d'épistémologie génétique*, 7:21-67. Paris: Presses Universitaires.

———— (1960), *The General Problems of the Psychobiological Development of the Child*, 4:3-27, eds. J. M. Tanner and B. Inhelder. London: Tavistock.

————, Apostel, L., Mays, W., and Morf, A. (1957), *Étude d'épis-témologie génétique,* Vol. 4. Paris: Presses Universitaires.

———— and Inhelder, B. (1941), *Le développement des qualités chez l'enfant.* Neuchâtel: Delachaux and Niestlé.

———— and ———— (1955), *The Growth of Logical Thinking from Childhood to Adolescence.* New York: Basic Books, 1958.

Piéron, H. (1951), *Vocabulaire de la psychologie.* Paris: Presses Universitaires.

Pinneau, S. M. (1955a), The Infantile Disorders of Hospitalism and Anaclitic Depression. *Psychol. Bull.,* 52:429-452.

———— (1955b), Reply to Dr. Spitz. *Psychol. Bull.,* 52:459-462.

Porot, A., ed. (1952), *Manuel alphabétique de psychiatrie.* Paris: Presses Universitaires.

Pratt, K. C. (1946), The Neonate. *Manual of Child Psychology,* ed. L. Carmichael. New York: Wiley, pp. 190-254.

Rank, B. (1949), Aggression. *The Psychoanalytic Study of the Child,* 3/4:43-48. New York: International Universities Press.

Rapaport, D. (1942), *Emotions and Memory.* New York: International Universities Press.

———— (1950), On the Psychoanalytic Theory of Thinking. *Int. J. Psychoanal.,* 31:161-170.

———— (1951), *Organization and Pathology of Thought.* New York: Columbia University Press.

———— (1954a), The Conceptual Model of Psychoanalysis. *Psychoanalytic Psychiatry and Psychology,* 1:221-247, ed. R. P. Knight. New York: International Universities Press.

———— (1954b), On the Psychoanalytic Theory of Thinking. *Psychoanalytic Psychiatry and Psychology,* 1:259-273, ed. R. P. Knight. New York: International Universities Press.

———— (1954c), On the Psychoanalytic Theory of Affects. *Psychoanalytic Psychiatry and Psychology,* 1:274-310, ed. R. P. Knight. New York: International Universities Press.

———— (1960), The Structure of Psychoanalytic Theory. A Systematizing Attempt. *Psychological Issues,* Monograph 6. New York: International Universities Press.

————, Reichard, S., et al. (1944), The Development of Concept Formation in Children. *Am. J. Orthopsychiat.,* 14:156-161.

Rheingold, H. L. (1961), The Effect of Environmental Stimulation upon Social and Exploratory Behaviour in the Human Infant. *Determinants of Infant Behaviour,* 1:143-171, ed. B. Foss. New York: Wiley.

Ribble, M. A. (1948), *The Rights of Infants*. New York: Columbia University Press.

Ritchfield, J. (1954), On the Scientific Status of Psychoanalysis. *Scientific Monthly*, 79:306-309.

Ritvo, S. and Provence, S. (1953), Form Perception and Imitation in Some Autistic Children: Diagnostic Findings and their Contextual Interpretation. *The Psychoanalytic Study of the Child*, 8:155-161. New York: International Universities Press.

—— and Solnit, A. J. (1958), Influences of Early Mother-Child Interaction on Identification Processes. *The Psychoanalytic Study of the Child*, 8:155-161. New York: International Universities Press.

Russell, D. H. (1956), *Children's Thinking*. Boston: Ginn.

Schachtel, E. G. (1959), *Metamorphosis*. New York: Basic Books.

Schaffer, H. R. and Callender, W. M. (1959), Psychologic Effects of Hospitalization in Infancy. *Pediatrics*, 24:528-539.

Schilder, P. (1950), *The Image and Appearance of the Human Body*. New York: International Universities Press.

Sears, R. R. (1936), Experimental Studies of Projection: I. Attribution of Traits. *J. Soc. Psychol.*, 7:151-173.

—— (1947), *Survey of Objective Studies of Psychoanalytic Concepts*. New York: Social Science Research Council.

—— and Wise, L. W. (1950), Relation of Cup Feeding in Infancy to Thumb Sucking and Oral Drive. *Am. J. Orthopsychiat.*, 20:123-138.

Seitz, P. F. D. (1950), Psychocutaneous Conditioning during the First Two Weeks of Life. *Psychosom. Med.*, 12:187-188.

Servadio, E. (1954), Le rôle des conflits pre-oedipiens. *Rev. fr. psychanal.*, 18:1-46.

Sewell, W. H. and Mussen, P. H. (1952), The Effects of Feeding, Weaning, and Scheduling Procedures on Childhood Adjustment and the Formation of Oral Symptoms. *Child Devel.*, 23:185-192.

Snedecor, G. W. (1950), *Statistical Methods*. Ames, Iowa: Iowa State University Press.

Spitz, R. A. (1945a), Diacritic and Coenesthetic Organization. *Psychoanal. Rev.*, 32:146-172.

—— (1945b), Hospitalism: An Inquiry into the Genesis of Psychiatric Conditions in Early Childhood. *The Psychoanalytic Study of the Child*, 1:53-74. New York: International Universities Press.

—— (1946a), Anaclitic Depression: An Inquiry into the Genesis of Psychiatric Conditions in Early Childhood. *The Psychoanalytic Study of the Child*, 2:313-342. New York: International Universities Press.

—— (1946b), Hospitalism: A Follow-Up Report. *The Psychoanalytic Study of the Child*, 2:113-117. New York: International Universities Press.

—— (1947), Emotional Growth in the First Year. *Child Study*, 27:68-95.

—— (1949), The Role of Ecological Factors in Emotional Development in Infancy. *Child Devel.*, 20:145-155.

—— (1950a), Anxiety in Infancy, A Study of Its Manifestations in the First Year of Life. *Int. J. Psychoanal.*, 31:138-143.

—— (1950b), Digital Extension Reflex. *Arch. Neurol. Psychiat.*, 63:467-470.

—— (1950c), Possible Infantile Precursors of Psychopathy. *Am. J. Orthopsychiat.*, 20:240-248.

—— (1950d), Psychiatric Therapy in Infancy. *Am. J. Orthopsychiat.*, 20:1-6.

—— (1950e), Relevancy of Direct Infant Observation. *The Psychoanalytic Study of the Child*, 5:66-73. New York: International Universities Press.

—— (1951a), Environment Versus Race-Environment as an Etiological Factor in Psychiatric Disturbances in Infancy. *Psychoanalysis and Culture,* eds. G. B. Wilbur and W. Muensterberger. New York: International Universities Press, pp. 32-41.

—— (1951b), Psychogenic Diseases in Infancy, An Attempt at their Etiologic Classification. *The Psychoanalytic Study of the Child*, 6:255-275. New York: International Universities Press.

—— (1951c), Purposive Grasping. *J. Personal.*, 1:141-148.

—— (1953), Aggression: Its Role in the Establishment of Object Relations. *Drives, Affects, Behavior,* ed. R. M. Loewenstein. New York: International Universities Press, pp. 123-138.

—— (1954), Genèse des premières relations objectales. *Rev. fr. psychanal.*, 28:479-575.

—— (1955a), A Note on the Extrapolation of Ethological Findings. *Int. J. Psychoanal.*, 36:163-165.

———— (1955b), The Primal Cavity. A Contribution to the Genesis of Perception and Its Role for Psychoanalytic Theory. *The Psychoanalytic Study of the Child,* 10:215-240. New York: International Universities Press.

———— (1955c), Reply to Dr. Pinneau. *Psychol. Bull.,* 52:453-459.

———— (1957), *No and Yes: On the Genesis of Human Communication.* New York: International Universities Press.

———— (1958), On the Genesis of Superego Components. *The Psychoanalytic Study of the Child,* 13:375-404. New York: International Universities Press.

———— (1959), *A Genetic Field Theory of Ego Formation. Its Implications for Pathology.* New York: International Universities Press.

———— (1960), Discussion of Dr. Bowlby's Paper. *The Psychoanalytic Study of the Child,* 15:85-94. New York: International Universities Press.

———— (1965), *The First Year of Life.* New York: International Universities Press.

———— and Wolf, K. M. (1946), The Smiling Response. *Genet. Psychol. Mon.,* 34:57-125.

———— and ———— (1949), Autoerotism. Some Empirical Findings and Hypotheses on Three of Its Manifestations in the First Year of Life. *The Psychoanalytic Study of the Child,* 3/4:85-120. New York: International Universities Press.

Stanton, A. H. (1959), Propositions Concerning Object Choices, An Attempt at the Systematic Restatement of the Libido Theory. *Annals N. Y. Acad. Sci.,* 76:1010-1037.

Stern, W. (1930), *Psychology of Early Childhood up to the Sixth Year of Age.* New York: Henry Holt.

Stevenson, O. (1954), The First Treasured Possession. A Study of the Part Played by Specially Loved Objects and Toys in the Lives of Certain Children. *The Psychoanalytic Study of the Child,* 9:199-217. New York: International Universities Press.

Szekely, L. (1954), Biological Remarks on Fears Originating in Early Childhood. *Int. J. Psychoanal.,* 35:57-67.

Tanner, J. M. and Inhelder, B., eds. (1956), *Discussions on Child Development,* Vol. I. New York: International Universities Press.

———— and ———— (1960), *Discussions on Child Development,* Vol. IV. New York: International Universities Press.

Waelder, R. (1937), The Problem of the Genesis of Psychical Conflict in Earliest Infancy. *Int. J. Psychoanal.*, 18:406-473.

Warren, H. (1943), *Dictionary of Psychology*. New York: Houghton Mifflin.

Werner, H. (1957), *Comparative Psychology of Mental Development*. New York: International Universities Press.

Winnicott, A. W. (1953), Transitional Objects and Transitional Phenomena. *Int. J. Psychoanal.*, 34:89-97.

Wolff, P. H. (1960), The Developmental Psychologies of Jean Piaget and Psychoanalysis. *Psychological Issues*, Monograph 5. New York: International Universities Press.

——— (1963), Observations on the Early Development of Smiling. *Determinants of Infant Behaviour*, 2:113-138, ed. B. M. Foss. New York: Wiley.